Picturing Christian Witness

Picturing Christian Witness

New Testament Images of Disciples in Mission

Stanley H. Skreslet

WILLIAM B. EERDMANS PUBLISHING COMPANY
GRAND RAPIDS, MICHIGAN / CAMBRIDGE, U.K.

Wm. B. Eerdmans Publishing Co.
255 Jefferson Ave. S.E., Grand Rapids, Michigan 49503 /
P.O. Box 163, Cambridge CB3 9PU U.K.

Printed in the United States of America

11 10 09 08 07 06   7 6 5 4 3 2 1

Library of Congress Cataloging-in-Publication Data

Skreslet, Stanley H.
   Picturing Christian witness: New Testament images of disciples in mission /
   Stanley H. Skreslet.
         p.   cm.
   Includes bibliographical references (p.   ).
   ISBN-10: 0-8028-2956-2 / ISBN-13: 978-0-8028-2956-6 (pbk.: alk. paper)
   1. Witness-bearing — Biblical teaching.   2. Evangelistic work — Biblical teaching.
   3. Missions — Theory — Biblical teaching.   4. Discipling — Biblical teaching.
   I. Title.

   BV4520.S57   2006
   266 — dc22

                                                                    2005033663

www.eerdmans.com

For John L. Anderson

H. McKennie Goodpasture

Paul N. Priest

Mentors, friends, and joyful witnesses to the gospel

Contents

CONTENTS

Acknowledgments

In a very real sense, this book is grounded in my own experience as an interpreter of mission. Whether in the academy or the congregation, I have consistently found that image-language often permeates and subtly shapes what we think about evangelization and witness. Fortunately, in both settings I have had the benefit of many thoughtful discussion partners, who were willing to probe and analyze with me some of the ways in which people inside and outside the church have envisioned the task of Christian mission.

Much of my research has been shared with a variety of audiences, including several groups of past Millard Scholars, who gathered on the Union-PSCE campus for week-long discussions of evangelism and mission. In addition, I have presented large parts of this material to the following congregations: White Memorial Presbyterian Church, Raleigh, North Carolina; St. Matthew's Episcopal Church, Richmond, Virginia; St. Gile's Presbyterian Church, Richmond, Virginia; and National Presbyterian Church, Washington, D.C. For the insights generated by these opportunities to wrestle in public with the theology and practice of mission, I am truly thankful.

Among those individuals whose contributions to this project I would like especially to acknowledge is Luther Seminary professor Mark Swanson, whose careful reading of a portion of the manuscript helped to clarify several important issues for me. I'm also grateful to my Union-PSCE faculty colleagues Dawn DeVries and Frances Taylor Gench for their willingness to critique the premises and methodology of my proposed research agenda from the perspective of their respective fields of study. Very early on, I much appreciated chances to discuss my ideas with Philip Clayton, Kenneth Bailey, and John G. Lorimer. Not soon to be forgotten either is the persistent industry of Union-PSCE serials librarian Pam Wells, whose efforts to obtain interlibrary loan materials on my behalf often extended well beyond the strict call of duty. I am likewise grateful for the assistance of Lou McKinney, a member of the Media Services staff at Union-PSCE, whose expert help has enhanced the visual quality of the illustrations included in these pages. Finally, I want to record my sense of gratitude for the sabbatical leave generously granted to me by the administration and trustees of Union-PSCE, without which this project would no doubt still be languishing, half-finished.

Above all, I'm indebted (again) to the careful editorial eye and loving support of my remarkable wife, Paula Youngman Skreslet, who now holds the position of reference librarian in the Morton Library at Union-PSCE. Thanks to her inimitable ability to detect weak prose, the written outcome of my efforts is much better than might otherwise have been the case. I am just as certain that without her gentle but persistent encouragement, I could not have seen this project through to its conclusion.

Abbreviations

ABD	*Anchor Bible Dictionary,* ed. David Noel Freedman et al., 6 vols. (New York: Doubleday, 1992)
ASNU	Acta Seminarii Neotestamentici Upsaliensis
BAGD	W. Baur, W. F. Arndt, F. W. Gingrich, and F. W. Danker, *A Greek-English Lexicon of the New Testament and Other Early Christian Literature,* third ed. (Chicago: University of Chicago Press, 2000)
BibInt	*Biblical Interpretation*
BJRL	*Bulletin of the John Rylands University Library of Manchester*
CBQ	*Catholic Biblical Quarterly*
DArt	*Dictionary of Art,* ed. Jane Turner, 34 vols. (New York: Grove, 1996)
DPL	*Dictionary of Paul and His Letters,* ed. Gerald F. Hawthorne and Ralph P. Martin, with Daniel G. Reid (Downers Grove, Ill.: InterVarsity, 1993)
EDWM	*Evangelical Dictionary of World Mission,* ed. A. Scott Moreau, with Harold Netland and Charles Van Engen (Grand Rapids: Baker, 2000)
ETL	*Ephemerides theologicae lovanienses*
HTR	*Harvard Theological Review*
IBMR	*International Bulletin of Missionary Research*
IRM	*International Review of Mission*
JBL	*Journal of Biblical Literature*

JETS	*Journal of the Evangelical Theological Society*
JSNTSup	Journal for the Study of the New Testament Supplements
LXX	Septuagint
NKJV	New King James Version
NRSV	New Revised Standard Version
NTS	*New Testament Studies*
NovTSup	Novum Testamentum Supplements
RSV	Revised Standard Version
SBLDS	Society of Biblical Literature Dissertation Series
SJT	*Scottish Journal of Theology*
TDNT	*Theological Dictionary of the New Testament,* ed. Gerhard Kittel and Gerhard Friedrich, trans. Geoffrey W. Bromiley, 10 vols. (Grand Rapids: Eerdmans, 1964-1976)
TDOT	*Theological Dictionary of the Old Testament,* ed. G. Johannes Botterweck and Helmer Ringgren, trans. John T. Willis et al., 11 vols. (Grand Rapids: Eerdmans, 1974-)
WUNT	Wissenschaftliche Untersuchungen zum Neuen Testament
ZNW	*Zeitschrift für die neutestamentliche Wissenschaft und die Kunde der älteren Kirche*

Illustrations

CHAPTER 3

CHAPTER 4

chapter 1

Images and Mission

The Power of Images

When Jesus called his earliest disciples to follow him, the Synoptic Gospels agree that he also handed them a symbolic task for the future: "I will make you fish for people" (Mark 1:17).[1] In this way, Jesus himself created the crucial link that continues to hold together figurative language and Christian mission.

The details of the disciples' commission would come later. In the meantime, Jesus had much to share with them concerning the nature of the commitment he had invited them to embrace. In this regard, the manner of Jesus' approach is instructive. His was a venture that began its public phase under the banner of a metaphor, with the announcement of God's reign having arrived: "the kingdom of God is at hand . . ." (Mark 1:15). Subsequent teaching would be infused throughout with the terminology of comparison, most notably in the parables, as Jesus attempted to explain and illustrate the significance of his words and deeds in ways that could connect with his hearers' experience. By these means, Jesus situated the whole of his ministry within a framework of meaning that was much larger than the sum of his precepts and actions. Only so could he properly relate what he was doing day-by-day to God's cosmic intentions, already made known in Israel's Scriptures.

---

1. Unless otherwise indicated, quotations from Scripture are drawn from the New Revised Standard Version translation of the Bible (NRSV).

Jesus' interpretive challenge has since devolved upon those who hope to follow him in mission. This is why church leaders and missionaries alike instinctively reach for image-language whenever they feel the need to clarify the conceptual basis on which ministries of evangelization rest. Images are also used to express visually the many different possible goals of mission and the means most appropriate for the realization of evangelistic aims. Throughout the modern period, the process of image-making, as it relates to missionaries and the work they do, has been a vital part of fundraising and the building of support networks needed to sustain these activities. One might argue further that the images used by churches to explain their theologies of mission have also, to a degree, shaped those theologies, sometimes inadvertently. It is certainly the case that most individuals, past and present, who have considered themselves to be missionaries have had a dominant image or set of images that has illustrated to themselves, first of all, and then to others the deeper intentions lying behind daily occupations. Not all Christian missionaries are theologians, to be sure, but each has had a theology of mission, even if unarticulated, and the images employed often speak volumes about the fundamental sense of vocation that guides and defines missionary praxis.

In this study, images of mission are taken to be visual expressions of one or another understanding of Christian outreach.[2] Whether presented graphically or verbally, they make manifest the underlying ideas and key concepts that decisively shape particular theologies and practices of mission. As products of the imagination, metaphors and images are related phenomena, which, nevertheless, may be distinguished from each other. If metaphors are heuristic lenses through which to view reality afresh, then images are more iconic portrayals of what one has perceived.[3] Like meta-

2. Cf. Paul Ricoeur, *The Rule of Metaphor: Multi-Disciplinary Studies of the Creation of Meaning in Language,* trans. Robert Czerny et al. (Toronto: University of Toronto Press, 1977), pp. 60-61, who, following the nineteenth-century scholar of rhetoric Pierre Fontanier, groups images with pictures and figures and then says about the figure: "[It is] the presentation of a thought in a sensible and tangible form." Further, "it is truly the figure that confers outward appearance on discourse by giving it contours, characteristics and exterior form, similar to the traits of physical bodies." Ricoeur's approach to the figure leads him to characterize the image as a "tableau." Echoing Ricoeur's conclusions, Janet Martin Soskice, *Metaphor and Religious Language* (Oxford: Clarendon, 1985), p. 55, has suggested that "image" is "a generic term for figures of speech," which also functions as a non-linguistic trope "used to designate mental events and visual representations."

3. On metaphors as lenses, see the remarks of G. B. Caird, *The Language and Imagery*

phors, images are transient in the sense that they arise out of and speak first to people living in specific times and places. That is to say, images are impermanent artifacts of culture. More will be said about this in the section to follow. First, I propose to explore some of the reasons why practitioners and theoreticians alike turn to images as a way to depict or represent their theologies of mission. How do images exert their power?

Images As Affective Motivators

Some images of mission demonstrate their vitality by moving hearts. In particular, these images are effective to the degree that they are able to evoke feelings of compassion. As affective motivators, poignant images are bound to figure prominently when the goal is to stimulate zeal for the cause of Christian mission or to lay before the church public a compelling summons to responsibility or sympathy for persons living beyond the ordinary reach of the gospel.

Leonard Woods, professor of theology at Andover Seminary, invoked just this kind of rhetoric when he preached an ordination sermon in 1812 for the first group of missionaries to be sent abroad by the American Board of Commissioners for Foreign Missions (ABCFM). Speaking more directly to the gathered congregation than to the missionary candidates themselves, Woods declared:

> On this new and very interesting occasion, my object is *to rouse you* to benevolent exertion. I would persuade you to act, decidedly and zealously to act under the influence of Christian love. I would excite you by motives which no follower of Christ can resist, to make the spread

---

of the Bible (London: Duckworth, 1980), p. 152. With regard to the differentiation of metaphors from images, I have found the work of Paul Avis, *God and the Creative Imagination: Metaphor, Symbol and Myth in Religion and Theology* (London: Routledge, 1999), especially insightful. Avis points out that images tend to be static, visual, and simpler than metaphors, which are inherently dynamic, verbal, and conjunctive (p. 97). The greater complexity of metaphors over images is assured, Avis reminds us, because a metaphor works by putting two dissimilar images in juxtaposition. I am grateful to my former Union-PSCE faculty colleague, William P. Brown, for bringing the work of Avis to my attention. See Brown, *Seeing the Psalms: A Theology of Metaphor* (Louisville: Westminster John Knox, 2002), esp. pp. 1-14.

of the gospel, and the conversion of the world, the object of your earnest and incessant pursuit.[4]

To heighten the emotional impact of his appeal, Woods went on, as many in the modern missionary movement after him would also do, to describe a non-Christian world entirely given over to moral degradation and despair. Put yourselves in their places, he suggested, and imagine how it would feel to "spend your life in a land of darkness, ignorant of God, slaves to the basest superstition and the most hateful vices."[5]

Seen from this perspective, mission means to mediate salvation to whole classes of destitute people, who are thought to be languishing without hope in faraway places because they lack sure access to eternal salvation. A number of now familiar modern images of mission were crafted and promulgated with just such a reading of the human condition outside of Christendom in mind. Thus, Leonard Woods went on to suggest in his historic address that the departing missionaries of the ABCFM were about to go abroad as beacons of light to benighted districts of encompassing gloom: "you will be burning and shining lights in regions of darkness and death."[6] A variation on this theme has depicted the missionary task as an attempt to cut "wide, deep channels through which the waters of life [could] flow" to billions perishing of thirst in the parched deserts of non-Christian lands.[7] An illustration drawn directly from Scripture that appeared with some frequency in the missionary literature of the nineteenth and early twentieth centuries invited readers and listeners to imagine great blocks of people in distant realms, who resembled in their profound state of decay the living dead described in Ezekiel 37. These were waiting for a prophet to arrive with the words of life, accompanied by an animating spirit that could resuscitate the dry bones littering the floor of their particular valley.[8] A different sense

4. Leonard Woods, "The Ordination Sermon," in *Pioneeers in Mission: The Early Missionary Ordination Sermons, Charges, and Instructions. A Source Book on the Rise of American Missions to the Heathen,* ed. R. Pierce Beaver (Grand Rapids: Eerdmans, 1966), p. 258 (emphasis in the original).

5. Woods, "Ordination Sermon," p. 259.

6. Woods, "Ordination Sermon," p. 267.

7. E.g., Donald A. McGavran, "Will Uppsala Betray the Two Billion?" in *The Conciliar-Evangelical Debate: The Crucial Documents, 1964-1976,* ed. Donald A. McGavran (Pasadena: William Carey Library, 1977), p. 233.

8. Woods makes only a passing reference to this passage (p. 263). Cf. Andrew Watson,

of geography shaped the rhetorical approach of James M. Thoburn, the celebrated Methodist pioneer missionary to India, who urged domestic audiences in America to envision a wretched and entirely helpless heathen world served by the missions as "the beggar at our gate," asking for help like Lazarus in front of the rich man's door.[9] In his own way, Bishop Thoburn was also attempting to overcome indifference to foreign missions among those back home who already enjoyed the benefits of the gospel.[10]

Images As Conceptual Focusing Devices

Sometimes, word-pictures are used to direct attention to certain aspects of evangelization or a particular approach to the methodology of mission that a writer wishes to emphasize. When this happens, images of mission become conceptual focusing devices. To highlight the crucial role to be played by domestic supporters of Protestant foreign missions, for example, William Carey is said to have professed his readiness in 1792 to descend into the deep "gold mine" that was India, provided that his senior Particular Baptist colleague Andrew Fuller was willing to stay behind and "hold the ropes."[11]

The American Mission in Egypt, second ed. (Pittsburgh: United Presbyterian Board of Publication, 1904), p. 58.

9. James M. Thoburn, *Missionary Addresses* (New York: Phillips and Hunt, 1888), pp. 127-47. Thoburn was careful to point out that he did not consider non-Christians to be completely "enbruted and debased" by nature, as though totally bereft of all goodness and virtue (p. 132). He insisted, however, that he had perceived in the course of his missionary service abroad a kind of spiritual destitution ruling over life in "heathen" nations, reinforced by the power of material poverty, two conditions which he thought rendered the most substantial benefits of the gospel "practically unknown" in those lands (p. 133). Thoburn exhorted what he considered to be a materially rich and spiritually blessed nation of American Protestants to share the whole of their God-given wealth with the needy multitudes put well within their physical reach by the advances of technology in the nineteenth century.

10. A twist on this motif has the non-Christian world calling out directly to Christians for help, in the manner of the man in Paul's dream who implored him to "come over to Macedonia and help us" (Acts 16:9). To see a pair of illustrations that very effectively represent this scene in contextualized terms, one may consult William R. Hutchison, *Errand to the World: American Protestant Thought and Foreign Missions* (Chicago: University of Chicago Press, 1987), pp. 10-11.

11. According to the popular story that circulated afterward, Fuller declared: "There is a gold mine in India, but it seems almost as deep as the centre of the earth, who will venture

The power of analogy to represent a key element of mission is likewise demonstrated in the figure of speech that Henry Venn used to describe the proper relationship of foreign mission societies to the native churches they were striving to create. Venn was general secretary of the Church Missionary Society (CMS) in Great Britain between 1846 and 1873. Throughout his influential career, Venn consistently pushed for the raising up of self-supporting, self-governing, and self-propagating indigenous churches as the ultimate goal of foreign missions. Thus, Venn urged the missionaries of the CMS to consider their work a necessary but temporary phase in the natural life cycle of mission, which he sometimes pictured as a long-term but finite construction project:

> Keep steadily before your minds what is the great object of a foreign mission. It is the raising up of a Native Church — self-supporting, self-governing, self-extending. The Mission is the scaffolding; the Native Church is the edifice. The removal of the scaffolding is the proof that the building is completed. You will have achieved the greatest success when you have taught your converts to do without you and can leave them, for fresh inroads into the "regions beyond."[12]

In this instance, Venn's image of mission is clearly more than a passing illustration. It sums up and vividly expresses a set of core convictions that essentially defined a vital part of the distinctive missiological stance he had adopted as his own. The same could be said of the sharply drawn image of mission advanced at the turn of the twentieth century by Presbyterian missioner Rena L. Hogg. Speaking especially to critics of American missionary practices in the Middle East, Hogg offered the following expla-

---

to explore it?" Carey reportedly replied, "I will go down, but remember that you must hold the ropes." I first encountered this anecdote in the suggestively titled (but anonymously written) *Vanguard of the Christian Army. Or, Sketches of Missionary Life* (London: Religious Tract Society, [1882]), p. 40. See also Gilbert Laws, *Andrew Fuller: Pastor, Theologian, Ropeholder* (London: Carey, 1942), p. 68.

12. Venn, "Instructions to Missionaries," *Church Missionary Intelligencer* 14, no. 5 [May 1863]: 112. On the identification of Venn as the author of these instructions, see Wilbert R. Shenk, "Henry Venn's Instructions to Missionaries," *Missiology* 5 (1977): 468. In other contexts, Venn referred to the last step of foreign mission work as the "euthanasia" of mission. For a thorough discussion of Venn's theory and the subsequent career of his most influential missionary principles, see C. Peter Williams, *The Ideal of the Self-Governing Church: A Study in Victorian Missionary Strategy* (Leiden: Brill, 1990).

nation of why she believed a Protestant message of salvation had to be offered first to the Orthodox Copts and then to the Muslim majority of Egypt:

> To turn the whole attack against Mohammedanism, to the neglect of these Copts, would be like attempting to cut down an oak with a sharp penknife while a blunt ax and a grindstone lay ready to hand. The early missionaries wisely planned to sharpen the blunt ax, stained with the rust of centuries, and then to guide its strokes towards the felling of that tree whose branches had so long spread darkness over the land and harbored every evil vice.[13]

Writing some twenty years later in the aftermath of the First World War, the Anglican Bishop of Jerusalem, Rennie MacInnes, chose to portray the situation of Protestant missions in the Middle East in quite different terms. According to MacInnes, Orthodox Christians in the Middle East were in truth active partisans and colleagues, not obstacles or liabilities, nor even passive tools, in the cause of Western missions to the Muslim world. Eastern Christians had had enormous tactical value, he asserted, as "soldiers who have guarded the outposts and suffered the first shocks and full force of the enemy's onslaught and, though all but exterminated and

13. Hogg's vivid figure is provided as an illustration within the biographical profile of fellow United Presbyterian missionary Martha J. McKown that Hogg contributed to a denominational mission study book. See Charles J. Watson, ed., *In the King's Service* (Philadelphia: Board of Foreign Missions of the United Presbyterian Church of North America, 1905), p. 60. The idea of Protestant missionaries using one or another of the ancient churches in the Middle East as a means to evangelize the Muslim world had been advanced long before Hogg wrote. See, for example, Eli Smith and H. G. O. Dwight, *The Researches of the Rev. E. Smith and Rev. H. G. O. Dwight in Armenia; Including a Journey through Asia Minor, and into Georgia and Persia, with a Visit to the Nestorian and Chaldean Christians in Oormiah and Salmas* (Boston: Crocker and Brewster, 1833), vol. 2, p. 265, who proposed that the Nestorians of Persia had the potential to become the "prop on which to rest the lever that will overturn the whole system of Muhammadan delusion." Elsewhere, Smith and Dwight characterized the "Oriental Christians" as an "open door," through which Western missionaries would find "an easy entrance into the heart of our enemy's territory" (vol. 2, pp. 334-35). A generation earlier, Claudius Buchanan had imagined a similar role for the Armenian community he found spread throughout the Middle East and Southwest Asia, provided that their "languid" zeal for mission could be properly stimulated. See Claudius Buchanan, *Christian Researches in Asia: With Notices on the Translation of the Scriptures into the Oriental Languages* (New York: Richard Scott, 1812), pp. 137-40.

cut off from all outside material support and moral encouragement, have yet held tight to their posts — such soldiers, however wounded and help-less, however limited in outlook and enterprise, and however lacking in re-source and initiative, can only inspire feelings of respect and veneration in the hearts of fellow-fighters in happier, more successful, and — let it not be forgotten — easier fields." In MacInnes's image of mission, constructed against the background of his wartime experience in the Middle East, the Protestant foreign missionary is the "younger, fresher fighter from the West," whose task it is to re-equip his "veteran brother fighter," these "worn and weathered pickets," who, thankfully, now find themselves in the condition of a "relieved garrison."[14]

Images As Narrative Intersections

The energetic prose of Rennie MacInnes points to a third way that mission images have typically functioned in the modern era. Sometimes, a given representation of mission attempts to capitalize on the synergy that can be generated when two or more stories are interwoven. Images of mission that operate in this manner could be called narrative intersections.[15] In the characterization of mission offered by Bishop MacInnes, at least three dif-ferent narrative components have been put into play. There is, first of all, the sequence of events that led to the establishment of his own ecclesiasti-cal position in Jerusalem, a century-long account of Anglican missionary activity in the region. Placed next to this story is a selective reading of the

14. Rennie MacInnes (in collaboration with Herbert Danby), "The Ancient Oriental Churches and Islam," in *The Moslem World of To-day,* ed. John R. Mott (New York: George H. Doran, 1925), pp. 263-65.

15. The work of Paul Ricoeur has sensitized me to this aspect of religious imagery. "Metaphorization," Ricoeur observes, can take place not only at the level of the sentence but also among texts, a phenomenon he calls "intertextuality." Ricoeur has explored the process of mutual interpretation that can take place between larger and smaller units of text (e.g., between parables and the genre of Gospel), a situation of interplay that allows each narrative strand to participate in a dynamic process of signification far exceeding the hermeneutical potential of any single one of them. Since visual images are a kind of text that must be inter-preted to discover their (possible) meaning(s), we can expect his analysis also to apply to them. See Ricoeur, "The Bible and the Imagination," in *Figuring the Sacred: Religion, Narra-tive, and Imagination,* ed. Mark I. Wallace, trans. David Pellauer (Minneapolis: Fortress, 1995), pp. 144-66.

history of Orthodox Christianity in the Middle East since the advent of Islam, which MacInnes understood to have been largely a chronicle of slow decline and increasing isolation from the rest of the Christian world. A third element surfaces in his reference to the Great War recently concluded in Europe, one major campaign of which had earlier swept through the Holy Land itself. MacInnes treated that conflict as a noble achievement — a story of heroism, fortitude, compassion, and camaraderie from which he apparently believed that supporters of Protestant mission efforts in the Middle East could learn much.

It is impossible to know now how many hearers in Bishop MacInnes's audience might have found insight or inspiration in this portrayal of mission. In any event, the impulse to interpret Christian mission through the rhetoric of war recurs so often in the literature (and hymnody!) of the modern missionary movement that it almost fails to surprise us today. It is not uncommon either to encounter visual explanations of mission from the last two centuries that eagerly borrowed from the stock vocabulary of imperialism and/or humanitarian uplift. When this happens, mission tends to be portrayed as a campaign of conquest, a crusade for progress, a means by which to refashion what are thought to be primitive cultures in the image of a more advanced West.

Some Graphic Examples of Narrative Intersections

I now will present several examples of graphic images or visual fields through which more than one narrative line seems to be passing. The first of these is a cover illustration published more than a century ago in *Harper's Weekly* (fig. 1).[16] The subject of the picture is a desert outpost of the White Fathers, a Roman Catholic missionary order founded in the nineteenth century by Charles Cardinal Lavigerie for the purpose of re-evangelizing North Africa. Lavigerie's passion for the whole of France's *mission civilisatrice* knew few boundaries, and often it was difficult to tell whether the Cardinal's diplomatic machinations in Algiers, Tunis, Paris,

---

16. *Harper's Weekly* 35, no. 1798 (June 6, 1891). On the inside of the magazine, F. Cunliffe Owen discussed the larger purposes of Lavigerie's plans for his missionary order; cf. "The Warrior Monks of the Sahara: A New Order of Chivalry" (p. 427). All the quotes in this paragraph come from Owen's one-page article.

9

HARPER'S WEEKLY
JOURNAL OF CIVILIZATION

Vol. XXXV.—No. 1798.
Copyright, 1891, by Harper & Brothers.
All Rights Reserved.

NEW YORK, SATURDAY, JUNE 6, 1891.

TEN CENTS A COPY.
INCLUDING SUPPLEMENT.

THE WARRIOR MONKS OF THE SAHARA.—Drawn by T. de Thulstrup.—[See Page 427.]

Fig. 1. Cover of *Harper's Weekly* (June 6, 1891), showing an outpost of the White Fathers in North Africa

and Rome were driven primarily by political or by religious motives.[17] As the article that accompanies this cover illustration explains, the Maltese cross embossed on the monks' tunics was deliberately meant to evoke the Crusaders' dream of re-establishing a robust form of Christianity in those places where it had been displaced by Islam centuries before. Suitably armed and trained for life in the desert, these "warrior monks of the Sahara" would be prepared "to fight for their lives," instead of "meekly bowing to receive the martyr's crown." Lavigerie's provisions for the missionaries' self-defense, however, were not devised solely to enhance their ability to survive in a hostile environment. His followers had already begun to establish a series of "fortified stations," strategically located astride the major caravan routes of North Africa. Lavigerie looked forward to the day when these would be ready to serve the two great philanthropic purposes he had in mind for them: the economic development of this vast barren wasteland and the interdiction of the slave traffic that incessantly passed through it. A nearly seamless interweaving of narratives is indicated in the declaration Lavigerie delivered at the consecration of the first postulants to join his order: "*En avant* for God, for France, and for humanity."

A second picture included here (fig. 2) at first glance seems not to have anything at all to do with Christian mission. In the mind of John R. Mott, however, this train-yard scene in China perfectly summarized the world missionary situation facing the Protestant churches of the West in 1910, and so it was included in the first book he published after the World Missionary Conference finished its work earlier that year in Edinburgh.[18]

---

17. J. Dean O'Donnell's study of Lavigerie's North African career highlights the way these two elements became mixed together in the course of the Cardinal's long career. See O'Donnell, *Lavigerie in Tunisia: The Interplay of Imperialist and Missionary* (Athens: University of Georgia Press, 1979). See also François Renault, *Cardinal Lavigerie, 1825-1892: Churchman, Prophet and Missionary*, trans. John O'Donohue (London: Athlone, 1994). It should be noted that militant imperialism by no means sums up or exemplifies the long and distinguished record of Christian witness given since Lavigerie's time by the Society of Missionaries of Africa, as the White Fathers are officially known. On this history, see Aylward Shorter, "Christian Presence in a Muslim Milieu: The Missionaries of Africa in the Maghreb and the Sahara," *IBMR* 28 (2004): 159-64.

18. This is the final illustration included in John R. Mott, *The Decisive Hour of Christian Missions* (New York: Student Volunteer Movement for Foreign Missions, 1910), facing p. 222. Several other industrial scenes are also reproduced in the book, and a foldout map attached to the back cover documents the worldwide "commercial expansion of the non-Christian world." A highlighted feature of the map shows a network of "existing and pro-

Fig. 2. "A Chinese Wheelbarrow and Its Rival" (early twentieth century)

For Mott, railroad technology epitomized the irresistible power of the culture that had produced it. The spiritual heart of that culture was assumed to be the Christian religion. The fact that a proud but backward nation had allowed this symbol of foreign intrusion into its cultural space signaled to Mott that the long-awaited transformation of China had begun, a wholesale movement of renovation that he anticipated would extend well beyond matters of commerce. Mott's generation of mission strategists fully expected the traditional religions of the East to share the certain fate of the primitive wheelbarrow pictured here. To Mott and other leaders of the Student Volunteer Movement he headed, these two stories of material and religious progress were not simply parallel developments. Indeed, they were thought to be closely and providentially intertwined.

A final example of narrative strands crossing paths in an image of mission comes from a contemporary (rather than historical) trend in thinking about cross-cultural evangelism. Much attention has been fo-

---

jected" railways in Europe, Asia, Africa, and Australia. Mott chaired the Edinburgh 1910 conference, a landmark gathering of the world's missionary leadership at which the strategic situation of the church was exhaustively discussed.

cused recently on the problem of how to conduct mission activities in countries whose governments severely restrict some or all forms of public Christian witness, usually in deference to the wishes of a non-Christian majority population. In one sense, such conditions have always been a part of the church's experience, reaching all the way back to its inception in the sometimes acutely hostile pagan environment of the Roman Empire. Four classic responses to this situation, by no means mutually exclusive, still obtain: quietude for the sake of social peace or to safeguard the institutional interests of the Christian community; intercessory prayer on behalf of non-Christian neighbors and governments; limited forms of social witness that demonstrate gospel values and community spirit without offending cultural sensitivities; attempts to proselytize in open defiance of the authorities, knowing that persecution or martyrdom may be the result.

A new wrinkle, introduced in the second half of the twentieth century, has appeared in the notion that mission in these circumstances could also be undertaken as an operation of covert resistance to non-Christian ideologies. In fact, it is becoming increasingly common, especially in conservative evangelical circles in the West, to envision foreign mission in so-called "restricted-access" countries as a kind of secret counter-intelligence campaign. The accompanying figure (fig. 3), published recently by the World Evangelization Research Center, illustrates the point well by pulling together in one place a distinctive set of terms for missionaries, drawn quite obviously from the thought-world of espionage.[19]

In this emerging image of mission, cross-cultural Christian workers are invited to conceive of themselves as "moles," "couriers," "smugglers," and "clandestine" agents. At the same time, their citizen-collaborators might take up the roles of "undergrounders," "messengers," "guerrillas," and "unregistered" operatives. We have here the raw material with which to fill out and extend Ralph D. Winter's picture of mission as a "lock-picking business," by means of which one penetrates or gets inside of strange and alien cultures that steadfastly resist more straightforward methods of evangelization.[20]

19. David B. Barrett and Todd M. Johnson, *World Christian Trends, AD 30–AD 2200: Interpreting the Annual Christian Megacensus* (Pasadena: William Carey Library, 2001), p. 61.

20. Ralph D. Winter, "Are 90% of Our Missionaries Serving in the Wrong Places?" *Mission Frontiers* 15, no. 5-6 (May-June 1993): 29-30. More recently, Winter has depicted the task of mission to unreached people groups as an exercise in "locksmithing" made necessary

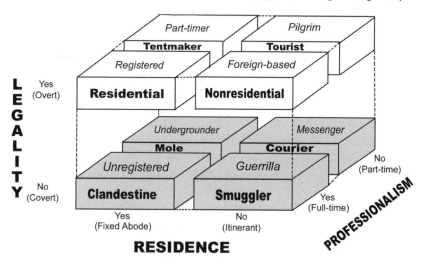

Fig. 3. "Intersecting Narratives: Mission and the Cold War"

The narrative roots of this approach to mission appear to reach back to the Cold War. A formative influence along the way, I believe, was supplied by the pseudonymous Brother Andrew, an ardent anti-Communist whose exploits behind the Iron Curtain were recounted in a best-selling tale of daring and intrigue published under the title of *God's Smuggler*.[21] With the collapse of the Soviet Union in 1991, those most likely to think of mission in terms of an underground battle to be waged against dark geopolitical forces began to turn their primary attention to China and the Muslim-majority nations that dominate the "10/40 Window" framing North Africa and South Asia.[22] One

_____

by closed cultural doors. See Ralph D. Winter, "Editorial Comment," *Mission Frontiers* 24, no. 6 (November-December 2002): 5.

21. A thirty-fifth anniversary edition of *God's Smuggler* was recently issued. The publisher claims on the cover that ten million copies of the book have been printed since its initial publication in 1967.

22. The "10/40 Window" is a geographical construct (10 degrees to 40 degrees north of the equator, from the west coast of Africa to East Asia) that was first applied to the goal of world evangelization within the Lausanne Movement. A majority of the world's "least evan-

is struck by how closely this shift has tracked the preoccupations of political conservatives in the United States since the fall of the Berlin Wall, a development that reinforces the sense that in this image of mission more than one powerful narrative is exerting its force.

Wanted: New Images of Mission

Modern-era images of mission of the kind featured in the first section of this introduction no longer exercise the same breadth of appeal they once did, despite the fact that certain parts of the church may still find them quite attractive. For this reason, an increasing number of missiologists today, representing a wide variety of denominational backgrounds, are calling for new forms of mission imagery. Representative of this trend is David Bosch's view that "mission must be understood and undertaken in an imaginatively new manner today."[23] According to Bosch, the church is being driven to generate new forms of mission imagery now because it faces a profoundly challenging "contemporary crisis."[24] "From all sides the Christian mission is under attack, even from within its own ranks," a fact that makes it necessary "to find an entirely new image today."[25] The "time of testing" confronting the church at the turn of the twenty-first century has brought with it a confusing season of uncertainty. If Bosch is correct in his belief that a "paradigm shift" in thinking about the church and its mission is already underway, then old assumptions and the images that represented them need to be re-examined, and new visual expressions of mission theology must be developed. In the context of an emerging postmodern world, Bosch contends, the church has no choice but to grasp and confront its new situation.[26]

Among the "old" assumptions that no longer seem sustainable to many in the church are an uncritical belief in human progress, a sense of self-assuredness regarding the superiority of Western culture (and of West-

---

gelized" ethnic people groups live in the area defined by this strategic concept. See Richard D. Love, "10/40 Window," in *EDWM*, p. 938, and Robert T. Coote, "'AD 2000' and the '10/40 Window': A Preliminary Assessment," *IBMR* 24 (2000): 160-66.

23. David J. Bosch, *Transforming Mission: Paradigm Shifts in Theology of Mission* (Maryknoll, N.Y.: Orbis, 1991), p. 367.

24. Bosch, *Transforming Mission*, pp. 1-8.

25. Bosch, *Transforming Mission*, p. 518.

26. Bosch, *Transforming Mission*, pp. 181-89, 349-67.

ern forms of the church), and an expectation that Christianity is about to overwhelm and completely crowd out all the world's other religious traditions. Such convictions undergirded and helped to sustain the great surge of energy in the West for mission that coalesced in the wake of the Enlightenment and thrived well into the twentieth century. A truly globalized Christian community has come into being as a result of these efforts. While few regret the wonderful diversity that now marks the world church today, many are raising questions about the historical processes by which this welcome outcome was realized. Also suspect are some of the attitudes concerning non-Christians and their cultures that were held by many Western foreign missionaries in the modern period. In the Orthodox church and in Catholic teaching since Vatican II, and for most ecumenical Protestants today, the pronounced ethnocentrism of many in the modern missionary movement casts serious doubt on the enduring validity of the theological perspectives that shaped earlier practices of Christian mission.

A similar change of fashion is underway with respect to images of mission. Objections are heard when figures of speech like the ones cited above are used today. On what basis could Christians imagine that entire populations are living in total darkness, without any knowledge whatsoever of God's reality? Is it now acceptable to think of mission, following William Carey, as a mining exercise in which those being evangelized are treated like precious but basically inert objects of Christian compassion? By what right could one church presume to select and use another as its willing or unwilling tool for evangelization, as Rena Hogg suggested that Protestants in Egypt were meant to do with respect to the Coptic Orthodox Church? Given the horrific legacy of armed conflict in the twentieth century, what would possess anyone today to associate warfare with the Good News of Jesus Christ? To the extent that questions like these hit home, the power of such images to sway and convict tends to evaporate.

Over the past decade, several creative efforts have been made to identify new images of mission that might speak more directly to the church's contemporary situation. Among these is a thoughtful article published by Stephen Bevans, in which he sets out to discover images for mission that could enable us to "speak in a more adequate way about who missionaries are and what they are supposed to do."[27] Reflecting on the U.S. Catholic

---

27. Stephen Bevans, "Seeing Mission through Images," *Missiology* 19 (1991): 46. The quotations that follow in this paragraph are taken from pp. 46-47 of Bevans's article.

Bishops' 1986 pastoral statement, "To the Ends of the Earth," Bevans argues that missionaries need to understand themselves and be understood by others through different images than those used in the past. This is necessary "because the world in which they do their service has fundamentally changed." Thus, instead of seeing missionaries as "apostles," "martyrs," "heroes," or the "shock troops" of the church, one might better understand the missionary as a "treasure hunter, teacher, prophet, guest, stranger, partner, migrant worker and/or ghost." So, for instance, the missionary as treasure hunter not only comes to another culture to give and dispense, but also expects to find things of great value. Or the missionary as partner does not just do good deeds *for* others, but works alongside them in ministry. Or the missionary as ghost is always aware of the fact that eventually his or her work will have to be surrendered into the care of others who may have a different vision for its future development. The missionary as ghost, Bevans suggests, does not hang on but prepares to move on when the time is right.

Donald E. Messer proposes that the overriding priority for Christian mission today is to avoid "world havoc" by creating "a world house."[28] Accordingly, he has sought to reconceptualize mission through images that promote good stewardship of the earth and the building of positive relationships among people of diverse backgrounds. In Messer's vision for mission, ministries of conversion, church-centered strategies, and all forms of triumphal, monarchical, and patriarchal language are to be avoided when visualizing Christian mission, because all of these contribute to division and acrimony among people (in other words, "world havoc"). In their place, the church is urged to adopt the hopeful symbol of the rainbow, the ideal of God's eternal reign, and a uniting ethic that promotes the doing of good deeds in defiance of oppressive powers (in other words, joining the "conspiracy of goodness"). The basic choice that must be made in the present age of nuclear threat, Messer asserts, is the one that requires Christians to set aside matters of salvation history in favor of a theology of creation that affirms the earth and all of its inhabitants. To opt for the latter means here to put oneself in "a covenant of global gardeners," "a collegiality of bridge builders," "a company of star[fish] throwers," and "a community of fence movers."[29]

---

28. Donald E. Messer, *A Conspiracy of Goodness: Contemporary Images of Christian Mission* (Nashville: Abingdon, 1992).

29. Messer, *Conspiracy of Goodness*, pp. 65-66. Messer is concerned most of all to see

Bruce F. Gannaway has put forward a third set of mission images, which he believes will be more appropriate for the church's changed context for mission.[30] This time, the presenting problem is identified as the persistent tendency of missionaries to inflate their own importance when imagining the roles they hope to fulfill as sharers of the gospel with non-Christians. In particular, Gannaway takes issue with any image of mission that carries with it "an aura of authority." Among the images no longer appropriate for the church to use are ones in which cross-cultural missionaries are shown assuming the roles of evangelist, teacher, healer, and church leader. Far more agreeable, Gannaway suggests, are images of the missionary as "partner," "[fellow] disciple," "diaconal [servant]," "co-worker," and "companion." As I have shown elsewhere, the determinative criterion that holds this collection of images together is the value of cooperation or partnership.[31]

An Attempt at Another Approach

My intention up to this point was to present two sets of data that pertain to the making of mission images today. In the first section of the chapter, I focused on the kinds of images that typically enjoyed wide support through the course of the modern missionary movement. At the same time, attention was given to the different ways in which images of mission generally have functioned as motivators and as interpretive constructs. Then, I turned to consider the views of some articulate critics of past trends in the depiction of mission. In response to a rising sense that new images are now needed because the church's context for mission is different from what it was in the nineteenth and early twentieth centuries, several specific proposals have been offered for the re-envisioning of Christian mission. Three of these were described in some detail, because I believe that together they tell us something important about current thinking on mission imagery, at least among those most committed to an ecumenical perspective on the theology of mission.

---

exclusivist theologies replaced by interreligious programs of social action based on environmental awareness.

30. Bruce F. Gannaway, "Mission: Commitment to God's Hopeful Vision," *Church and Society* 84, no. 1 (September/October 1993): 42-50.

31. See Stanley H. Skreslet, "The Empty Basket of Presbyterian Mission: Limits and Possibilities of Partnership," *IBMR* 19 (1995): 98-106.

For my own part, I agree with those critics who say it is impossible for the church today simply to take over an earlier age's approach to mission. I am not surprised that in ecumenically-engaged churches (the perspective from which I write), diminishing constituencies now respond to images of the missionary as explorer, pioneer, hero, adventurer, founder of institutions, and civilizer of barbarian races. The problem is not just a matter of shifting visual tastes. The once-venerable conceptual foundations on which these and similar images used to rest have substantially eroded over the past half-century among conciliar Christians. I count myself among those who cannot use many of the images that so moved hearts and captured imaginations in a bygone Romantic era of Christian mission, because several key assumptions that these images expressed so vividly then no longer seem to fit. More specifically, I cannot affirm the premise that Christianity is a territorial religion, such that mission could be pictured as an act of expansion from Christian nations to non-Christian lands. Nor do I agree that missionaries have a right to impose on new communities of faith a foreign hierarchy of normative cultural values (a prerogative implicitly claimed by all would-be civilizers, religious or secular). Further, in light of the sometimes-heavy legacy of mission history, I believe it inappropriate as a rule to apply military language to the concept of Christian mission.[32] To do so means to link the mission of the church to acts of coercion and violence. Mission images drawn from warfare, even when attempts are made to spiritualize them, inevitably communicate values at odds with the gospel. On this point especially, the integrity of what we attempt to do in the name of Christ is at stake.

To agree with the critics' diagnosis of the problem, however, does not necessarily commit one to any of the remedies that have been prescribed thus far. As I see it, the three groups of images briefly described above (from Bevans, Messer, and Gannaway) function most effectively as responses to the mistakes of the past. They do not seem to me to represent foundations substantial enough to sustain a fully rounded theology of Christian mission capable of carrying the church into the future.[33] The re-

32. On this issue, I am in agreement with the "Statement on Mission Language" recently formulated by the Evangelical Fellowship of India. See *IRM* 90 (2001): 190-91.

33. In the case of Bevans, it may be that his treatment is just too brief to allow for the development of the deeper foundations he may be assuming for this set of images. I, for one, hope that he will return to this subject in the near future and expand on his initial analysis and reflection.

active quality of the proposals offered by Gannaway and Messer is especially pronounced. As each has explained, their preferred images of mission have been derived on the basis of what they negate.

Thus, Gannaway reaches for images of cooperation because these stand in opposition to earlier images that seemed to imply autonomous missionary authority. This may be a sound move to the extent that it helps to correct for the abuse of power by missionaries in the past, but will this procedure lead us to a positive grasp of the fullness of Christian mission in the present? Likewise, Messer begins by forswearing approaches to mission that might result in interfaith conflict or otherwise detract from efforts to promote world peace. His particular aim is to dissociate the church from destructive forms of proselytism, a goal that should be widely embraced by all who hope to practice faithful witness in the way of Jesus Christ. One has to wonder, though, what might be left of the church's *distinctive* calling once it has been determined that potentially divisive issues of salvation history are moot in the twenty-first century, that a concern for the establishment and growth of the church is entirely beside the point in mission, or that conversion to a living personal relationship with Jesus Christ could be practically a matter of indifference to contemporary missioners. From the days of the apostles until now, such considerations have served to distinguish Christian mission from more general programs of benevolence and altruism.

A desire to participate in the renewal of mission imagery lies at the heart of this book. Some misgivings about the results achieved thus far, just noted, have prompted a search for another method by which to carry out this crucial task. I am particularly keen to see the New Testament play a more direct role in the generation of mission images, believing that this set of foundational texts has been underutilized in the recent past with respect to this objective. My hope is that a way could be found for the New Testament to suggest an initial framework for theological reflection on Christian mission, which might then be developed and interpreted in a variety of contexts, with specific cultural and historical considerations in mind. To the extent that such a framework might be inherently visual, its potential to nourish the revitalization of mission imagery will undoubtedly be enhanced.

Why privilege the New Testament in this way? First of all, because the ties that bind the New Testament and Christian mission are uniquely deep and enduring. Although it would be misleading to characterize this group of writings as a set of missionary tracts or sermons, it is nevertheless true that they were prepared especially for nascent communities of faith that understood themselves to be set in highly charged contexts of missionary challenge. If nothing else, the dynamic encounter taking place everywhere around the first-century church between the gospel and Hellenistic culture may be recognized as a missionary factor that decisively shaped Christianity and its emerging canonical corpus in the apostolic and sub-apostolic eras.[34] Just as important was the need of the early Christian community to determine its relationship to Judaism and the basis on which missionary appeals to the synagogue could be offered.

Thus, the New Testament can be seen as a *product* of mission, but, at the same time, we can appreciate how it has served the church as the preeminent *means* of Christian witness over the past two millennia. No other text on earth has been translated so many times into such a wide variety of languages as the New Testament, and almost always the initial spur for this activity has been a desire to communicate the Good News across cultures. Along the way, the entire Bible (Old and New Testaments) has provided the church with a self-renewing source of faith language and inspiration for mission that has proved so far to be inexhaustible. As the biblical scholars Donald Senior and Carroll Stuhlmueller have observed, the capacity of Scripture "to suffuse the mind and heart of the church with a vision" for mission, undertaken in hope, is one of its most vital functions.[35] Indeed, the ability of the Bible to stimulate the theological imagination of the church as it moves across every kind of cultural boundary and through time has been demonstrated too often to count. As we engage the problem of reconceptualizing mission suggested by Bosch and others, there is every reason to expect that the New Testament will confirm once again its continuing relevance and poietic vigor.

Of course, there is more than one possible way to approach the New Testament as a primary resource for images of mission. The particular interpretive device I propose to use here will focus on the missionary praxis of Jesus' followers, whose stories are included in the New Testament. Hence the particular wording of the subtitle given to this book: "New Testament Images of *Disciples* in Mission." My chief concern will be to identify and then to illustrate the leading roles in mission assumed by the first

---

34. Here and elsewhere in this study, "sub-apostolic" refers to the first generation in the church to come after the time of the apostles.

35. Donald Senior and Carroll Stuhlmueller, *The Biblical Foundations for Mission* (Maryknoll, N.Y.: Orbis, 1983), p. 343.

few generations of Jesus' disciples, as these have been made known to us through the writings of the New Testament.

I know of no other study devoted to the New Testament and mission that has employed this strategy of investigation. It is far more common for surveys of mission in the New Testament to proceed on a book-by-book basis in order to distill a series of New Testament perspectives on mission ("the mission theology of Matthew," and so on), which are then usually synthesized by means of a unifying theme or particular definition of mission. The work of Donald Senior already cited above remains a widely respected, although not unchallenged, example of this approach.[36] Ferdinand Hahn conducted a similar kind of analysis for an earlier generation of biblical scholars.[37] In just the last few years, another three volumes have been published that more or less apply the same methodology to the whole of the New Testament, albeit with a variety of ends in view.[38] Additionally,

36. To clarify, Senior wrote the New Testament section of *The Biblical Foundations for Mission,* while Carroll Stuhlmueller analyzed the Old Testament material. The concluding chapter of the book was co-authored. Senior and Stuhlmueller anchor their complete set of "biblical foundations" for Christian mission in the idea of universal salvation, which they see most fully realized in the church's mission to the Gentiles. As they put it in the book's introduction, "we are concerned with how the universal mission became an accepted part of the Christian scriptural perspective" (p. 4). A major aim of their work, therefore, is to show how the Old Testament prepared the way for a more explicit application of this principle in the aftermath of Jesus' crucifixion. A critical view of *Biblical Foundations* is offered in Andreas J. Köstenberger, "The Place of Mission in New Testament Theology: An Attempt to Determine the Significance of Mission within the Scope of the New Testament's Message As a Whole," *Missiology* 27 (1999): 354-56.

37. Ferdinand Hahn, *Mission in the New Testament* (Naperville: Allenson, 1965). Hahn was less concerned than Senior and Stuhlmueller to bring the various perspectives on mission he found in the New Testament under one thematic roof. In order to unify his study, he pointed instead to recurring problems that the church in mission had to face in the apostolic era, like the Jewish-Gentile question and the relationship of the church to its mission. Of course, the diversity of views within the New Testament on the theology of mission that Hahn, in the end, leaves side by side constitutes an implicit theme on its own. Legrand and Bosch, cited below, will develop this idea more fully after Hahn.

38. In William J. Larkin Jr. and Joel F. Williams, eds., *Mission in the New Testament: An Evangelical Approach* (Maryknoll, N.Y.: Orbis, 1998), the verbal proclamation of the Word is characterized as the "primary task" of New Testament mission (pp. 241-44). Johannes Nissen's survey, *New Testament and Mission: Historical and Hermeneutical Perspectives* (Frankfurt am Main: Peter Lang, 1999), begins and ends with questions about dialogue (both between missiology and biblical studies and among the religions). Andreas J. Köstenberger and Peter T. O'Brien, *Salvation to the Ends of the Earth: A Biblical Theology of*

the missiologists Lucien Legrand and David Bosch have put forward substantive proposals for evaluating biblical data on mission, although neither attempted to treat each book in the New Testament.[39] Most comprehensive of all is the massive historical and exegetical study of mission in the New Testament recently published by Eckhard J. Schnabel.[40]

Given the sheer number of general surveys devoted to the Bible and mission already in circulation, one may perhaps be excused for not immediately wanting to add to this collection. Another disincentive that pertains more directly to the goals and methods of the present study is that this angle of approach tends to remain highly abstract and analytical, rather than visual. This is the case even with Bosch, in spite of his professed intention to seek after new images of mission. What he eventually draws out of the New Testament is a series of "salvific events" that are centered on Christ: the incarnation, the cross, the resurrection, the ascension, Pentecost (understood as Christ's continuing presence through the Spirit), and the Parousia.[41] Bosch's concern to represent Christian mission as a

---

Mission (Downers Grove, Ill.: InterVarsity, 2001), seek to confirm by their analysis that "God acts coherently and purposefully in history" (p. 20), meaning in their case that God has a definite plan of salvation in mind.

39. After examining "the twin poles of Israel's mission" (i.e., election, on the one hand, and concern for the nations, on the other), Lucien Legrand provides an account of Jesus' pre-resurrection mission in the Synoptics, next to which he puts the outlooks found in Acts, the letters of Paul, and the Gospel of John. Bosch, *Transforming Mission,* is even more selective, choosing to concentrate his discussion on Matthew, Luke-Acts, and Paul as "representative" New Testament texts (pp. 54-55). For different reasons, Legrand and Bosch both seek to establish that a variety of still relevant perspectives on mission are contained in the New Testament. In Legrand's case, the fact of this diversity is put into conversation with several other elements that point to the unity of God's mission in the New Testament, like the singular Word that creates and sustains one consecrated people, who together constitute the body of Christ. Legrand's overall purpose is nicely captured in the title given to the English translation of his work: *Unity and Plurality: Mission in the Bible,* trans. Robert R. Barr (Maryknoll, N.Y.: Orbis, 1990) (originally published as *Le Dieu qui vient: la mission dans la Bible*). For Bosch, the several approaches to mission he finds juxtaposed to each other in the New Testament point forward to the phenomenon of shifting paradigms in the church's theology of mission, a major organizing idea in his book.

40 Schnabel, *Early Christian Mission,* 2 vols. (Downers Grove, Ill.: InterVarsity, 2004). This is an exhaustive review of the relevant historical data that pertain to mission in the apostolic era, presented in the style of Adolf von Harnack's classic study of a century ago, *The Mission and Expansion of Christianity in the First Three Centuries.*

41. Bosch, *Transforming Mission,* pp. 512-18.

multifaceted undertaking is well served by the comprehensive interpretive framework based on the New Testament that he adopts, but the approach does not seem to suggest anything specific about how to portray mission.

A second well-traveled scholarly pathway connecting the New Testament to mission passes directly through the district of ecclesiology. Studies of the church and its background in the New Testament naturally touch on issues of mission, since the Christian community has, from the beginning, understood itself not only in terms of a distinctive identity but also with reference to its purpose in the world.[42] An advantage of this approach to the question of mission and the New Testament is immediately felt in the wealth of evocative scriptural imagery that becomes available to the interpreter of mission once the decision is made to focus one's hermeneutical spyglass on the sails of the church.[43]

John Driver and Robert Kysar are two scholars who have recently attempted to capitalize on this methodology in order to spark their own re-evaluations of the church's self-understanding. Driver sees the "true identity and role" of the church as "God's contrast-society in the world," indicated in the biblical concepts of pilgrimage, the new order, peoplehood, and transformation.[44] Kysar proposes looking at the church as a "community of faith on the way home stumbling in the light," a composite image he constructs out of a series of key New Testament metaphors.[45] Kysar agrees with Driver that a changed context in the world requires the church to update its use of imagery. Notably, both reach back to the Bible to begin this process of renewal.[46]

A different kind of inquiry is implied in the decision to feature here disciples in mission rather than the church as a whole. Instead of highlight-

42. A classic study of the Bible and mission undertaken as an exercise in ecclesiology is Johannes Blauw, *The Missionary Nature of the Church: A Survey of the Biblical Theology of Mission* (New York: McGraw-Hill, 1962).

43. Paul S. Minear, *Images of the Church in the New Testament* (Philadelphia: Westminster, 1960), estimates that there are between eighty and one hundred different images of the church provided in the New Testament (p. 28).

44. John Driver, *Images of the Church in Mission* (Scottdale: Herald, 1997), p. 22.

45. Robert Kysar, *Stumbling in the Light: New Testament Images for a Changing Church* (St. Louis: Chalice, 1999).

46. Besides the work of Driver and Kysar, we also have a series of articles by Donald Senior, Norman E. Thomas, and Janet Carroll on "Images of Church — Images of Mission," which was the theme chosen for the 1994 annual meeting of the American Society of Missiology. See *Missiology* 23 (1995): 3-42.

ing corporate images of outreach in the apostolic era, our concentration will focus on embodiments of mission depicted in the New Testament that took place at a more personal level. This is not an attempt to promote individualism in mission. The church as a gathered community of faith has its own distinctive calling that is more than the sum of its members' individual efforts. Yet, within the comprehensive framework suggested by the church's identity as the body of Christ, there are specific roles to be played by disciples, who act in the name of Jesus on behalf of the community. In my view, these two perspectives on the church's mission in the New Testament, communal and individual, are complementary.[47] Each has something important to contribute to a biblical theology of mission. For our purposes, the chief difference between these two kinds of New Testament mission images lies in the fact that they have not received an equal amount of scholarly attention recently. The analysis that follows will attempt to rectify this imbalance. My aim is to bring into view a broad selection of distinctive New Testament images of mission in which disciples of Jesus are shown carrying on the work that he began, albeit in light of the resurrection and in circumstances he did not seem entirely to have anticipated.

For the sake of clarity, a few other matters of procedure and definition require some comment before our discussion can move forward to its next step. The first concerns the designation "disciple." To whom does this term apply? As a rule, when reference is made here to disciples of Jesus in the New Testament, the assumption will be that this category includes more than the innermost core of those who followed after him.[48] The "twelve disciples" referred to in the Gospels represent a specific and important subset of this larger group. Among all those drawn to Jesus during the public phase of his ministry, "the Twelve" were the ones to whom he granted the privilege of observing his behavior at close range and with whom he shared the greatest degree of intimacy. On occasion, these few even received special instruction from Jesus to which the larger crowds of

47. In 1 Corinthians 12, Paul shows how different spiritual gifts empowered a variety of particular ministries within the early church (e.g., of apostles, prophets, teachers, and so on), which together were encompassed by the figure of one body.

48. My approach here resembles the position adopted by John P. Meier, *A Marginal Jew: Rethinking the Historical Jesus,* vol. 3: *Companions and Competitors* (New York: Doubleday, 2001), pp. 1-285, where he describes three "concentric circles" (p. 5) within the mass of those who followed after Jesus: crowds — disciples — Twelve. I will develop this idea further in Chapter Three.

devoted followers and curious onlookers were not privy. It should not be supposed, however, that only those disciples who would later be reckoned apostles by the church were capable of emulating Jesus' missionary example, either by participating in his activities while he still lived or by carrying on his cause after the crucifixion. The story of the mission of the seventy (or seventy-two) recorded in Luke 10, if reliable, would be enough to establish that Jesus himself thought in terms of an apostolate that encompassed many more than just a select company of experts and specialists in the field of evangelism.[49] In any event, the literature associated with the early Christian movement shows many lesser-known figures working beside or in support of the heroes of apostolic faith, whose achievements and leadership functions are so obviously featured in the Gospels and Acts. The contributions of these so-called "minor" disciples to the mission of the church should not be overlooked.

Yet, not everyone in the New Testament who attached herself or himself to Jesus or joined the fellowship of the earliest church may be said to have been a missionary. For this reason, I do not intend to give equal attention to all the stories of those in the New Testament who appear to have been followers of Jesus' Way. My interest falls more particularly on a smaller group of New Testament characters, the ones shown demonstrating trust in Jesus by sharing their faith with others. Such are the followers of Jesus I have in mind when I suggest looking at New Testament images of *disciples in mission.*

---

49. I am assuming that this story is not a complete fabrication on the part of Luke, who alone among the four Evangelists included it in his Gospel. The historicity of a missionary-sending event during Jesus' lifetime involving more than the Twelve, however, is not easy to prove. For example, Joseph A. Fitzmyer understands this episode to have come to Luke via the sayings-source he shared with Matthew (i.e., "Q"), but considers it to be a second form (parallel to Mark 6:6-13) of a single missionary discourse, which was connected with the sending of the Twelve. See Joseph A. Fitzmyer, *The Gospel according to Luke (10–24): Introduction, Translation, and Notes* (Garden City, N.Y.: Doubleday, 1985), pp. 81, 842. If Fitzmyer is correct, then the number of those sent out by Jesus in Luke 10 (seventy or seventy-two) is an invention of the Third Evangelist, created in order to preserve both traditional versions he received of the same story of missionary sending. On the other hand, no one has been able to prove that Jesus did *not* send out a second group of disciples on mission, as asserted in Luke's Gospel. This is acknowledged in Meier, *A Marginal Jew,* vol. 3, p. 163, leading him to formulate the following carefully worded conclusion: "I think it more probable than not that *at least* the Twelve were sent out on mission, whether or not other disciples were dispatched as well" (emphasis in original).

The question of exactly how these disciples put their own under-standings of mission into practice may be left somewhat open at this stage, since this is precisely the subject of the study that follows. Nevertheless, a preliminary definition of Christian mission can and should be provided now, in order for the reader to know how I intend to sift through the New Testament data and then highlight some of the materials found there. By "mission," I mean acting in the name of Jesus Christ with the intention of communicating or demonstrating to others something substantive about the Good News that defines the believing fellowship of the church. At the center of this Good News is a *message* about what God has done for all hu-manity through the life, death, and resurrection of Jesus Christ and a *com-mitment to live* in ways that publicly affirm the transforming power of God's love. Such communications could be verbal, in which case acts of gospel proclamation might figure prominently, but the idea of *demonstrat-ing Good News* extends well beyond this narrower definition of missionary action. Mission in the New Testament is also understood here to include the element of *invitation* — whether by word or deed — whereby followers of Jesus extended his call to others to be in relationship with him and to celebrate his sovereignty as Lord over the whole creation.

On the basis of this definition, a multifarious picture of early Chris-tian mission will emerge from the exegetical work presented in the chap-ters that follow. Complexity is to be expected, since progress in the spread of Christianity did not proceed everywhere at the same rate and, in differ-ent circumstances, first-century efforts at outreach to Jews and Gentiles certainly took on more than one tightly controlled form. Significantly, early Christian believers shared their faith while functioning in a variety of contexts and overlapping social relationships, including business, govern-ment, travel, friendship, kinship, and the extended household of the fam-ily. Fortunately, the literature of the New Testament is subtle enough to convey more than just a hint of the exciting and unpredictable atmosphere of possibility that surrounded mission in the most intense period of wit-ness and growth the church has ever known. The challenge here will be to capture the dynamic and pluriform character of mission in the New Testa-ment, while also recognizing that certain patterns of interaction recurred and so lend a discernible shape to apostolic-era missionary encounters.

The several mission images that follow will not be arranged accord-ing to any hierarchy of relative validity or importance. I begin with the ac-tion of announcement only because I suspect that this idea lies at the heart of what a majority of people inside and outside the church has long assumed to be an essential feature of mission. In other words, I intend to start where I think many of my readers already find themselves. Likewise, the last of the images presented here is not meant to be taken as the capstone of the series. In the end, what we will have in front of us is a diverse array of mission images, a collection of approaches to Christian witnessing, each one of which can lay claim to substantial support in the New Testament. The theological implications possibly indicated by this result will be discussed at the conclusion of this study.

Finally, a few words more regarding methodology may now be added to explain how this particular collection of New Testament mission imagery came together. That is to say, what will these different images have in common? Several key criteria account for the selection that has been made. As noted already, my intention has been to emphasize the personal dimension of faith-sharing, as practiced by followers of Jesus in the New Testament. Thus, at the center of each mission image is the figure of a disciple, meaning a person committed to Jesus, who is engaging others in Jesus' name with the claims and promises of the gospel. These interactions did not unfold in a haphazard or random fashion. Certain social roles assumed by disciples in mission appear to stand out and so are highlighted here. Care has been taken to ensure that each image is framed broadly in terms of an action, which can be represented, if not entirely explained, by an underlying verbal idea (thus announcing, sharing, interpreting, shepherding, and building/planting). I am convinced that by giving priority to actions and patterns of human communication the resulting images will be more sharply drawn, more vivid, and more visual than would have been the case had I focused on values and attitudes, which tend to remain abstract.

I have also paid attention to the distinctiveness of each image. It is not my intention to offer a series of small variations on the same basic theme. In order for an image to be included here, it must be possible to distinguish it in a fundamental way from the rest of the collection. To enhance this aspect of the presentation, a different perspective on social space is developed for each image of mission. Thus, for example, mission as an act of announcement seems to imply a face-to-face orientation among the parties involved, while the notion of sharing Christ with friends is probably best pictured as a side-by-side encounter. To the extent that each image can be distinguished from the rest, the collection as a whole becomes more comprehensive and, therefore, a more adequate description of New Testament patterns of mission. If even a fair degree of the rich texture of mission portrayed in the New Testament can be represented by these means, then this project will have achieved at least a small measure of success.

In the Chapters That Follow . . .

It may prove helpful now, before concluding these preliminary remarks, to provide a brief overview of the five images of disciples in mission around which this book is organized. I propose also at this point to indicate with broad strokes how these images will be treated in the following chapters, so that the reader will have an idea in advance how each one fits roughly into the larger point of view being put forward. The introduction will then draw to a close with some comments about the different tasks (exegetical, theological, and illustrative) that must be engaged in each chapter, if these various images of mission are to become anything more than quick sketches without texture.

Five Images of Disciples in Mission

1. Announcing Good News   Like heralds dispatched by an authoritative ruler, some disciples in the New Testament clearly understood their missionary vocation to be a call to follow Jesus' example by announcing Good News. Theirs was a role of public proclamation that assumed confidence in the Christian message of redemption and reconciliation. For many who have preferred to see mission in these terms, the commissioning texts of the New Testament (Matt. 28:16-20 and parallels) are taken to be crucial and sufficient warrants that authorize and, perhaps, mandate this missionary role. Visually, however, it is Luke, through the Acts of the Apostles, who has given this image its most familiar form. Here, the reader meets the missioner as powerful orator, who skillfully declaims the message of the gospel to large but potentially hostile audiences.

First-century announcers of Good News sought to spread their message far and wide. Therefore, large-scale meetings and mass baptisms are the stuff of these stories. As commissioned agents of the risen Christ, these disciples developed into bold witnesses, who claimed to act on the authority of one greater than themselves. Not unnaturally, the idea of fearless

evangelizers engaging crowds of strangers with the gospel often led to heroic, larger-than-life portrayals of the apostles and other famous missionaries. Less often appreciated in the New Testament materials we will review
in this chapter is the factor of vulnerability in mission. To assume the role
of Good News announcer can also mean to risk rejection, humiliation, and
even mortal danger.

2. Sharing Christ with Friends   Quite a different picture of mission
emerges in Chapter Three, where Christian outreach is essentially defined
by the idea of sharing Christ with friends. Mission in this scenario is not a
matter of mass appeals, but primarily an act of interpersonal communication, a sharing of the gospel's riches with one's kin, friends, and close
neighbors. This image is, without a doubt, the most inclusive of the five
that will be examined in this study. All that is required here is a heartfelt
conviction that what one has experienced as faith is worth sharing. Obviously, any disciple could function as a missionary in this sense and, indeed,
may have done so, but often without the public recognition customarily
accorded to the "pillars" of the church and the giants of Christian faith.

It is in connection with this image that one can begin to appreciate
how far removed Jesus' call to mission is from compulsion. One does not
share the gospel with friends and family because it is commanded or required. A feeling of obligation is hardly needed where joy is present. It is
refreshing also to (re)discover that mission can be a spontaneous act,
rather than having to be a product of our own calculation and planning.
This is, perhaps, the characteristic that most strongly links together the
primary New Testament texts discussed in this chapter: the calling of Peter
by Andrew recorded in John 1:35-42, the actions of the Samaritan woman
recounted in John 4:1-42, and Mark's story of the paralyzed man healed by
Jesus (2:1-12).

3. Interpreting the Gospel   That the Good News is not a prepackaged
commodity in fixed form to be dispensed everywhere *semper eadem* is,
theologically, what underlies image number three: mission as an act of interpreting the gospel. To see mission as interpretation is to recognize that
when the gospel crosses over into new cultural contexts it meets people
with particular frames of reference and closely held convictions of their
own. This image suggests that missioners are not sent into a void; nor do
they carry their message into some kind of amorphous world culture in

order to apply it like salve to a wound whenever they come across sufferers of the human condition. Interpreters, like simultaneous translators at a summit meeting, are facilitators who enable communication to take place between two living realities.

One can hardly claim that demonstrating respect for foreign cultures and non-Christian religions was a dominating concern of the early church, yet there are some signs that such a sensitivity was not entirely absent. In particular, four episodes from the Acts of the Apostles have spurred me to think about this image of mission: Philip and the Ethiopian eunuch (8:26-40), Peter and Cornelius (10:1-48), Paul and Barnabas in Lystra (14:8-20), and Paul's visit to Athens (17:16-34). Many have seen in these passages examples of a dialogical orientation to mission. What I see in them is a series of encounters in which new hearers and an explicit form of the gospel appear to meet for the first time. In each case, an apostolic figure is present but does not control the action of the story. The role of these missionary interlocutors is to interpret and translate, to link and facilitate, more than it is to represent or embody a "Christian" point of view. I do believe that this image of mission makes manifest a crucial insight often revealed in the course of sustained interfaith dialogue: the realization that God may be active not only within but also beyond the sphere of the church. It is quite possible for God's Spirit to lead the way into mission.

4. Shepherding   In Chapter Five, the missionary nature of shepherding will be examined, first of all, on the basis of John 21. This chapter, an epilogue to the Gospel proper, will be approached as an illustration or clarification of what may be implied in John's "Great Commission" text in chapter 20: "As the Father has sent me, so I send you." This analysis, in turn, will lead to a consideration of John's portrait of Jesus as the Good Shepherd in chapter 10 and of the Old Testament material that informs and inspires his treatment, since all of this, I believe, forms the immediate background to Jesus' pastoral charge to Peter given in John 21:15-17 ("Feed my lambs. . . . Tend my sheep. . . . Feed my sheep.").

As a metaphor for pastoral leadership, shepherding is a flexible concept, able to bear a variety of interpretations, not all of them consistent with each other. Indeed, through the ages a majority within the church has imagined shepherding to be primarily a task of conservation. According to this way of thinking, pastoring means to tend and guard whatever fate has delivered into one's hands and to keep it under control. But this is not the only path by which to approach the concept of shepherding. It may be argued that proficient shepherding also implies a willingness to seek out lost or disoriented sheep, including those not of "this fold." On the basis of John 10, the earliest church certainly understood shepherding in this way. Accordingly, to be a pastor today could mean to act on the assumption that God's flock is much larger than the empirical reality sitting in the pews every Sunday. It is this more dynamic and mission-minded understanding of pastoral leadership that will be traced out here.

5. Building and Planting   No study of this kind could be complete without at least one image of mission coming directly from Paul, who epitomizes for many Christians the very model of a New Testament missionary. It seems almost inevitable that Paul's most vivid mission imagery would arise in the midst of the Corinthian correspondence. In Corinth, Paul's claim to leadership was openly challenged by rivals, among whom were those he characterized, ironically, as "super-apostles." This induced Paul to reflect on the nature of his own missionary practice, within the broad context of his entire theology. In other words, Paul was forced by circumstances to reconsider his methodology and how he conceived of his role with respect to the Corinthian church he purported to lead.

The results of Paul's thinking about mission, I believe, are encapsulated in two images presented together in 1 Corinthians 3. Just what did Paul think he was doing? According to these figures of speech, mission is building and planting. It is undertaken not as a solo act, but in cooperation with others like Apollos, under the aegis of God, who alone can grant success to the whole of their activity. Particularly stimulating is the way Paul, by his use of these metaphors, relates his understanding of mission to the content of the gospel he is preaching. In the letters to Corinth, there seems to be a conscious effort to correlate the medium (his missionary practice) with the message; this aspect of Paul's approach will be highlighted in the course of the discussion presented in Chapter Six.

Several Vital Tasks: Exegetical, Theological, Illustrative

At the end of this study, what I hope to have produced is a fresh way to conceptualize the New Testament foundations of Christian mission. In order to begin to reach toward this goal, three different tasks will have to be entered into for each of the five images of mission I have just briefly described. The first of these tasks is exegetical. Thus, I intend to analyze certain of the New Testament data in detail, with particular attention paid to the passages indicated above. At times, this discussion will become somewhat technical, as critical issues of language present themselves and significant views within the history of interpretation connected to these passages are taken into account.

Since this study passes over a rather wide expanse of scriptural territory, however, it has not been possible in every instance to recreate and document the extensive scholarly debates that surround and inform virtually every assertion a contemporary interpreter might wish to make today. In most cases, I have had to be satisfied with a citation or two in the notes that indicate where more detailed information or additional support for the exegetical position taken here may be readily found. On the other hand, where the work of particular New Testament scholars has substantially influenced my own reading of a given passage, I have sought to incorporate their insights more directly and extensively into the text proper. In part, my purpose is to share with fellow missiologists some of the scholarly riches currently on offer in biblical studies that most tellingly bear on our specific concern for the biblical foundations of Christian missionary practice and theory. Within the limits imposed by the scope of this project, I have sought especially to make use of literary studies and social analyses that might help us to understand better how followers of Jesus in the first century understood and interacted with the world around them.

At the same time, I believe that missiologists have significant contributions to make to parallel investigations taking place elsewhere within the theological curriculum. On this basis, I have presumed to write in hopes of participating in the flow of biblical scholarship. In a general way, of course, the interests of my field (mission studies) stand as a constant reminder to every interpreter of the New Testament that the dynamic communities for whom these texts were first written were engaged in powerful ministries of outreach and witness throughout and beyond the period of the canon's formation. Thus, to a degree perhaps not always fully recognized, early Christians expressed the core values of their distinctive identity through mission. Sometimes, more specialized hermeneutical benefits may also be realized, as familiar passages are re-examined from a missiological point of view.

Among the observations on mission in the New Testament offered in this volume, several intersect with issues likely to be of interest to New Testament scholars as well as to missiologists. These include the question of minor characters in the Gospels and Acts and the missionary roles they take up in those books, usually without fanfare of any kind. In this, I attempt to build on recent New Testament studies that have treated the minor characters in the Gospels as exemplars of faithful discipleship or as important dramatic personae, but my overriding concern is to show how these followers of Jesus participated in and extended the reach of his ministry. Potentially significant as well is the idea of social space as that appears to have defined the different types of missionary encounter found in the New Testament documents. Also worth our mutual attention is the missionary character of pastoral leadership, which comes into view in connection with the image of shepherding. Finally, I join with others in urging that Paul's apostolic edge not be obscured or eclipsed by the seminal role he came to play in the history of Christian theology. More specifically, I will argue that Paul used the paired roles of planter and master-builder to sum up and represent visually his own very complex sense of missionary vocation. Except for the rather more abstract notion of apostleship, no other self-designation employed by Paul seems to me to capture so completely his capacity to function simultaneously as an evangelist, strategist, and theologian of mission.

Half or more of each chapter to come is devoted to exegetical matters. A second undertaking ventured here is more strictly theological. Once it has been established that a given approach to mission has solid scriptural support, questions immediately arise concerning the implications of this or that New Testament image for the theology of mission. As we will see, issues of missionary authority and motivation surface repeatedly. Picturing Christian witness as an act of interpretation, for example, will naturally lead to reflections on the cross-cultural factor in mission, plus some thinking about the problem of interreligious encounter. Likewise, when mission is considered as a kind of shepherding, one is prompted to look again at the nature of pastoral ministry in general, including its practice in thoroughly domestic circumstances. Perhaps the most important theological questions raised will not be addressed directly until the end of this study, when an assessment is made regarding the adequacy of these images of mission as a collection. At that point, we will want to know not only about the capacity of these five images of disciples in mission together to represent how the earliest generation of Christians engaged in mission, but also something about how this collection of images might function as a New Testament basis for Christian outreach today.

It is my intention, finally, to explore in each chapter how these different images of mission have been or might be depicted visually and to do so in a multicultural manner. The graphic representations incorporated below will range from Chinese paper cuts to Byzantine ivories, from catacomb drawings to cathedral decorations, from student art produced in East Africa to commissioned masterpieces of European Baroque extravagance. Besides religious art, a few secular images will also be included, because these illustrate one or another important feature that distinctively marks these New Testament images of mission on which our attention will be focused.

The artwork used in this study is intimately related to one of its central purposes, which is to stimulate new thinking about how we conceive of mission. I anticipate that the illustrations will strengthen my argument in at least two ways. First, by moving in the direction of the graphic, I believe it becomes possible to clarify further what some of our many words about mission might actually mean. This could help to overcome a difficulty that routinely impairs our attempts to reflect theologically, both inside and outside of missiology proper, about the mission or purpose of the church. The root problem is that the same concepts do not communicate the same message to all people, even within the same culture. An author might lift up the notion of "servanthood," for example, confident that it expresses a noble ideal of sacrifice with which no one could take issue. Yet it is possible that another might perceive in servanthood instead an abject and unworthy servility that is neither appealing nor persuasive. The same might be said of shepherding, which could be understood at base to be either a benevolent or coercive act. The point here is that often when an idea is represented visually, added transparency can be achieved, and the underlying issues thought to be critical by the speaker or writer are sometimes placed less ambiguously before hearers and readers.

A second reason to direct our attention to pictures of mission is that this approach respects the power of images to describe, as ideas do, but also to move. Imagery can explain *and* engage the one who perceives the image in ways not always possible for un-enfleshed concepts. People who respond to a "call" to mission (whether temporary or lifelong) are not, I believe, ultimately swayed by arguments and axioms. Rather, they "see" a need and want to respond to it, or they "feel" a pull to cross a boundary that defines the believing community, in order to engage another part of their world in the name of Christ. A confessional statement or set of doctrines may provide a macro-framework of theory by which concrete actions may be evaluated, but I doubt that dogma alone or even primarily can account for the inner *motivation* that impels disciples of Jesus to take the next step by following him into mission.

Thus, in the chapters to follow we will deliberately move along the "continuum of religious language," as theologian Sallie McFague has put it, away from the purely conceptual and toward the metaphorical and visual, while trying to remain connected to the biblical text.[50] A successful presentation will balance an appreciation for the subtle vigor and perceptive clarity of images with an awareness of the limited capacity of *any* image to represent completely what it means to be a Christian disciple in mission. Above all, I hope by these means to address the intellectual problem of describing what constitutes Christian mission today by exploring in an imaginative way how it might actually look when actively embodied in life.

50. Sallie McFague, *Metaphorical Theology: Models of God in Religious Language* (Philadelphia: Fortress, 1982), p. 23.

chapter 2

Announcing Good News

The Social Setting of Christian Witness

From the beginning, Christian mission has assumed a wide variety of forms. Among the factors that have given shape to these various expressions of outreach, perhaps none is more crucial than the question of social setting. Do we imagine that our efforts to communicate or demonstrate the gospel to others will take place on intimate terms, as might occur naturally among friends or relatives, for example? If so, then many things may be left unsaid, since a common frame of reference is likely to be shared from the outset. Close individual relationships also imply an acknowledged social location or place to stand, meaning the right to speak and sometimes even an expectation that one will share those parts of personal experience that have meant the most to oneself. In familiar surroundings, like the home, or within the amicable bonds of friendship, faith-sharing can be a private affair, an informal act of communication that proceeds in a relaxed manner among people who have already grown accustomed to one another's ways.

When the missioner does not yet participate in an established network of close social ties involving those with whom she or he hopes to share the gospel, a completely different set of conditions arises. In this case, nearly everything connected to the event of Christian mission has to be explained or negotiated, not least the identity of the one bearing witness and that one's motives. On what grounds does this person presume to speak or act on behalf of the gospel here? Does this one intend good or ill for my community and family? Must previous commitments and loyalties be completely abandoned, if we accept this new point of view? Are there political implications or other interests embedded in this appeal to faith? Such questions find partial answers in the social roles taken up by would-be evangelizers who attempt to carry on their activities outside the snug confines of private life.

This chapter will examine one way that some prominent first-century disciples of Jesus chose to conduct themselves in the *public* domain, as they sought to present the claims and promises of the gospel to groups of people, most of whom they did not know well or at all beforehand. The primary action that stands behind this image of mission is announcement. Above all, this image nurtures the impression that the Good News grounded in Jesus Christ is a message that requires proclamation. These disciples supposed that it was their prerogative to address others in Jesus' name with their declarations, in order to extend the range of his influence and to assert for his teaching and activities the widest possible significance. In this way, they hoped to fulfill the trust Jesus had placed in them at the time of their initial commissioning as his associates in mission, while creating new opportunities for others to become disciples of the Risen Lord.

The first of those who stepped forward to make announcements on Jesus' behalf were, to some extent, imitators of his personal example. Just as Jesus had spoken forthrightly of God's in-breaking reign, they would preach their message to every kind of public audience, including (by implication) Caesar himself. In this respect, their mission of proclamation was a continuation of Jesus' ministry and their methodology would be crucially informed by the earlier pattern of his public conduct. Yet, so far as we know, these disciples in mission did not presume to act as replacements for their absent leader. In the immediate post-ascension period, for example, even the greatest of the apostles declined to appropriate for themselves any of the potent titles the community ascribed so willingly in their preaching and writings to Jesus the Messiah. In addition, those who led the way in the cause of Christ after his death faced circumstances that were in some ways quite different from what Jesus himself had experienced.

Any investigation into the New Testament roots belonging to this image of mission will thus need to pay attention to a double set of reference points. Mission as an act of announcing the Good News reflects something of Jesus' distinctive imprint on the vocational self-understanding of his earliest disciples. At the same time, this image as it finally developed in the New Testament period was able to account for some rather substantial adjustments in practice and theological perspective that attended the apostles' evolving vision of their public ministry. Accordingly, we will look first at several groups of passages drawn from the Synoptic Gospels, all of which seem to contemplate some kind of public missionary role for Jesus' disciples, either during his lifetime or soon after his death. Subsequently, a selection of relevant material from Acts will be examined, in order to establish the ultimate shape assumed in the New Testament for this image of disciples in mission. Then, on the basis of this exegetical work, our focus will shift to the question of how announcers of the gospel have been and might be depicted visually.

An Apprenticeship in Mission

According to the Synoptic Gospels, Jesus began to assemble around himself a group of disciples almost as soon as he separated from the company of those who followed after John the Baptist. The Synoptics also agree that among the first of those called to his side were two sets of brothers, all of whom were known to have earned their livings as fishermen on the Sea of Galilee before meeting Jesus for the first time (Mark 1:16-20; cf. Matt. 4:18-22). The second half of the summons Jesus issued to Andrew and Peter on that occasion, the part that pointed to their future work as "fishers of people," is peculiar to this scene. In the New Testament, no other follower of Jesus is called in this way (not even James and John), and, in fact, no evidence exists to suggest that Jesus used this designation again with reference to any other of his disciples. An interesting variation in wording occurs in Luke 5:10, where the more finely focused idea of capturing one's prey alive (ζωγρῶν) is substituted for the broader term applied to all those who catch fish, regardless of technique (ἁλιεύς).[1]

1. On the semantic range of ἁλιεύς and the practice of fishing in biblical Palestine, see Wilhelm H. Wuellner, *The Meaning of "Fishers of Men"* (Philadelphia: Westminster, 1967), esp. pp. 11-63. Luke also differs from Mark and Matthew in that Simon Peter alone is addressed when Jesus promises a future ministry of "catching people."

Only in the most general way does this initial call to discipleship and vocation suggest what the missionary task of the apostles might look like in the future. Indeed, Jesus' promise that the disciples will one day catch people as they used to fish for food raises more questions about the methodology and purpose of Christian mission than it answers. The grotesque possibilities implied in this figure of speech plainly qualified its potential value as a means by which to picture mission, and so it is not surprising to learn that the concept of "fishing for people" largely failed to catch on in the early church as a living metaphor for evangelism.[2] A more enduring — but indirect — connection between mission and the profession of fishing is indicated in the mention of the casting-nets with which these Galilean fishermen all apparently plied their trade. Without a doubt, the action of gathering belongs to the conceptual world of mission in the Bible, and the fisherman's net is potentially a powerful symbol of such work. In this particular case, however, the hermeneutical point is surely weakened, if not sacrificed entirely, by the obvious weight given in all three Synoptic Gospels to the radical break with the past Jesus demanded of his new followers. This act of renunciation is the final emphatic note on which Matthew, Mark, and Luke alike conclude their accounts of the first disciples' call to mission. At the end of the episode, the reader is given to understand that these disciples had to *leave* their nets and boats completely behind, not to mention their co-workers and family, in order to respond fully to Jesus' command to follow him.

Once they had accepted Jesus' invitation to accompany him, his closest disciples (symbolically designated in all of the Gospels as "the Twelve") began a rather extraordinary period of internship. As Jesus' everyday traveling companions, they would have been able to observe his activities at very close

---

2. What cannot be ignored is the fact that humans ordinarily catch fish in order to consume them. The potential for misunderstanding is nearly as high with Luke's choice of vocabulary, since the trapping of animals by hunters and the capture of prisoners in battle (these are the contexts most readily suggested by ζωγρέω) are not necessarily exercises that connote benevolent intent. No such difficulty seems to have attended the use of the fish symbol for Jesus, and so one finds it more commonly employed by the early Christians in their catacomb art. On the background and use of ζωγρέω in Jesus' era, see Ceslas Spicq, *Theological Lexicon of the New Testament*, ed. and trans. James D. Ernest (Peabody: Hendrickson, 1994), vol. 2, pp. 161-63. John P. Meier observes in his study of the historical Jesus, *A Marginal Jew: Rethinking the Historical Jesus*, vol. 3: *Companions and Competitors* (New York: Doubleday, 2001), p. 160, that the early church shunned "fishers of people" language until the end of the second century.

range and so witness first-hand many of the incidents from Jesus' life that would later be recounted in the Gospels (plus many other events, presumably, that have not been preserved in the record). On occasion, Jesus seems to have offered additional explanations or special teaching to his innermost circle of followers that he did not impart to the crowds.[3] He also allowed his most privileged understudies to ask questions about the deeper meanings that lay behind his actions and words (cf. Matt. 13:10, 36; 17:10; 24:3).

The proximity of the Twelve to Jesus throughout the period of his public ministry would have afforded them an unparalleled opportunity to see how Jesus interacted with a wide variety of interlocutors. Among these were the desperate ones who sought Jesus out, hoping to benefit directly from his charismatic power. Others came looking for a definitive word or sign from Jesus, something that might have made clear the significance of the man and his actions. At the same time, certain scribes and Pharisees approached him in order to conduct their own forms of assessment. Using very carefully worded questions, these representatives of Jewish religious authority tested the limits of Jesus' knowledge, while probing his intentions. Itinerating as they were with Jesus on a daily basis over an extended period of time, the Twelve were thus perfectly situated to see how Jesus responded to the many entreaties and challenges that came his way.

The problem of how to characterize what the Twelve experienced while in the presence of Jesus is substantially solved by his reply to the disciples of John (Matt. 11:2-6; Luke 7:18-23). The Baptist's emissaries came with a question on behalf of their master that pressed Jesus to identify himself: "Are you the one who is to come, or are we to wait for another?" Significantly, Jesus responded by drawing attention to his actions, rather than by laying claim to one or another of the Jewish messianic titles that the Baptist would have recognized immediately:

> "Go and tell John what you have seen and heard: the blind receive their sight, the lame walk, the lepers are cleansed, the deaf hear, the dead are raised, the poor have good news brought to them [εὐαγγελίζονται]. And blessed is anyone who takes no offense at me." (Luke 7:22-23; cf. Matt. 11:4-5)

3. Thus, we read in Mark 4:34, for example: "he did not speak to [the crowds] except in parables, but he explained everything in private [κατ' ἰδίαν] to his disciples." Cf. Luke 10:23-24.

For our purposes, the crucial point here lies in the balance struck in Jesus' own description of his missionary activities. In order to gain a proper understanding of his identity and purpose, Jesus is saying, an observer has to pay attention both to what he does and to what he says. In this regard, the bringing of good news to the poor is an extremely compressed reference to the whole of his teaching and preaching activity up to this point in the story of his ministry. The list of miraculous cures Jesus cites for John's benefit (extending even to the resurrection of the dead), on the other hand, serves to highlight his growing reputation as a healer. The fact that Jesus, in this saying, provides much more detail about the miracles he was performing than about his preaching does not indicate an emphasis on the one activity at the expense of the other. Such a reading would contrast with the basic approach taken in the Synoptic Gospels to the overall shape of Jesus' ministry. Matthew, Mark, and Luke seem to agree that Jesus conducted himself as an authoritative teacher who was constrained above all to communicate something about the character of God's reign and the need of humankind to respond to it with repentance. This implies a substantial and sustained ministry of public proclamation. The function of the miracles was to demonstrate the already-arrived presence of the reality that Jesus was announcing in his sermons, parables, and other teaching.

That Jesus invited at least a few of his followers in the course of his ministry to participate directly in his missionary activities is well attested. The character of their involvement is set forth by means of several stories we find embedded in the larger narrative of Jesus' career as recounted in the Gospels. In these closely related accounts, Jesus is shown designating particular groups of people to be his missionary agents for a time. Included here are the sending stories centered on the Twelve that are recorded in all three Synoptic Gospels (Matt. 10:1, 5-15; Mark 6:7-13; Luke 9:1-6), to which Luke has added a separate missionary report involving a larger group of seventy (or seventy-two) disciples (Luke 10:1-20).[4]

4. Whether Luke has passed on two completely different stories of sending or two versions of the same story is discussed in Risto Uro, *Sheep among the Wolves: A Study on the Mission Instructions of Q* (Helsinki: Suomalainen Tiedeakatemia, 1987), pp. 25-72. As noted in the previous chapter (see chap. 1, n. 49), it is possible that Luke received two traditions based on the same incident, one via Mark and the other through the Q source he shares with Matthew. If so, Matthew appears to have integrated all of this information into one story, while Luke decided to keep separate the two different traditions at his disposal.

Many of the most intriguing details mentioned in these stories apparently did not survive as permanent features of the missionary vocation in the apostolic era. For example, the practice of sending out missionary laborers in pairs, explicitly noted in Mark 6 and Luke 10, recurs rarely in Acts. Likewise, the strict regulations laid down by Jesus regarding dress and comportment seem not to have taken hold broadly within the early church as behavioral norms for Christian missionaries.[5] A particularly awkward theological challenge is posed by the absolute prohibition given in Matthew 10:5 against all missionary activity among non-Jews: "Go nowhere among the Gentiles, and enter no town of the Samaritans. . . ." As the book of Acts clearly demonstrates, the first generation of church leaders chose another path. In fact, it seems that conscious efforts (albeit under the influence of the Holy Spirit) were made relatively soon after the resurrection to evangelize both Samaritans and Gentiles. Despite a fair number of scenes in the Gospels that might justify this change of ethnographic focus as a shift foreseen and prepared for by Jesus himself (e.g., Matt. 28:19 and parallels; cf. also John 4), the tension felt between Jesus' stark command in Matthew to focus only on the Jews and the church's subsequent practice is not easily resolved.

Short-lived details aside, the Synoptic sending stories, taken together, do communicate several important values that relate directly to the image of mission under discussion in this chapter. The first is that in all of these stories Jesus initiates and authenticates the mission of those who go forth on his behalf. That is to say, Jesus not only chooses those whom he will send but also empowers them by granting them the authority they will need to speak and perform extraordinary deeds in his name: "Then Jesus summoned his twelve disciples and gave them authority over unclean spirits, to cast them out, and to cure every disease and every sickness" (Matt. 10:1). Since Jesus throughout retains the initiative in mission, the disciples are consistently portrayed as subordinate characters, even when it is claimed that they are able to exercise authority (ἐξουσία) over demons and disease. As a result, the disciples remain students of their master in these

---

5. In Mark 6:8-9, for example, Jesus tells the disciples "to take nothing for their journey except a staff; no bread, no bag, no money in their belts; but to wear sandals and not to put on two tunics." As for lodging, he tells them: "Wherever you enter a house, stay there until you leave the place" (6:10). One does hear about first-century missionaries whose itinerant lifestyles seem to resemble this description (e.g., *Didache* 11), but it is striking that in neither Acts nor the letters of Paul are such details featured.

stories rather than becoming fully independent actors. Their mission is essentially an extension of what Jesus is already doing.

A second point to be noted is that Jesus instructs the disciples to prepare for resistance to their activities and even the possibility of persecution. In its least threatening form, this warning anticipates that some who hear the disciples' words will not accept them, in which case the missionaries are to give a dramatic sign (wiping or shaking the dust off their feet before leaving that house or village) that publicly acknowledges the fact of their rejection (Mark 6:11; Luke 9:5; cf. Matt. 10:14-15; Luke 10:10-16). Matthew goes further than this when he includes a prediction that outright persecution awaits the disciples as a consequence of their missionary activities. In the extended discourse presented in Matthew 10 (esp. vv. 16-23), for instance, Jesus tells the disciples to expect not only unresponsiveness from certain of their hearers but also hate-filled antagonism that will not be satisfied until his witnesses are silenced. This then becomes an opportunity for Jesus in Matthew to counsel steadfastness and confidence in the face of violent opposition, advice that may have been particularly well suited to the later circumstances of the Evangelist's own community.[6]

The forms of missionary service envisioned here for the disciples' first foray into public ministry are also worth examining. Through the sending stories, we learn that the disciples are to do two basic things. One is to heal in the manner of Jesus, which means in Matthew's amplified rendering to "cure the sick, raise the dead, cleanse the lepers, cast out demons" (10:8).[7] At the same time, they are to proclaim a message, whose content is variously described as the need for people to repent (Mark 6:12), the fact of God's reign (Luke 9:2), or the nearness of the New Age (Matt. 10:7; Luke 10:9).

---

6. For an exegetical treatment of the First Gospel that puts the situation of Matthew's community in the foreground, see Robert H. Gundry, *Matthew: A Commentary on His Handbook for a Mixed Church under Persecution,* second ed. (Grand Rapids: Eerdmans, 1994).

7. Mark reports that the disciples cast out many demons, adding that they also healed many who were sick by anointing them with oil (6:13). Luke is the least specific of the first three Gospels with respect to the wonders wrought by Jesus' disciples. For example, it says only that the Twelve healed "everywhere" in the villages they visited (9:6). As for the experience of the seventy/seventy-two, they and Jesus rejoiced together over the authority that had been exercised over the demons upon their return, but no details are provided regarding the kinds of exorcisms and/or acts of healing that had been performed.

How are the disciples to communicate their missionary message? The key word used in all three Gospels to describe this part of the disciples' task is κηρύσσω, a verb that means to announce or proclaim, that is, to declare in public a matter of critical importance to the community. A royal or municipal context often lies behind the use of κηρύσσω.[8] The kind of person who might be expected to carry out this action is the king's herald, as in Daniel 3:4. In the Gospels, very few persons besides the Twelve are explicitly referred to by means of vocabulary derived from κῆρυξ/κηρύσσω. John the Baptist is one of these, not surprisingly, since all of the Gospel writers interpret his primary function to be one of announcement in preparation for the coming of the Messiah (e.g., Mark 1:4, 7). In two stories of healing in Mark, we read about grateful recipients of Jesus' ministrations who cannot restrain the urge to share broadly the good news of their healing (1:45; 5:20; cf. Luke 8:39). In many more instances, it is Jesus himself to whom the verb κηρύσσω is applied (fourteen times in Mark), leaving the impression that he was acting as a herald dispatched by God when he preached about the impending arrival of God's rule. Significantly, Jesus is portrayed as an announcing figure in the Synoptic Gospels not only when the dramatic circumstances call for it (for example, his first sermon in Nazareth in Luke 4), but also when the Evangelists want to summarize and describe the essential character of his ministry (as at Matt. 4:23; 9:35; 11:1).

Of utmost importance is the scope of the action indicated by the verb κηρύσσω when it is used in the Gospels. Typically, commissioned announcers do not direct their remarks to individuals. Instead, they address whole communities or groups of people who represent larger social realities. The story of John the Baptist provides a classic illustration of this dynamic, when it is said that he proclaimed his message to "the whole Judean countryside and all the people of Jerusalem" (Mark 1:5; cf. Matt. 3:5) by preaching to the crowds that came out to him in the wilderness. In a similar spirit, it is claimed in Mark that the impetuous testimony of the healed demoniac from Gerasa caused "everyone" in the region of the Decapolis to marvel at what Jesus had done (Mark 5:20). Not without a practical reason did Jesus in Matthew's missionary discourse tell the disciples to proclaim their message "from the housetops" rather than whispering it in secret (Matt. 10:27; cf. Luke 12:3). By so doing, the size of their potential audience

8. On the Hellenistic and Jewish background of this word-group, see Gerhard Friedrich, *TDNT* 3:683-718.

would be maximized. In corresponding fashion, Jesus in Luke issues the command to the seventy/seventy-two disciples that we noted earlier, telling them to demonstrate their intention to quit an unfriendly town by going "into its streets" and wiping the dust off their feet (Luke 10:10-11), presumably in full view of the local inhabitants. The public character of these actions associated with κηρύσσω is unmistakable. We have uncovered a foundational insight that obviously relates to the mission image under development in this chapter.

Before moving on to Acts, one more group of sayings and stories drawn from the Gospels must be considered. These are the Synoptic accounts of Jesus' Great Commission, to which should be added a small collection of logia uttered by Jesus (Mark 13:10; 14:9; and parallels) that point at least indirectly to the kind of public ministry he seemed to expect the disciples to take up over the long term. No attempt will be made here to dissect each part of this material exegetically, since many scholars have already performed this task, with a great deal of attention having been focused especially on the final commissioning scenes in the Gospels.[9] My sole objective is to gather together and present whatever additional information there might be in the Synoptic Gospels that could help us to envision a New Testament image of disciples engaging in mission by announcing Good News.

One point on which these passages strongly concur is that the disciples' coming mission would transcend the boundaries of Israel, both ethnically and geographically. The earlier restrictions Jesus had placed on the missionary activities of the Twelve ("Go nowhere among the Gentiles, and enter no town of the Samaritans . . ."), for example, do not surface again in any of the Great Commission texts. Theirs is to be a universal mission, which is described in two ways. The first of these makes reference to "the nations," a broad cultural designation that may or may not include the Jews.[10] Thus, we find Jesus at the end of Luke telling the disciples "that re-

9. Besides the commentaries, I have in mind here studies such as David Bosch, "The Structure of Mission: An Exposition of Matthew 28:16-20," in *Exploring Church Growth*, ed. Wilbert R. Shenk (Grand Rapids: Eerdmans, 1983), pp. 218-48; Mortimer Arias and Alan Johnson, *The Great Commission: Biblical Models for Evangelism* (Nashville: Abingdon, 1992); and Peter Stuhlmacher, "Matt 28:16-20 and the Course of Mission in the Apostolic and Postapostolic Age," in *The Mission of the Early Church to Jews and Gentiles*, ed. Jostein Ådna and Hans Kvalbein, WUNT 127 (Tübingen: Mohr Siebeck, 2000), pp. 17-43.

10. As an ethnographic term, "τὰ ἔθνη" can be used to refer collectively to all non-

pentance and forgiveness of sins is to be proclaimed in his name *to all nations,* beginning from Jerusalem" (24:47). In Matthew's parallel account (28:19), the resurrected Jesus likewise directs the Eleven to address themselves to "all nations" (πάντα τὰ ἔθνη) as they seek to make new disciples by teaching and baptizing. We do not find this precise wording at the conclusion of Mark, but earlier, at 13:10, similar phrasing occurs with reference to the role Jesus' witnessing disciples will play in the apocalyptic scenario he outlines for their benefit: "the good news must first be proclaimed *to all nations.*"

In several other places, a kind of cosmic universality is asserted or implied for the disciples' future labors. Thus, it is said in connection with the unnamed woman who poured out a jar of expensive ointment over Jesus that her story would be told in perpetuity, "wherever the good news is proclaimed *in the whole world*" (Mark 14:9; Matt. 26:13). Similarly, in the longer ending of Mark (16:9-20), Jesus is shown sending the disciples into "all the world," so that they might preach the gospel "to the whole creation." This they began to do, according to Mark's version of the Great Commission, which does not end with Jesus' command but concludes instead with a report of its fulfillment: "And they went out and proclaimed the good news *everywhere*" (16:20). Finally, in the context of Matthew's apocalyptic discourse, Jesus speaks of the entire created order (ἐν ὅλῃ τῇ οἰκουμένῃ) as the proper setting for the disciples' impending mission, while identifying "the nations" as the particular objects of their attention. The result is a doubly expansive vision for mission, unmistakably wide-open in scope: "And this good news of the kingdom will be proclaimed *throughout the world,* as a testimony to *all the nations;* and then the end will come" (Matt. 24:14).

Jews, in which case it is usually translated "Gentiles." On the other hand, if one construes "all nations" to mean the whole of humanity in all its cultural diversity, then Jews, too, are certainly meant to be included. Douglas R. A. Hare and Daniel J. Harrington, "'Make Disciples of All the Gentiles' (Matthew 28:19)," *CBQ* 37 (1975): 359-69, make a case for the former interpretation of the term in Matthew 28, while John P. Meier, "Nations or Gentiles in Matthew 28:19?" *CBQ* 39 (1977): 94-102, pushes for the latter. For a more recent argument, see Ulrich Luz, "Matthew's Anti-Judaism: Its Origin and Contemporary Significance," *Currents in Theology and Mission* 19 (1992): 405-15, and the articles of Luz, Peter Stuhlmacher, and Hans Kvalbein in *Mission of the Early Church,* ed. Ådna and Kvalbein, pp. 17-68. Of course, behind this question of semantics lies a major theological issue, namely, whether the early church's embrace of the Gentiles also implied a turn away from the Jews.

Less consistency is shown in these passages with respect to the form of the apostolic mission they anticipate. In other words, it is not altogether clear how the disciples are to go about fulfilling the final charge given to them by the resurrected Christ. Apart from the idea of proclamation, indicated once again by the presence of the verb κηρύσσω in nearly all of these passages (Matthew 28 is the single exception), little else remains constant as we move once more through the material quoted above. In Luke 24, for example, Jesus specifies that the disciples' preaching will feature a call to repentance and the forgiveness of sins in his name, an emphasis not found in any other version of the Great Commission.[11] For his part, Matthew stresses the teaching function the disciples will exercise on behalf of Jesus, an approach that corresponds to his portrayal of Jesus as an authoritative teacher like Moses. In the longer ending of Mark, attention is drawn to a series of "signs" or miracles that will be performed as a result of apostolic preaching, at least one of which has no counterpart elsewhere in the New Testament.[12] In short, the peculiar concerns of each Gospel seem to be reflected in the wording they report for Jesus' farewell speech to his disciples. Except for the general notion of announcement and a shared conviction that the resurrected Jesus intended his apostles to engage the whole of humanity with the gospel after Easter, the shape and form of the disciples' mission resist simple definition when viewed from within the Synoptic horizon.

Proclaimers of Good News in Acts

The gospel materials we have been examining thus far suffer from a major limitation: despite the obvious interest shown in the disciples as Jesus' mis-

---

11. Luke 24:47. Luke may be intending to recall with this phrasing the "baptism of repentance for the forgiveness of sins" that John the Baptist preached (cf. Luke 3:3//Mark 1:4; cf. also Acts 13:24; 19:4).

12. The claim that believers will be able to drink poisonous liquids without harm (Mark 16:18) is not reported anywhere else in the canon. The other miracles listed in verses 17-18 (the casting out of demons, outbreaks of tongues, an ability to pick up snakes, healing the sick by the laying on of hands) have parallels in the New Testament, but not in any of the other Great Commission texts. The sources behind the longer ending of Mark's Gospel and many other related matters are discussed in great detail by James A. Kelhoffer, *Miracle and Mission: The Authentication of Missionaries and Their Message in the Longer Ending of Mark* (Tübingen: Mohr Siebeck, 2000).

sionary protégés, the extent and character of their participation in his program of public outreach is left rather undeveloped. As we have seen, one is forced, in large part, to imagine the missionary deeds performed by the disciples while under Jesus' direct supervision, since the Evangelists themselves provide no more than scant accounts. In Matthew's treatment of the sending of the Twelve, for example, Jesus is shown teaching the group at great length about how to act and clothe themselves and what to expect on their first missionary journey, but nothing is said about the actual sending.[13] Mark and Luke are content to summarize in just a verse or two the activities of the disciples on mission (Mark 6:12-13; Luke 9:6). They also allude to a scene in which the twelve disciples report back to Jesus, but this is so briefly described that the narrative has almost no texture.[14] Luke seems to venture a bit further than Mark or Matthew when he tells of the seventy or seventy-two disciples returning to Jesus and celebrating with him the success of their mission (10:17: "Lord, in your name even the demons submit to us!"). Yet, here again, no stories are included that might help us to picture the circumstances of the disciples' actions. The reader is left wondering: how exactly did the disciples relate to those with whom they came in contact while fulfilling the missionary responsibilities given to them by Jesus?

In Acts, of course, the disciples as apostles finally emerge as major dramatic figures in their own right. They do so by becoming Jesus' leading

---

13. Somewhat incongruously, Matthew picks up Jesus' narrative immediately upon the conclusion of the missionary discourse in chapter 10: "Now when Jesus had finished instructing his twelve disciples, he went on from there to teach and proclaim his message in their cities" (11:1).

14. In Mark 6:30, it is put this way: "The apostles gathered around Jesus, and told him all that they had done and taught." As viewed from the perspective of narrative criticism, the comments of Sheila Anne Klassen-Wiebe regarding Luke 9:1-11 seem to apply equally well to Mark: "Although the twelve return, apparently having successfully completed their mission, the overall impact of their mission does not meet readers' expectations. The report of their return is so brief and unilluminating as to be disappointing. They have simply done what Jesus did with no evident ramifications or results. On the whole, their mission has little impact on the reader's construction of a portrait of the disciples. At the end of this account the implied reader continues to look for new ways in which the disciples will carry out their mission of 'catching people alive.' . . ." See Klassen-Wiebe, "Called to Mission: A Narrative-Critical Study of the Character and Mission of the Disciples in the Gospel of Luke" (Ph.D. diss., Union Theological Seminary and Presbyterian School of Christian Education, 2001), p. 202.

witnesses in Jerusalem, Samaria, and beyond (cf. Acts 1:8). Peter and Paul dominate the action, but other characters also find their way into the great story Luke has woven together to explain how the church of his day came into being. Running through this material are certain motifs that lend coherence to the overall narrative. One of these centers on the Holy Spirit, an invisible but active agent of divine will that Luke understood to be a crucial means by which God and God's Son continued to guide the apostles (cf. Acts 8:29; 10:19; 11:12; 13:4; 16:6; 21:4). Another overarching idea concerns the mission to the Gentiles — how it began and then came to overshadow the church's initial efforts to evangelize the Jews. A third key motif revolves around the question of the community's relationship to the governing authorities. A fourth is suggested by the many scenes of speech-making that punctuate the plot of Acts. The speeches represent, in capsule form at least, some of the content of the apostles' early preaching. They also indicate something about the methodology of Christian mission highlighted in Acts. Nowhere else in the New Testament is the idea of announcing Good News so vividly portrayed.

The primary image Luke constructs in Acts of the disciples' approach to mission resembles in several important ways the picture that had begun to form in the Synoptic Gospels. In Acts, for example, as in the Gospels, Jesus is identified as the initiator of the missionary program carried out by his followers. He is, throughout, the ever-active sender, whose enabling role must be assumed every time the word "apostle" (literally, "sent one") is applied to one of his disciples. At no point in the story of the community's origins recounted in Acts can it be said that Jesus ceased to lead the church in its mission. From first to last, the disciples who offer testimony to the work of salvation wrought through Jesus assiduously pay heed to his authority over them. They demonstrate their obedience to Jesus by continuing to call him Lord, by urging others to place their trust in him (not them) and to be baptized in his name, by directing their prayers to him, and by acknowledging him to be the source of the Holy Spirit and other divine messengers. In these and other ways, the book of Acts confirms the impression created in the Gospels that even fully empowered missionary representatives of Jesus remain completely dependent on him.

The Gospels and Acts also overlap with each other in the matter of response to the apostles' preaching. In the abstract, as we have seen, Jesus in the Gospels prepared the disciples for more than one reaction to their missionary efforts by suggesting that some would receive them gladly, while others would remain indifferent or set themselves in active opposition. In Acts, these different outcomes are brought to life by means of narratives that show how different groups of people in specific circumstances of evangelistic encounter responded to the apostles and their message. Scenes of great success are balanced by situations of grave danger and predicaments in which a variety of threatened interests seek to impede the Christian mission. The apostles do not always overcome the resistance they face. Persecution and even death are also part of the story, just as Jesus in the Gospels suggested they would be. The possibility of failure adds tension to the narrative of Acts by providing a background of peril against which the apostles' courage and fortitude stand out in even higher relief. Luke's editorial hand is evident each time he draws attention to the "boldness" (παρρησία) with which apostles proclaimed the gospel, in season and out.[15] Whether understood as bravery or as an expression of self-confidence, this is certainly not how the disciples conducted themselves *before* Jesus' ascension. The situations of adversity depicted in Acts, which could only be hinted at in the Gospels, allow Luke to describe in dramatic terms how this new character trait began to emerge among the disciples of Jesus.

The verbal aspect of the disciples' mission is similarly enhanced in Acts. This does not mean that other forms of outreach disappear altogether. Indeed, in keeping with the pattern set by Jesus in the Gospels and the expectations of their age, the apostles in Acts are shown performing a steady stream of miracles, most of which involve incidents of extraordinary healing (e.g., 3:1-10; 5:15-16; 9:33-35; 28:7-10).[16] Also, Luke reports situations in which conversions and faith followed directly upon demonstrations of power by the apostles. Such would seem to have been the case, for example, after Tabitha's miraculous restoration to life by Peter: "Then . . .

15. Luke applies the verbal and substantival forms of this word to the apostles twelve times in Acts. In none of the Gospels are Jesus' disciples so described.

16. Apart from healings and exorcisms in which they are involved, the apostles are also shown to benefit repeatedly from divine interventions on their behalf. Three such incidents are related in which one or more of the apostles is miraculously released from prison (Acts 5:19-21; 12:6-11; 16:25-26). Paul's survival after being bitten by a poisonous snake (28:3-6) could be considered a miracle of nature. In two other situations (5:1-11; 13:6-12), Peter and Paul each participate in God's punishment of others by pronouncing different forms of prophetic judgment against their false actions.

he showed her to be alive. This became known throughout Joppa, and many believed in the Lord" (9:41-42).[17]

While not hiding his conviction that wonder-working was a mark of true apostleship, Luke nevertheless found ways in Acts to put this activity into a more comprehensive framework dominated by the word. In some cases, the apostles' miracles are shown to need preaching before they could become meaningful and compelling with respect to faith. At Pentecost, for example, the loud noise produced by the arrival of the Spirit drew to the disciples a bewildered crowd that may have heard them speaking in their own languages but still could not make sense of what was happening around them: "All were amazed and perplexed, saying to one another, 'What does this mean?'" (2:12). In this situation, Peter's announcement of Good News is the means by which the crowd's experience is finally rendered intelligible and a proper response to it becomes possible.

A similar relationship of word to miraculous sign is described in the story of Peter and John at the temple, when they heal the man who had been lame from birth (Acts 3:1-10). Their feat produces wonder (θάμβος), amazement (ἔκστασις), and astonishment (ἔκθαμβος) among the eyewitnesses, but apparently no faith. Peter summarizes the flawed response of the crowd to what they had seen in these terms: "You Israelites, why do you wonder at this, or why do you stare at us, as though by our own power or piety we had made him walk?" (3:12). At the end of the episode, after the authorities intervened and placed the apostles under arrest, faith does manifest itself. Tellingly, Luke gives the credit to Peter's sermon, while ignoring entirely the miracle event with which the story had begun: "But many of those who heard the word believed; and they numbered about five thousand" (4:4).[18]

---

17. In light of this story and several others in Acts where miracles either seem to produce faith or to substantially prepare the way for faith to develop (9:34-35; 13:12; 16:30; 19:17), Paul J. Achtemeier has concluded: "It is rather clear in Acts that miracles were an effective device for turning people to faith." See Achtemeier, "The Lucan Perspective on the Miracles of Jesus: A Preliminary Sketch," *JBL* 94 (1975): 553. On the miracles in Acts, see also Frans Neirynck, "The Miracle Stories in the Acts of the Apostles: An Introduction," in *Les Actes des Apôtres: Traditions, rédaction, théologie,* ed. Jacob Kremer (Gembloux: Leuven University Press, 1979), pp. 169-213, where Achtemeier is quoted (p. 202).

18. The incident of Paul and Barnabas at Lystra (14:8-18) resembles in some respects this story about Peter and John in Solomon's Portico. In both cases, observers witness a miracle of healing and then misinterpret what they saw. Thus, Paul's sermon at Lystra, like Pe-

When Peter and John go before the Sanhedrin, another insight is offered concerning the importance of the spoken word within the developing mission of the apostles. The charge against the two apostles is not that they contravened some rule of society by curing the crippled man of his lameness, although that is an embarrassing fact with which their accusers have to contend. The council wants to know instead, "by what power or by what name did you do this?" (4:7). This is a way of asking them to explain the significance of their actions, which Peter is only too happy to do once again by preaching about "Jesus Christ of Nazareth, whom you crucified, whom God raised from the dead, by whose name this man is standing before you in good health" (4:10).[19]

A vital detail is slipped into the record of the council's verdict. The apostles are released after being warned not to preach or to teach ever again in the name of Jesus (4:17-18), but nothing whatsoever is said about their miracle working. In the many trial scenes to come in Acts after this, the central issue will always be the apostles' compulsion to proclaim salvation in Jesus' name and the commotion sometimes caused when they answer this prompting.[20] The ability of the apostles to work miracles does not seem to have troubled any of the religious authorities or secular tribunals before which they were made to appear with some frequency. The governing powers apparently had little interest in or incentive to attempt to regulate this activity, a result, perhaps, of the broad acceptance of miracle-mongering within the apostles' social environment.

In other ways, too, the priority of preaching in the apostles' ministry is repeatedly underscored in Acts. More than any other activity in which they engage, this seems to be what defines the vocation of an apostle, as Luke understands it. We see this demonstrated very clearly in the story of the seven Hellenists, who are chosen at a point of crisis to serve the com-

---

ter's in Jerusalem, is meant to clarify the meaning of the miracle, but this time no faith or baptisms are reported, only the restraint of the crowd that attempted to fete the apostles as gods come to earth.

19. This translation is my own.

20. Luke is very consistent on this point. For example, when the apostles are arrested a second time in the vicinity of the temple after having performed many signs and wonders, the high priest opened the proceedings against them by recalling the terms of the earlier verdict: "We gave you strict orders not to teach in this name . . ." (Acts 5:28). At the end of the incident, virtually the same sanction is imposed (and again ignored), without any mention being made of the miracles worked by the apostles.

munity by overseeing the daily distribution of food to the poor (6:1-6). The crucial issue, from the standpoint of the Twelve, was whether or not the accrued obligations of leadership would be allowed to distract them from their central task — the proclamation of the word — as the affairs of the fellowship grew more complex. In the end, they decided not to let this happen:

> It is not right that we should neglect the word of God in order to wait on tables. Therefore, friends, select from among yourselves seven men of good standing, full of the Spirit and of wisdom, whom we may appoint to this task, while we, for our part, will devote ourselves to prayer and to serving the word. (Acts 6:2-4)

Accordingly, Luke proposes at several points in the narrative of Acts to measure the success of the apostles' efforts by charting the progress of God's word. Thus, indications are given that the word "advances" and the number of disciples "increases" as the apostles fulfill their calling (12:24; 6:7), that the word "spreads" throughout whole regions in the course of their visits (13:49), or that it "grew mightily" when the name of the Lord Jesus was extolled where it had not previously been recognized (19:20). Again, one is struck by how often deeds of proclamation stand behind these evaluations of the apostolic mission. Above all, what matters to Luke is that the influence of the word continues to extend ever outward from Jerusalem to the ends of the earth. He leaves no doubt that the preaching ministry of Jesus' disciples was the primary means by which this happy outcome was to be realized.

Thus, we are prompted, finally, to consider the speeches of Acts, since this is the literary device by which Luke most often portrays the apostles as announcers of Good News. The number of speeches included in Acts and the length of the remarks sometimes reported (cf. Stephen's address in 7:2-53) are notable facts of Luke's compositional style, which serves to draw attention to the presumed oratorical skills of the apostles.[21] It may be asked, what is gained theologically by giving over nearly a third of the book to speech-making? As Marion Soards has observed, the

21. G. H. R. Horsley, "Speeches and Dialogue in Acts," *NTS* 32 (1986): 609-14, compares Luke's use of speech material with the technique of several ancient historians and finds a much higher density of speeches in Acts than in any of them.

speeches in Acts contribute in a major way to the book's overall purpose. Their role is "to tell the story of the witness — of its articulation, acceptance, or rejection — and to do so in such a way that through repetition the unified witness is emphasized and articulated in a manner greater than the capacity of any single speech."[22] One way the speeches achieve this effect is by assisting the reader to visualize different members of the community acting as witnesses to Jesus Christ and the God who raised him from the dead.

Subtle signs of interpretive activity may be detected in the way Luke has handled the speech materials. It is important that these be identified, because once recognized, they can help the reader to appreciate more fully just how the apostles have been depicted in Acts. We may begin with the settings in which the various speeches have been placed.[23] While a few of the speeches are associated with secluded surroundings appropriate to in-group gatherings, more commonly the setting described is fully public and the audience is obviously dominated by nonbelievers with whom one or more of the disciples hopes to share Good News.[24] Among the public venues specified for the speeches given by the apostles in Acts are the temple precincts in Jerusalem, numerous synagogues, a marketplace, a city gate, and a variety of courtrooms and council chambers, both religious and sec-

22. Marion L. Soards, *The Speeches in Acts: Their Content, Context, and Concerns* (Louisville: Westminster/John Knox, 1994), p. 199.

23. I am proceeding here on the assumption that sometimes the circumstances of a speech are part of the earlier tradition Luke inherited and so could reflect the actual situation of the speaker in history. At other times, however, it may well be that Luke the redactor added details of setting, either because the tradition he had received lacked these altogether or because he wanted to adapt the different scraps of traditional material at his disposal to fit the requirements of his overall narrative. In either case, the general impression created of the apostles as public speakers through the speeches related in Acts can be described. This is what I intend to do in the next few paragraphs, without conducting a historical-critical analysis of each speech to determine the level of its historicity with respect to setting or content. For a quick review of the scholarly debates that have, since the nineteenth century, swirled around the historiographical intentions and literary methods of Luke, see Soards, *Speeches in Acts,* pp. 1-17.

24. Peter's speech to the rest of the fellowship, delivered just before the election of Matthias (Acts 1:15-22), is an example of apostolic speech-making that assumes a gathering of believers. The meeting of the so-called Jerusalem Council (Acts 15) is another occasion at which leaders of the community speak to fellow insiders. See also 11:5-17 (Peter's speech to the advocates of circumcision within the church), 20:18-35 (Paul's farewell address to the Ephesian elders), and 21:20-25 (James's remarks to Paul and the elders of Jerusalem).

ular. It is not unusual for the dramatic situation of a given speech to include an element of confrontation or potential violence, as the apostles repeatedly faced crowds in the open, some of which were clearly predisposed to reject their message. In any event, all this public speaking has a cumulative effect, which is to establish, as Paul will point out, that the Christian movement was not some kind of secret society or subversive association doing its business "in a corner" (26:26). By showing the apostles so energetically at work in the public square, Luke leaves the reader in no doubt that the early church meant to engage the entire creation with Jesus' word, rather than retreating in fear from the world around it.

Also worth some scrutiny are the presentational aspects of the speech scenes. That is, having been placed in narrative situations where Good News could be proclaimed, how did the apostles in Acts acquit themselves as characters? This is, first of all, a matter of stance and gesture and then an issue of rhetorical style. As for physical positioning, public speakers in Acts quite often signal an intention to deliver a formal address by rising to their feet.[25] Once, it is said that Peter also raised his voice as he stood up and began to preach (2:14). Three times Paul is described as having made a motion with his hand, in order to gain the attention of an audience at the outset of a speech (13:16; 21:40; 26:1).[26] Peter must do likewise to quiet the excited crowd gathered for prayer on his behalf at the house of Mary (12:17). The significance of these details is not readily apparent, when considered apart from questions of rhetorical form. It is intriguing to note in passing, however, that Paul stands up to speak in the synagogue at Antioch of Pisidia (13:16), while Jesus is specifically described as having sat down in the synagogue at Nazareth before offering his comments on the Scripture he had just read (Luke 4:20). Also, the gesture Paul makes at the start of his speech in Antioch seems out of place in the environment of the synagogue.[27]

25. Thus, Peter (Acts 1:15; 2:14; 15:7) and Paul (13:16; 17:22; 21:40; 26:22; cf. 27:21), but also Gamaliel (5:34), Agabus (11:28), and some scribes of the Pharisees (23:9). There is also the story of the apostles' miraculous release from prison in Jerusalem, when an angel of the Lord tells them, "Go, stand in the temple and tell the people the whole message about this life" (5:20).

26. A leader of the Jews in Ephesus, Alexander, is also described using this gesture in an attempt to quiet the crowd that had gathered in the city's theater (Acts 19:33).

27. Cf. Ernst Haenchen, *The Acts of the Apostles: A Commentary,* trans. Bernard Noble et al. (Oxford: Basil Blackwell, 1971), p. 408, who calls Paul's wave of the hand "superfluous" in this setting.

Moving on to the form of the remarks delivered by the apostles, it is widely agreed that the speeches in Acts reflect an awareness of Greco-Roman rhetorical practice. As Philip Satterthwaite has observed,

> At point after point Acts can be shown to operate according to conventions similar to those outlined in classical rhetorical treatises. There are some aspects which it is hard to explain other than by concluding that Luke was aware of rhetorical conventions: the preface; the layout of some of the speeches; and the presentation of legal proceedings in chapters 24–26.[28]

This is not to say that the speeches are slavish reproductions of Greek oratory. After all, the main subject matter to which the apostles return again and again in their speeches — the gospel of repentance and Jesus' resurrection from the dead — are not part of the classical repertoire of standard topics. Also, in their remarks the apostles rarely draw directly on sources or literary examples that secular Greco-Roman audiences would have found most persuasive, preferring instead to reference the Jewish Scriptures. Even so, it is hard not to conclude that the speeches in Acts consistently show deference to patterns of practice widely accepted in Luke's context for deliberative and forensic rhetoric especially. This seems to hold true whether the speaker being portrayed is a Galilean fisherman or a Hellenized Jew like Paul.[29] When this information about rhetorical style is combined with

---

28. Philip E. Satterthwaite, "Acts against the Background of Classical Rhetoric," in *The Book of Acts in Its First Century Setting,* ed. Bruce W. Winter and Andrew D. Clarke, vol. 1 (Grand Rapids: Eerdmans, 1993), p. 378. Soards, *Speeches in Acts,* p. 143, comes to a similar conclusion, stating that "there is a clear relationship between the form and style of speeches in Hellenistic historiography and the form and style of the speeches in Acts, although there is no exact correspondence in these matters." At the same time, Soards is keen to show how the *content* of the speeches in Acts differs substantially from what one is likely to encounter in Hellenistic historiography. See also Ben Witherington III, *The Acts of the Apostles: A Socio-Rhetorical Commentary* (Grand Rapids: Eerdmans, 1998), esp. pp. 39-51, where the rhetorical dimension of Acts is explored with marked persistence.

29. This does not mean that the backgrounds and immediate circumstances of the different speakers in Acts are completely ignored or that their separate personalities are entirely effaced. As Henry J. Cadbury, *The Making of Luke-Acts* (New York: Macmillan, 1927), pp. 70-75, pointed out long ago, the early chapters of Acts, which focus on the activities of the reconstituted group of twelve disciples in Jerusalem, contain relatively more Semitisms than the later chapters. Similarly, Paul tends to express himself in ways that would be com-

the data presented above regarding gesture and stance, the resulting image quickly snaps into clear focus. As speech-makers, the apostles in Acts are presented in the guise of Greco-Roman orators.

It remains now to summarize very briefly what has been learned about the New Testament background that belongs to this first image of disciples in mission. Whether considered from the standpoint of Acts or the Synoptic Gospels, it is clear that announcers of Good News go forward in the name of Jesus Christ, the authoritative sender and source of whatever spiritual power his emissaries might be able to exercise in his name. Theirs is a public function, which cannot be accomplished at home or among friends. They seek to engage new audiences with the gospel, an aim that requires them to risk rejection, humiliation, or worse. Within the New Testament, proclaimers of Good News are most often described as making declarations or in some other way vocalizing their message, although other forms of service, like healing, can accompany or prepare the way for verbal announcements. In Acts, a more fully realized visual form of announcement is encountered, which seems to owe something to the historical circumstances of Luke and his presumed readership. By choosing to depict the apostles as accomplished public speakers in the Greco-Roman tradition, the author of Acts achieved a degree of vividness not evident elsewhere in the New Testament. At the same time, his literary strategy raises an implicit question about the cultural dimensions of this and other mission images and the matter of their representation. It is to just this set of issues that we must now direct our attention.

Representing an Idea: Announcers of Good News

The illustration with which I propose to begin this section is widely acknowledged to be a masterwork of the early Italian Renaissance, set in a venue where the history of European art took a relatively sudden and decisive turn. Yet, it was not for reasons of reputation that I chose this painting.

---

patible with an increasingly Gentile constituency (cf. esp. his speeches at Lystra and Athens). Witherington, *Acts of the Apostles,* pp. 43-44, shrewdly hypothesizes that this variation in style within the book may be yet another indication that Luke is following the rhetorical conventions of his day. In this case, however, instead of Atticizing his narrative as a first-century Greek historian might be expected to do, Luke is archaizing the initial chapters of his text by introducing Septuagintal vocabulary and phrasing.

What drew my interest instead was the rather straightforward way by which the idea of announcing Good News has been rendered in *The Preaching of St. Peter* (fig. 4; plate 5). My intention is to use Masolino's fresco scene as a baseline representation of this image of mission, against which several other visualizations of the same concept will then be compared.

The Preaching of St. Peter is part of an extensive series of frescoes added in the early fifteenth century to a small private chapel belonging to the church of Santa Maria del Carmine in Florence.[30] The Italian painter Masolino (1383–c. 1436) probably began work on the ceiling by himself, but a compatriot, Masaccio (1401-1428), soon joined him, and the pair seems to have devised a joint compositional plan for the wall decorations.[31] The two artists worked under a commission most likely provided by Felice Brancacci, a silk merchant and scion of the prominent Florentine family whose name has become permanently attached to the chapel. The apostle Peter was the main subject of the frescoes. In all, seventeen different episodes out of his life were depicted on the walls of the Brancacci chapel, drawn either from the Gospels and Acts or from noncanonical stories recounted in *The Golden Legend*.[32] *The Preaching of*

30. I am indebted especially to the following books and articles for information relating to the frescoes of the Brancacci chapel: Diane Cole Ahl, "Masaccio in the Brancacci Chapel," in *The Cambridge Companion to Masaccio*, ed. Diane Cole Ahl (New York: Cambridge University Press, 2002), pp. 138-57; Keith Christiansen, "Masolino (da Panicale)," in *DArt* 20:553-59; Paul Joannides, *Masaccio and Masolino: A Complete Catalogue* (London: Phaidon, 1993); Hellmut Wohl, "Masaccio," in *DArt* 20:529-39.

31. The two painters collaborated in an unusual way, with each taking primary responsibility for alternating picture fields while sometimes adding elements to the other person's work. A more cohesive result was achieved by this approach than might have been possible had the artists simply decided to assign themselves separate halves of the total working space. It appears that the younger Masaccio influenced the style of the more established Masolino, rather than the other way around. On this, see Joannides, *Masaccio and Masolino*, pp. 61-80, 101-12. A broad consensus of expert opinion regards Masaccio as the first true Renaissance painter, whose innovations included a new approach to perspective that was modeled on the breakthrough achieved by Brunelleschi in architecture, his use of bright colors, and a realistic style. Filippino Lippi completed the decoration of the chapel in 1481 to 1482. The reason why Masolino and Masaccio left their decorative scheme unfinished is unknown.

32. Ahl, "Masaccio in the Brancacci Chapel," pp. 146-47, discusses the sources of information on which the painting cycle was probably based and notes that even the biblical materials may have been mediated to the artists by means of liturgical resources like *The Golden Legend*, a lectionary compiled by Jacobus de Voragine, bishop of Genoa, in the mid-

Fig. 4. *The Preaching of St. Peter*, Brancacci Chapel, Florence. Fresco painting by Masolino, with background details added by Masaccio (1425)

St. Peter is one of four scenes painted on the south wall of the chapel. The other three depict the apostle baptizing new believers, healing with his shadow (Acts 5:15), and distributing charity to the poor over the corpse of Ananias (Acts 4:32–5:11).

Masolino's rendering of *The Preaching of St. Peter* expresses in visual terms much of what was learned above through exegesis about this New Testament image of mission. We have here a scene in which a disciple of Jesus is shown addressing a small crowd of strangers with the gospel. Despite the hillside painted into the background, most interpreters take Peter's speech at Pentecost in Jerusalem (Acts 2:14-40) to be the underlying text on which the picture is based.[33] With an upraised arm, Peter assumes the pose of an orator. His mouth is open. He faces his audience to speak, and it is obvious from the rapt attention most of them are giving to his words that a successful act of communication is underway. Various faces in the crowd stand out with recognizable features, adding to the impression that the apostle was trying to engage a group of individuals and not an undifferentiated mass of people with his message in an effort to persuade and convince them. Peter's stature as an apostle is asserted with restraint. He has a halo, but it is tilted down and located partly behind his head and so appears to be slightly truncated. More than half of the crowd is portrayed kneeling on the ground, but the standing figures located toward the margins of the picture appear to be the same height as the apostle. As a witnessing disciple, Peter seems to be establishing eye contact with virtually everyone in the audience who is standing or kneeling in front of him.

Two Carmelite friars, identifiable by their distinctive white outer garments, are included in the crowd that listens so intently to St. Peter's

---

thirteenth century. Also important in this regard is a set of frescoes, no longer extant, that used to adorn the portico of Old Saint Peter's Church in Rome. These depicted the lives of Peter and Paul and became an authoritative point of reference for later artists. Ahl calls the Old Saint Peter's frescoes "the illustrious prototype" of the Brancacci chapel paintings (p. 146).

33. On the relationship of this fresco scene to a specific text from Acts, see Joannides, *Masaccio and Masolino*, p. 328. Obviously, the open setting indicated by the hillside weighs against this interpretation, but most experts understand the hillside to be an aesthetic rather than exegetical element in the composition, the purpose of which was to relate this scene to the one painted next to it on the lateral wall (Masaccio's *Tribute Money*). Masaccio is widely thought to be the one who painted the hillside in Masolino's *The Preaching of St. Peter,* while Masolino is usually given credit for the landscape elements in Masaccio's nearby *Baptizing the Neophytes.*

preaching.[34] In addition, the woman in the foreground dressed in black may be a tertiary belonging to the same religious order.[35] A simple — but not entirely adequate — explanation is available to account for this glaring anachronism. Since the church of Santa Maria del Carmine belonged to the monastic foundation of the Carmelites, the artist surely meant to honor the order by placing a few of its members among the background figures in the fresco. It may be that by following this artistic convention Masolino also intended to buttress the fervent claims of the Carmelites to an ancient origin that predated their establishment in the Middle Ages, as some art historians have speculated.[36] When viewed from the perspective of the twenty-first century, however, the effect of this compositional detail is quite the opposite of what may have been intended in the artist's own era. Instead of pulling a few of the painting's minor figures back into the time of the apostles, Masolino seems to have brought St. Peter forward as an announcer of Good News, whose witness was still active in the fifteenth-century context provided by the Brancacci chapel. This interpretation is supported by the fact that very few of the characters depicted in this picture are wearing the kind of clothes one might naturally associate with the first century. Besides the Carmelites, for example, we find a number of other figures whose tunics, distinctive headgear, and overall appearance fit the Quattrocento far better than they do a Greco-Roman milieu. Most profoundly, what *The Preaching of St. Peter* may be saying is that Christ's Great Commission to the apostles extended even beyond the physical boundaries of geography ("to the ends of the earth"). Indeed, as fifteenth-century contemporaries of the artists who created these frescoes symbolically participated in the event of Peter's announcement of Good News, it also stretched across time.

The apostle Paul is the subject of this chapter's second illustration (fig. 5). The image shown is one of several thousand medallion-shaped scenes that adorn the Toledo manuscript of a thirteenth-century *Bible*

34. Similarly clad figures are also inserted into one of Masaccio's frescoes, *The Raising of the Son of Theophilus and St. Peter Enthroned.*

35. For this claim, see Joannides, *Masaccio and Masolino*, p. 328.

36. Ahl, "Masaccio in the Brancacci Chapel," pp. 140-41, discusses the ongoing controversies that surrounded the foundation of the Carmelite order in the late Middle Ages. Joannides, *Masaccio and Masolino*, p. 334, accepts this explanation, while adding that the insertion of several Carmelites into the scene of St. Peter's enthronement also signaled the order's strong support for the doctrine of papal primacy.

Fig. 5. Illustration for Hebrews 4:12, Toledo *Bible moralisée* (thirteenth century)

moralisée.[37] In the *Bibles moralisées*, each roundel is part of a complex system of exegetical interpretation that combines a short biblical passage or paraphrase with a snippet of commentary (the "moralization"), both of which are portrayed visually. The biblical materials do not always control the iconographic and textual commentaries with which they appear. Quite often, by the time one encounters the illumination provided for the nonbiblical text, the original sentence(s) of Scripture with which the sequence began may no longer be readily discerned. Whether or not this is a legitimate way to approach the exegesis of the Bible is not our concern.

37. The process by which these justly celebrated books were created is described in John Lowden, *The Making of the Bibles Moralisées*, vol. 1: *The Manuscripts* (University Park: Pennsylvania State University Press, 2000). The Toledo manuscript, in three volumes, is one of four extant fully illustrated exemplars of the genre, all of which date from the first half of the thirteenth century. Lowden has calculated (pp. 4-5) that the Toledo manuscript (so named because it belongs to the archive collection of the Roman Catholic Cathedral at Toledo, Spain) contains 4,896 medallions like the one shown here.

The point is that each of the illustrations contained in the *Bibles moralisées* was executed within the context of a dynamic project of scriptural interpretation, where the capacity of the biblical text to inspire vivid, evocative, and culturally resonant visual images was explored with a maximum of creative energy.

The single image reproduced here from the Toledo *Bible moralisée* clearly represents a scene of preaching. The figure on the left can be identified as Paul on the basis of his physical appearance, which is consistently portrayed in medieval art as it is in this illustration: balding and bearded.[38] The two objects Paul holds in his hands seem to recall different aspects of his life and career. The book, of course, conventionally represents the epistolary legacy of the apostle. In the setting of this picture it also probably stands for the substance of his evangelistic message, since he seems to be proffering it to the group of people who stand opposite him in the roundel. The sword, often used in portraits of Paul as a symbol of his martyrdom, is perhaps better explained, at least in a preliminary way, by the biblical text with which the picture appears. That text is Hebrews 4:12, which famously describes the word of God as "living and active, sharper than any two-edged sword."[39] As for Paul's interlocutors, an informed reader could not fail to identify them. Bearded, with long cloaks, and wearing cone-shaped hats on their heads, these must be Jews.[40]

38. On the physical features regularly attributed to Paul in Christian art, see Luba Eleen, *The Illustration of the Pauline Epistles in French and English Bibles of the Twelfth and Thirteenth Centuries* (Oxford: Clarendon, 1982), pp. 2-3.

39. A similar notion is encountered in Ephesians 6:17, where the word of God is identified as "the sword of the Spirit." In that context, the sword is considered to be part of the "whole armor of God" (Eph. 6:11-17), with which Christians should clothe themselves in order to resist the demonic powers of the present age. Not to be ignored is the fact that the one who offers up the martial imagery highlighted in Ephesians, presumably Paul, describes himself as "an ambassador in chains" (6:20) and not as a military figure. Equally significant is the fact that Paul prays for more boldness in speaking at the end of this passage, not for an increase in weaponry.

40. In *Images of Intolerance: The Representation of Jews and Judaism in the* "Bible moralisée" (Berkeley: University of California Press, 1999), pp. 15-21, Sara Lipton discusses the different markers by which Jews were often identified in medieval Christian art. An important study on which Lipton draws is the massive investigation of Ruth Mellinkoff, *Outcasts: Signs of Otherness in Northern European Art of the Later Middle Ages,* 2 vols. (Berkeley: University of California Press, 1993). As Lipton observes (p. 16), the pointed hat *(pileum cornutum)* had become by the thirteenth century the "standard Christian iconographic convention for identifying Jews." Perhaps the most convincing illustration of this conclusion in-

Perhaps the most striking feature of this illustration lies in what it suggests about the relationship of Paul to the group of people standing in front of him. There is more than a hint in this scene that the apostle's function is not so much to invite the Jews to salvation as it is to declare them condemned as a result of their rejection of the gospel. Several clues point toward this reading of the picture. One comes from the larger literary context supplied by the book of Hebrews, in which the superiority of Christ's priesthood over the old dispensation given to Aaron and Moses is asserted with intense rhetorical force.[41] More specific to the picture itself is the fact that the front-most individuals in the group are shown raising their left hands in what appears to be a gesture of defensiveness or refusal. Their expressions, characterized by art historian Luba Eleen as "remorseful," certainly give no indication of openness to Paul's message.[42]

If the illuminators have chosen here to highlight the recalcitrance of the Jews, a major and persistent theme within the *Bibles moralisées,* then a reinterpretation of the sword in Paul's hand may be in order.[43] On the basis of Hebrews 4:12, as noted above, it is plausible that the book and the sword are presented as synonyms, with each attribute standing for God's word. Equally possible, and perhaps more likely in the thirteenth-century crusading context assumed by the *Bibles moralisées,* is the notion that the sword represents armed militancy in the presence of obduracy on the part of heretics and other enemies of Christ. It could be that a sequence of actions has been rendered in this scene of Paul preaching, with the sword coming into play at last as a response to the Jews' rejection of Paul's offer of the gospel.

---

cluded in Lipton's study is one she selects from a *Bible moralisée* in which a Jew in the process of conversion is shown taking off his distinctive hat while the man next to him discards a scroll that most likely signifies the old law (fig. 56; p. 78). Beards and long cloaks could also function as signs of Jewish alterity, but these overlapped with Christian habits of grooming and dress and so are less reliable indicators of a non-Christian religious identity in these works of art.

41. The book of Hebrews, widely accepted in the pre-modern period as a composition written by Paul for the benefit of a Jewish or Jewish-Christian audience familiar with the ritual provisions of the Old Covenant, relentlessly argues that these have been rendered meaningless by Christ's sacrifice and so are abolished (see, for example, Heb. 10:9).

42. Eleen, *Illustration of the Pauline Epistles,* p. 70. Oddly, Eleen does not attempt to interpret the gesture of the Jewish figures in this scene.

43. The works of Lipton and Mellinkoff cited above show how pervasive this motif was to become within the visual world imagined by the artists and theologians who created the *Bibles moralisées.*

What are we to make of this, in light of the exegetical work presented earlier? Remove the sword and one would have a scene in which Good News was announced but not accepted, a possibility clearly anticipated in the New Testament materials we examined. The suggestion, however, that Paul and other witnesses to the gospel have been authorized by the risen Christ to threaten or punish those who refuse to heed their call to Christian faith surely lies outside the bounds of this image of disciples in mission.

Another kind of distortion to which this image of mission seems often to have been susceptible is given visual form in the following set of illustrations (figs. 6-8). While our primary subject here may not be an apostolic figure drawn from the pages of the New Testament, he is nevertheless still widely regarded as a giant in the history of Christian mission. The particular monument to be analyzed is Ferdinand Maximilián Brokof's statue of St. Francis Xavier, which sits atop the southern parapet of Prague's most famous span across the Vltava River. The Charles Bridge itself is a jewel of late medieval European architecture, begun in 1357 at the direction of Charles IV, ruler of the Holy Roman Empire from 1355. Construction of the bridge was just a small part of an extensive building campaign that included the founding of central Europe's first university (Charles University in 1348), new fortifications for several sections of the old city, the establishment of an entirely new city quarter (New Town), and the erection of what would become a magnificent cathedral dedicated to St. Vitus (begun in 1344). By the time Emperor Charles IV died in 1378, Prague had been transformed into a visually impressive, culturally vibrant, and prosperous city, the new capital of a far-flung multinational empire and emblem of a rising sense of Bohemian national pride.

Brokof's statue would not grace the Charles Bridge for another three centuries. In the intervening period, Praguers were to witness no less than two famous defenestrations amidst a lengthy struggle to define the religious identity of their nation. At the beginning of the conflict, Jan Hus and the Taborites fought principally for religious reform, aided by partisan heroes like the palcat-wielding Jan Žižka. Later, the issue was territorial Protestantism, such as had been adopted elsewhere in northern Europe. In the end, a successful alliance of papal and German-leaning imperial interests was able to subdue Bohemia militarily (the decisive battle being fought in 1620 at the White Mountain, just outside of Prague). An extended campaign then followed to attract and deepen support in Bohemia and Moravia for the Catholic faith of their Hapsburg rulers, who exercised political control from Vienna.

The first statue to be placed on the Charles Bridge was that of St. John of Nepomuk. Jan Brokof, the father of F. M. Brokof, created it in 1683. Within the context of the ideological clash of Protestants and Counter-Reformation Catholics then still underway in the region, this choice of subject was extremely significant. For Catholics, John was a martyr, most particularly for having been thrown from the bridge into the Vltava to drown in 1378 by the emperor Wenceslas IV, who later became a supporter of Hus. There is little doubt that Jan Brokof's statue was meant to serve the cause of the Counter-Reformation in Bohemia by promoting the cult of St. John of Nepomuk, who was eventually canonized in 1729. In any event, it is known that Jan Brokof himself converted to Catholicism from Lutheranism while working on this project.[44] In this most public of venues, Jan Brokof's statue was a reminder to all who passed that Catholics had a worthy alternative to offer for the devotion many in Prague still harbored for the memory of that other example of steadfast Czech faith, Jan Hus.

Eventually, a total of thirty different monuments came to line the two sides of the Charles Bridge, the last one of Saints Cyril and Methodius being added in 1938. Ferdinand Maximilián Brokof contributed to or was solely responsible for eight of these statues, which he carved in stone or marble between 1707 and 1714. One of the remarkable features of F. M. Brokof's sculptures is that they are group compositions, rather than individual studies of the saints. Sometimes this means that several principal figures are presented together (for example, the statues of Saints Barbara, Margaret, and Elizabeth, or those of Saints Vincent Ferrer and Procopius). As a variation, Brokof also depicted single saints in the company of other characters, many of whom are clearly identifiable as non-Christians. In the latter case, the stone grouping becomes a missiological statement that can be read with respect to Brokof's understanding of evangelism and mission.

The statue of Francis Xavier that F. M. Brokof completed in 1711 was actually one of two commissioned for the bridge by the Jesuit faculties of theology and philosophy of Charles University in 1709. The other — a composition with St. Ignatius Loyola as its central subject — survives in

---

44. See Ivo Kořán, "Jan Brokof," in *DArt* 4:843.

Fig. 6. Copy of St. Francis Xavier statue, Charles Bridge, Prague, by Č. Vosmík, after Ferdinand Maximilián Brokof (1913)

Fig. 7. Detail

Fig. 8. Recovered fragment of the original statue of St. Francis Xavier, Charles Bridge, Prague, by Ferdinand Maximilián Brokof (1711)

complete form as a wooden model only (fig. 9).[45] The two groupings share many of the same characteristics of style and approach, which is not surprising given their common author, shared historical provenance, and similar theme. These are unmistakably baroque creations, which is to say that each presents a busy tableau of sensory uplift that draws the attention of the viewer heavenward. In both cases, the figure of the saint crowns the sculpture group, emerging into three-dimensional clarity out of a somewhat confusing mass of less-than-fully-realized characters and background elements.

More specific to the statue-group of Francis Xavier, one encounters three separate vertical zones. At the bottom of the piece, there are four non-European figures, atlas-like, bearing a stone slab on their shoulders or backs (cf. fig. 7). One reading of the sculpture holds that these figures personify "the four continents" and are, therefore, analogous to the four female characters one finds in the St. Ignatius group, who together support a globe on which the saint stands.[46] Actually, the racial or national background of each figure under Francis Xavier can probably be established more precisely than this on the basis of dress and physical features. The four pedestal-bearing figures in the lowest register appear to be a black African, an Indian of the subcontinent, a Central Asian native of China, and a Japanese warrior. If these identifications are correct, then the figures represent the primary populations with whom Francis Xavier came into personal contact as a Jesuit missionary or for whom he was responsible as the papacy's officially appointed "Visitor to the East."[47] Three more figures are located on top of the slab, in the middle zone of the sculpture. One of these is commonly identified as an "Oriental king" or "prince." He is shown kneeling at the feet of the saint, attended by three pages. Finally, a tower-

45. Both statues fell into the river as a result of the great flood of 1890. Pieces of each were later recovered from the water and are now on display in the national Lapidarium. The statue of Francis Xavier one finds on the bridge today was sculpted by C. Vosmík in 1913, using Brokof's design. The Cyril and Methodius sculpture erected in 1938 stands in the place originally occupied by the St. Ignatius group.

46. This is the interpretation given in Ivo Kořán, "Ferdinand Maximilián Brokof," *DArt* 4:843.

47. Francis Xavier's career in the East is carefully reviewed in Andrew C. Ross, *A Vision Betrayed: The Jesuits in Japan and China, 1542-1742* (Maryknoll, N.Y.: Orbis, 1994). In the course of his groundbreaking missionary career, Xavier engaged in evangelistic work for extended periods of time in Madagascar, India, and Japan. Although he did not actually reach China himself, Xavier did advocate and plan for Jesuit missions to that land.

Fig. 9. Model for a statue of St. Ignatius Loyola, Charles Bridge, Prague.
Ferdinand Maximilián Brokof (c. 1711)

ing, fully upright missionary figure, in whose raised left hand is held a cross, completes the sculpture.

The missiological message of F. M. Brokof's rendering of St. Francis Xavier is ambiguous. On the one hand, Brokof appears deliberate in an attempt to draw the viewer's attention to the cross. He does so by positioning the cross at the end of Francis Xavier's outstretched arm, an effect made stronger by virtue of the fact that the saint's right hand also points upward toward it (cf. fig. 8). In short, all the movement in this statue is from below to above (in keeping with the spirit of baroque art in general), and Brokof has taken care to present the cross as the final destination point for the viewer's upward sweep of attention. A complementary spiritual statement may be perceived in the ironic detail of Eastern potentates (the "Oriental king" and Japanese nobleman girt with ceremonial swords, in particular) submitting to an unarmed missioner, whose only weapon is an uplifted cross.

There is, however, another theme at work in this sculpture, which threatens to overwhelm it. Francis Xavier may be pointing to the cross of Christ, but the statue, as a whole, is also clearly about the exaltation of the hero-saint himself. At what price is this moment of missionary apotheosis achieved? There is in this composition a strong suggestion — to borrow Kamil Novotný's phrase — of the vanquished bearing aloft their conqueror.[48] If so, then F. M. Brokof has put in front of the viewer a scene of humiliation rather than liberation. When the sculpture is considered from the standpoint of those to whom supposedly Good News has been announced, hardly any other conclusion is possible. One finds no joy in the faces of the kings and commoners who represent the objects of Francis Xavier's and his fellow Jesuits' missionary efforts. Worse, it is almost as if the converted cannot get out from under the weight of the ambassador who would call them to faith in Christ. But this effect, too, may have been deliberate. If Francis Xavier and Ignatius Loyola could promise to subdue with God's help the better part of the known world, might not other heroes also soon arise, as in the days of St. John of Nepomuk, who would finally put an end to Protestant resistance back in Europe?

48. In Kamil Novotný and Emanuel Poche, *The Charles Bridge of Prague,* trans. Norah Robinson-Hronková (Prague: V. Poláček, 1947), p. 73. Novotný also points out that F. M. Brokof employed a similar approach to the figurative group he created to honor St. Vincent of Ferrara and St. Procopius. In the sculpture dedicated to Vincent and Procopius, the defeated parties Brokof carefully positioned beneath the saints may be identified as a Turk, a rabbi, and a demon.

Striking an Evangelical Posture

As the first part of this chapter attempted to show, a solid foundation exists in the New Testament for an image of mission centered on the concept of announcing Good News. In the Gospels, as we have seen, close followers of Jesus participated in his ministry of proclamation and healing by emulating their leader's own practice. When groups of disciples went out to announce the arrival of God's reign and to demonstrate its reality, they did so under Jesus' authority and at his explicit direction. The missionary efforts of the apostles continued after the ascension but showed signs of some crucial modifications having been made in the meantime. An exclusive focus on the Jews was exchanged for a theology of mission that more explicitly encompassed the whole world in all its cultural complexity. The verbal component of the apostles' missionary program was increasingly emphasized. In the speeches of Acts, Luke presents a series of announcement scenes he has shaped in ways that his presumed audience would likely find appealing. Thus, we find the apostles in Acts as a group seeming to behave and speak more like Greco-Roman orators than like Galilean peasants.

Whether in Acts or the Gospels, a few defining features of this image of mission remained constant. Announcers of Good News operated in public. Their declarations were a primary means by which large numbers of people not otherwise connected to the believing fellowship first learned about this new way of faith. Proclaimers of the gospel could speak with justified confidence, so long as they relied ultimately on Christ's power and the Spirit's presence rather than their own strength. Nevertheless, bold witnesses had to prepare for the possibility of rejection, since even Good News could be refused by those to whom it had been offered.

The works of art discussed in this chapter were included as a means by which to reflect on how this New Testament image of disciples in mission could be represented visually. We began with a Renaissance-era depiction of Peter engaged in the act of preaching. In this picture, Peter assumes a declamatory pose resembling that described in Acts for some of the apostles when they addressed sizable gatherings of people in the open. The public setting of the encounter, the face-to-face orientation of the speaker to his audience, and the sense that Peter is attempting to persuade them of something are all details in the composition that serve to tie it directly to the biblical materials we analyzed initially.

The other two works of art reviewed above appear to have introduced significant variations into the idea of Christian mission as announcement. In the *Bible moralisée* illumination of Paul preaching to the Jews, for example, a hint of compulsion or intimidation has been injected into the mission image that was not there before. Further, the artists have unnecessarily distanced Paul from his audience in the illustration by creating a sharp-edged boundary of social difference between them. This occurs because the Jews are presented in visual terms that emphasize their pariah status within the Western medieval society that produced the *Bible moralisée,* while a sainted Paul bears two symbols (the book and sword) that indicate the church's power within that same social matrix. F. M. Brokof's tribute to Francis Xavier likewise posits a kind of social relationship between the evangelizer and those to whom he had been sent to announce Good News that diverges substantially from what we saw in the New Testament (and perhaps also from Francis Xavier's own example). In this retrospective glorification of the missionary and his work, we encounter an assertion of dominance that borders on triumphalism, if not outright condescension. The apostle of Christ is shown honoring the cross but finds himself in no position to speak in gospel terms to the unevangelized, whom in this case he cannot even see, as they are literally beneath his feet.

Finally, it is necessary to mention one element in this New Testament image of mission that is missing in all of the portrayals examined thus far. This is the idea that even bold announcers of Good News, acting confidently in response to Jesus' mandate, sometimes have to risk becoming vulnerable, which means facing the prospect of setbacks, humiliation, and the appearance of social weakness.[49] From the historical perspective available to Luke and the other Evangelists, success could hardly have seemed a foregone conclusion. They knew something about the blood of the martyrs, to be sure, but could only begin to perceive the fruit that would eventually issue from the faithful sacrifice of so many steadfast witnesses. Missionaries in the pre-Constantinian church often found themselves in

---

49. David J. Bosch emphasized just this point in his perceptive study of "The Vulnerability of Mission," republished in James A. Scherer and Stephen B. Bevans, eds., *New Directions in Mission and Evangelization,* vol. 2: *Theological Foundations* (Maryknoll, N.Y.: Orbis, 1994), pp. 73-86. More recently, Stephen B. Bevans and Roger P. Schroeder have insisted that those who proclaim the gospel should expect to suffer, if theirs is to be an authentic form of mission as "prophetic dialogue." Cf. Bevans and Schroeder, *Constants in Context: A Theology of Mission for Today* (Maryknoll, N.Y.: Orbis, 2004), pp. 360-61.

precarious circumstances, yet this reality is rarely reflected in the artwork that purports to represent the life of apostolic-era Christianity.

Thus, one more illustration (fig. 10) will be provided in an attempt to plug this last crucial interpretive gap. Paul the apostle is again at the center of the picture, but the equation of social power implied in this scene is not like anything we have seen heretofore. William J. Linton's nineteenth-century engraving (after H. Anelay) is not fine art, but it does capture a spiritual truth about New Testament proclaimers of Good News that ought not to be overlooked.[50] Shorn of his saintly corona and looking slightly disheveled, the apostle speaks from below his audience, rather than dominating them from on high. Paul has been demilitarized. A soldier standing guard over him wields the only weapon shown in the scene. The main party, clothed in finery that contrasts with Paul's simple costume, sits on the dais, while retainers located to either side of them hold the fasces, which are emblems of Roman authority. Clearly, they are judging the apostle and not the other way around, just as the story line in Acts 25–26 would require. The crown on King Agrippa's head indicates his high rank, while the chain dangling from the wrist of Paul symbolizes his weak and dependent physical state.

In no position to threaten anyone, Paul is free to declare the truth about Jesus Christ, even in the face of royal prerogative, as an "ambassador in chains" (Eph. 6:20). Unencumbered by the trappings of power, his invitation to faith can be taken for what it apparently was, a guileless call to Christian discipleship: "Whether quickly or not, I pray to God that not only you but also all who are listening to me today might become such as I am — except for these chains" (Acts 26:29). In this situation, Luke's figure of Paul becomes a model announcer of Good News, whose bold but vulnerable public witness through the power of the Holy Spirit is aptly portrayed as an attempt to convince and persuade anyone who would listen.

50. Linton was just one of many engravers whose work was incorporated into *Cassell's Illustrated Family Bible* (London and New York: Cassell, Petter, and Galpin, [c. 1859-1871]). A respected craftsman whose politics also attracted a fair amount of critical attention in his day, Linton's life is recounted in F. B. Smith, *Radical Artisan: William James Linton, 1812-1897* (Manchester: Manchester University Press, 1973).

Fig. 10. "Paul before Agrippa" (Acts 26:29), illustration by William James Linton in *Cassell's Illustrated Family Bible* (c. 1859-1871)

chapter 3

Sharing Christ with Friends

From Public to Private

In this chapter, we will move from an image of mission centered on the idea of public proclamation to one that assumes an entirely different social setting. Rather than mass meetings and great gatherings, where apostles and other high-profile witnesses hold forth eloquently in front of large groups of strangers, this image of mission envisions a more relaxed environment for one's testimony and a ready willingness to consider kindly whatever expression of faith might be on offer.

Sharing Christ with friends is what happens when followers of Jesus open up to loved ones or others with whom they are already in relationship and share their experience of faith in personal terms. This is a matter of speaking and acting from within some kind of defined community, as an accepted member of a recognized "we." Polished speech is not needed in this social zone. Here we find everyday, informal, and more spontaneous methods of communication pushing aside the refined rhetorical styles normally associated with public speaking. This is mission conceived on a small scale, where the authority of the speaker to address others on behalf of Christ is simply not an issue.

The initial burden of this chapter will be to demonstrate how the idea of disciples sharing Christ with friends was active from the beginning of Jesus' own ministry. As we will see, this approach to mission surfaces with some regularity in the Gospel of John, so much so that one suspects it to have been among the ordinary ways by which new disciples were introduced to the company of Jesus. While not as prominently on display outside the Fourth Gospel, this pattern of disciple-making was also at work in Matthew, Mark, and Luke. Once the scriptural basis of this mission image has been established, we will focus on the challenge of representing it visually. This is no easy task, since the type of missionary encounter under consideration in this chapter rarely takes place in dramatic circumstances and so has not often figured as a subject worthy of artistic attention. Our discussion will conclude with a summary review of the particular features that describe mission as an act of sharing Christ with friends.

Three Paths to Discipleship

How did Jesus come to have disciples? This is a deceptively simple question, but one with deep implications for understanding Jesus' practice of mission. Jesus lived in a world where the making of disciples was a common part of life. The Pharisees had their disciples and so did John the Baptist (cf. Mark 2:18; John 1:35). The great teachers of Jesus' age, whether of the Torah or of the leading Greek philosophies of the day, likewise attracted dedicated followings, some of which grew to be recognized as "schools" that survived the passing of their patronymic founders. Then there was the long tradition of prophetic leadership in Israel that included within it several examples of groups gathered around a central figure (like the bands of prophets around Samuel or the "sons of the prophets" in the time of Elijah), plus the idea of individual prophetic succession, as with Elijah and Elisha.

In these different cases, "following after" could mean many things, including conversion to a set of ideas, personal identification with a renowned teacher, or complete separation from one's family. The call to discipleship might even mean withdrawing from common society altogether, in order to join a new community of like-minded individuals (as with the Essenes). Whatever the meaning of discipleship in these different contexts might have been, the question of enrollment remains an equally important issue. Did new disciples come of their own accord or were they recruited? Were extraordinary acts of power decisive or was it the message that established the reputation of the leader and drew followers to him or her? Did initiates identify themselves primarily with a person, a cause, or a commu-

nity? Others will have to explore these questions with reference to the contemporaries of Jesus who also gathered followers.[1] Here we will concentrate on the disciples of Jesus and how they came to be associated with
him. This will set the stage to explore more fully a second way by which
followers of the historical Jesus participated in his disciple-making activities.

In the Gospels, three distinct pathways to discipleship seem to stand
out. First, we know the stories of a few individuals who adhered to Jesus
because he explicitly called them to himself. Others, most of them unknown to us by name, were attracted to Jesus by his growing reputation
and so, apparently, chose on their own to begin to follow him. A third
group is comprised of those followers who were introduced to Jesus by ac-
quaintances, friends, and kin. Like those drawn by hearsay reports, these,
too, ultimately had to choose to become disciples after their initial encounter, but the possibility of this happening depended, in the first instance, on the witness of someone else who had already committed herself
or himself to Jesus.

In the Synoptic Gospels, the first two of these three patterns clearly
predominate. Indeed, as we have seen, in the description of the beginning
of Jesus' ministry laid out by Mark (followed closely by Matthew), Jesus
had no followers until he decided to call Peter and Andrew and then James
and John from their nets to a new vocation (Mark 1:16-20; Matt. 4:18-22)
(see fig. 11). In this scene, the initiative belongs entirely to Jesus. He sees the
brothers at work on or near the Sea of Galilee and draws close enough to

---

1. A foundational study of Jesus' radical demand to leave all and follow him (cf. Matt.
8:21-22) in the context of his first-century Greco-Roman milieu is Martin Hengel, *Nachfolge
und Charisma* (Berlin: Walter de Gruyter, 1968) (English trans. by James Greig, *The Charismatic Leader and His Followers* [New York: Crossroad, 1981]). R. Alan Culpepper discusses a
wide range of operative first-century teacher-disciple relationships, both Hellenistic and
Jewish, in *The Johannine School: An Evaluation of the Johannine-School Hypothesis Based on
an Investigation of the Nature of Ancient Schools*, SBLDS 26 (Missoula: Scholars, 1975). More
recent examples of comparative analysis are offered by Whitney Taylor Shiner, *Follow Me!
Disciples in Markan Rhetoric*, SBLDS 145 (Atlanta: Scholars, 1995), and Michael J. Wilkins,
Discipleship in the Ancient World and Matthew's Gospel, second ed. (Grand Rapids: Baker
Books, 1995). In *Mission and Conversion: Proselytizing in the Religious History of the Roman
Empire* (Oxford: Clarendon, 1994), Martin Goodman not only evaluates the possible roots
of the church's first-century universal mission in pagan and Jewish practices but also con-
siders the effect that successful Christian efforts to proselytize may have had on Judaism after 100 CE.

Fig. 11. *The Call of Peter and Andrew,* early Christian mosaic (sixth century),
S. Apollinare Nuovo, Ravenna

be heard. Significantly, his first words to those who would become the nucleus of his inner circle are a command. In Mark's and Matthew's versions of the story, Jesus declares simply, "Follow me," and the two sets of brothers in turn do just that, leaving work and family behind in order to become attached to the one who had summoned them.

Luke proposes a slightly different setting for the call of the first disciples than that offered by the first two Evangelists. Jesus is said here to have encountered Peter, James, and John washing their equipment at the end of a fruitless session on the lake (rather than while fishing, as in Matthew, or before starting out, as Mark seems to assume). In Luke 5:1-11, Jesus begins by teaching a crowd of people while sitting in Peter's boat. Then he instructs Peter to resume fishing, a suggestion that Peter considers ill-advised, but which he nevertheless follows. The result, of course, is a miraculous catch of fish that requires another boat and the help of James and John in order to haul the "great shoal of fish" (Luke 5:6 RSV) onto the shore.

As numerous commentators have pointed out, the scene in Luke 5 and the dialogue between Jesus and Peter recorded there bring to mind not only Mark's and Matthew's accounts of the first disciples' call narrative but also the resurrection appearance of Jesus to the disciples at the Sea of Galilee recounted in John 21.[2] Be that as it may, Luke still exhibits here the basic pattern of disciple-making by direct command established for Jesus' earliest ministry by Mark. The first step in the call of the Twelve in Luke is still Jesus' own, just as it is in the other Synoptic Gospels. It is Jesus who seeks out those who will become his closest associates and bids them to follow as "fishers of people." And, in the end, these initial followers demonstrate their commitment to Jesus in the same way reported by Mark and Matthew, by leaving behind their former life as catchers of fish in order to follow him.

The story of the call of Levi (or Matthew) the tax collector, reported in all three Synoptic Gospels, is enough to establish that Jesus continued to call disciples directly to himself, in the same way he summoned Peter (and Andrew) and the sons of Zebedee.[3] Countless more persons, however, plainly undertook to follow Jesus on their own. All four of the Gospels make clear that as Jesus moved through Galilee and then on to Jerusalem, teaching and healing, large groups of people were drawn to him. At certain points in the narrative, the "crowds" came to number in the thousands, which explains why Jesus occasionally had to resort to teaching from hillsides or boats.

At the beginning of his ministry, Jesus' spreading fame as a teacher and healer is what attracted the multitudes to him from "Galilee, the Decapolis, Jerusalem, Judea, and from beyond the Jordan" (Matt. 4:25; cf. Luke 6:17 and Mark 1:28). We may assume that most of those who followed

2. The chief similarities that suggest some kind of relationship between John 21 and Luke 5:1-11 are Jesus' instructions to fish after a night of toil without result, the size of the extraordinary catch that ensues, and the enhanced role given to Peter in Luke when compared to the call accounts reported in Mark and Matthew. The similarities and differences between Luke 5 and John 21 are efficiently summarized in Joseph A. Fitzmyer, *The Gospel according to Luke (1–9): Introduction, Translation, and Notes* (Garden City, N.Y.: Doubleday, 1981), pp. 560-62.

3. Cf. Mark 2:13-14; Matthew 9:9; Luke 5:27-28. Except for the variation in the name of the called disciple, the correspondence of these accounts to each other is unmistakable. In each case, Levi/Matthew abandons his work without discussion at Jesus' terse command: "Follow me."

did no more than observe Jesus at a distance from within the anonymity of the throng, merely curious in a neutral way about what they were hearing and seeing. Others obviously came with a particular need in mind, and some of these presented themselves to Jesus with a specific request for help. Examples of this latter category abound in the Gospels. A well-known example would be the intertwined stories of Jairus's daughter and the woman who touched Jesus' garment in order to be healed of her persistent flow of blood (Mark 5:21-43). Of course, one finds mixed in with the inquisitive and the hopeful another group of considerably less sympathetic figures — the lawyers, scribes, and Pharisees — whose questions and responses to Jesus were meant to challenge and embarrass him in front of the multitude and so expose what they considered to be the false, demonic basis of his words and actions.

Certainly, not everyone who trailed after Jesus for a time became a devoted disciple. The merely curious would soon find another object for their passive attention. The implacably hostile would eventually retire to plot Jesus' demise. Of the more fervent from among Jesus' followers, even many of these turned away when the full implications of discipleship became more evident.

A poignant example of shallow fidelity to Jesus is presented in the Synoptic story of the rich young man. Even in the scant account offered by Mark (10:17-22), the reader is given an attractively drawn character who appears ready to enroll himself among Jesus' followers. With no apparent prompting from Jesus, the rich young man presented himself to the one whom he called "Good Teacher" in order to ask about how he might inherit eternal life. The respectful tone of his address and the young man's posture (kneeling), plus the eagerness signaled by his running to meet Jesus and the rectitude of his life up to the point of this encounter ("Teacher, I have kept all these [commandments] since my youth"), are details that together seem to indicate a sincere attempt to align himself with Jesus' program.[4] But Jesus' response, uttered in the context of his own tragic journey to Jerusalem already announced in the first two Passion predictions (Mark 8:31-33; 9:30-32), asked for a greater sacrifice than the rich young man was willing to give. When Jesus articulated the full implications of his Way ("Sell what you own, and give the money to the poor, and

---

4. The suggestive details of running and kneeling are reported only in Mark's rendering of the story. Cf. Matt. 19:16-22 and Luke 18:18-30.

you will have treasure in heaven; then come, follow me"), the would-be disciple abandoned his quest in sorrow, unable to continue on the difficult path marked out by Jesus for himself and his own.[5]

Others from the crowd came away from their encounters with Jesus neither indifferent nor disappointed but with hopes fulfilled and lives transformed. In a few cases, those healed in mind and body give unmistakable evidence of faith and demonstrate disciple-like behavior.[6] The clearest example of self-initiated enrollment from among Jesus' followers is found in the story of blind Bartimaeus, who thrusts himself onto Jesus from the side of the Jericho road (Mark 10:46-52). Undeterred by the crowd's attempt to silence him, Bartimaeus implores Jesus for mercy and then asks for the gift of sight. Like the rich young man, Bartimaeus is importunate and eager in Mark's account (10:50: "throwing off his cloak, he sprang up and came to Jesus"). The surprise in this encounter lies not only in the

---

5. Another explicit reference to disaffection among those drawn to Jesus is recorded in John 6. Jesus' "difficult teaching" about eating his flesh and drinking his blood causes offense, with the result that "many of his disciples turned back and no longer went about with him" (John 6:66). Likewise, Luke 9:57-62 offers several examples of qualified affiliation that Jesus rejects (e.g., "first let me go and bury my father").

6. A strict definition of "following after" the historical Jesus will insist on an explicit call to discipleship, taken at Jesus' initiative, followed by a period of intensive training with the master. Thus, John P. Meier, "The Circle of the Twelve: Did It Exist during Jesus' Public Ministry?" *JBL* 116 (1997): 636-37, and Hans Weder, "Disciple, Discipleship," *ABD* 2:207-8, among others. Seen from this perspective, other followers not called directly by Jesus may be designated, at best, "devoted adherents." Meier has since refined his position in *A Marginal Jew: Rethinking the Historical Jesus,* vol. 3: *Companions and Competitors* (New York: Doubleday, 2001), pp. 19-285. While continuing to stipulate the necessity of a call from Jesus, taken at his initiative, as a *sine qua non* of discipleship in the Gospels, Meier nevertheless allows for the possibility that Jesus "actively accepted and cooperated" with some who sought to follow him (p. 78). In this way, Meier is able to affirm that Jesus had women disciples among his most dedicated followers, despite the fact that the Evangelists do not actually designate them as such and no explicit call narratives are recorded for any of them. This important clarification seems to bring Meier into agreement with the view adopted here, which is also that of James D. G. Dunn, *Jesus' Call to Discipleship* (Cambridge: Cambridge University Press, 1992). Dunn's position is that there were "circles of disciples" recognized by Jesus, some of whom initiated their relationship to him. Elizabeth Struthers Malbon, *In the Company of Jesus: Characters in Mark's Gospel* (Louisville: Westminster John Knox, 2000), p. 77, nicely sums up the relationship between "following" and "discipleship" in these terms: "It would appear that following, while central to discipleship, is not limited to 'disciples.' The category of 'followers' overlaps with the categories of 'the disciples' and 'the crowd.' . . . Being 'for' Jesus is not defined by membership among the twelve disciples. . . ."

healing of the blind beggar, but equally in the story's conclusion that after receiving his sight Bartimaeus immediately "followed [Jesus] on the way." This appears to be an explicit use of technical disciple-making language, even though the initiative clearly lay with Bartimaeus and not Jesus himself.[7] Paul Achtemeier goes so far as to characterize Mark's story of Bartimaeus as another call narrative, on a par with the accounts offered earlier in the Second Gospel that describe how the first of the twelve disciples began to follow Jesus.[8]

One finds in the Synoptic Gospels a host of other, mostly minor characters who are not directly called by Jesus as followers, but who act like disciples nonetheless.[9] These would include figures like the woman who anointed Jesus at Bethany (Mark 14:3-9) and Joseph of Arimathea (Mark 15:42-46), a man of some prominence who provided for Jesus after his death as the disciples of John did for their leader (cf. Mark 6:29). Then there is Mary Magdalene, who with two women companions is described in Mark 15:40-41 as one of those who had "followed" Jesus in Galilee and "provided" for his needs. These three and "many other women" had gone up to Jerusalem with Jesus. The deep quality of their discipleship is evident in the fact that they continued to accompany Jesus even to the cross and then to the tomb (Mark 16:1). Their loyalty to Jesus stands in vivid contrast

7. One has to be careful not to leap too quickly to the conclusion that Bartimaeus became a disciple of Jesus in the fullest possible sense. Certainly, the possibility exists that he became just another one of the hangers-on in Jesus' larger entourage, albeit a grateful one. For some very good reasons, Jack Dean Kingsbury concludes for Matthew's parallel account of the two blind men healed outside of Jericho that a literal following along behind Jesus as a part of the crowd was all that developed from this encounter. See Kingsbury, "The Verb *Akolouthein* ('to Follow') As an Index of Matthew's View of His Community," *JBL* 97 (1978): 56-62. In Mark, however, three details seem to tip the scale decisively in the direction of actual discipleship as the ultimate result of the story: Jesus' recognition of Bartimaeus's faith, the reference to his following Jesus "on the way" (which, at this point in the Gospel, can only mean to the cross), and the lack of a reference to a crowd that follows Jesus at the beginning of the story (as at Matt. 20:29).

8. Paul J. Achtemeier, "'And He Followed Him': Miracles and Discipleship in Mark 10:46-52," *Semeia* 11 (1978): 115-45.

9. Cf. Joel F. Williams, *Other Followers of Jesus: Minor Characters As Major Figures in Mark's Gospel*, JSNTSup 102 (Sheffield: JSOT, 1994), and the summary of his findings offered in Joel F. Williams, "Discipleship and Minor Characters in Mark's Gospel," *Bibliotheca Sacra* 153 (1996): 332-43. Malbon, *In the Company of Jesus*, pp. 198-205, draws attention to these characters as "exemplars" of faith, who more often than not outshine the innermost circle of Jesus' disciples.

SHARING CHRIST WITH FRIENDS

to the behavior of the crowds that had long since disappeared, but especially to the Twelve, all of whom had by this time abandoned their leader.[10]

One would like to have more details to fill out the fragmentary picture we have of these minor characters who exhibit disciple-like devotion to Jesus. This much is known: Mary Magdalene was apparently drawn to Jesus as a supplicant, possessed by demons (Luke 8:2; cf. Mark 16:9). Joseph of Arimathea, a respected member of the Sanhedrin, is described as a seeker after the kingdom of God (Mark 15:43). The woman who anoints Jesus at Bethany simply appears in the narrative without explanation. The key common circumstance of their encounters with Jesus is this: all three risked something in order to honor Jesus and identify themselves with him at the time of his (approaching) death. Mary Magdalene and the other women risked the shame of being associated with a convicted criminal on the occasion of his execution. Perhaps that is why they only drew near enough to view the crucifixion "from a distance." In the case of Joseph of Arimathea, the reader of Mark's Gospel is told that Joseph needed courage in order to approach Pilate to ask for the body.[11] Ironically, the woman at

---

10. According to the shorter ending of Mark, these followers also appear to desert Jesus at the last by not fulfilling the command of the heavenly messenger to inform the disciples of what they had seen and heard (Mark 16:7-8). Not all interpreters accept this conclusion, however. Cf. the brief summary of the problem offered in Larry Hurtado, "Following Jesus in the Gospel of Mark — and Beyond," in *Patterns of Discipleship in the New Testament,* ed. Richard Longenecker (Grand Rapids: Eerdmans, 1996), pp. 23-24. In support of a more generous reading of the women's actions, we may also note that the other Gospels credit them with having reported to others what they had witnessed at the empty tomb (cf. Matt. 28:8; Luke 24:8-11; John 20:1-2). Additionally, in the longer ending of Mark (16:9-11), Mary Magdalene is said to have told a disbelieving group of disciples that Jesus appeared to her immediately after the resurrection.

11. John 19:38 will add that Joseph came to Pilate secretly, "because of his fear of the Jews." Exactly how much Joseph might have risked by requesting the body of Jesus is a matter of some contention among the exegetes. For example, on the basis of Joseph's standing as a leader of the Jewish community in Jerusalem, Gottfried Fitzer, "τολμάω," *TDNT* 8:183, concludes that nothing at all "venturesome" is indicated in Joseph's actions. It is difficult to accept, however, that Joseph's decision to associate himself publicly with the corpse of a condemned criminal carried no *potential* consequences. In contrast to Fitzer, the latest edition of BAGD recognizes at Mark 15:43 an element of possible danger lying behind the Greek verb τολμάω, with the result that Joseph is understood to have exercised a measure of bravery, courage, or (at least) daring by approaching Pilate with this request. Raymond E. Brown carefully reviews the evidence provided in each Gospel concerning Joseph of Arimathea in *The Death of the Messiah: From Gethsemane to the Grave; A Commentary on the Passion Nar-*

Bethany had to endure the scorn of Jesus' other disciples when she "wasted" her costly nard by pouring it over Jesus' head in preparation for his death (Mark 14:3-9). Whatever else might be learned from these minor characters, their example confirms that Jesus in the Synoptics had at least some followers who began their journey to faithful discipleship without the benefit of a direct call from Jesus himself.

Disciple-Making in John

One detects from the start a different perspective on the making of disciples in the Gospel of John than that found in the Synoptics. Not only is the call of the first disciples handled in an entirely new way, but the whole approach to disciple-making seems to have shifted. In a relatively few instances, Jesus will initiate the calling of individual disciples. At the same time, there appear to be no examples of self-initiated enrollment among the followers of Jesus in the Gospel of John.[12] In this Gospel, Jesus' earliest followers will most often come to him by means of another disciple's introduction. This, of course, is what sharing Christ with friends is all about.

---

ratives in the Four Gospels (New York: Doubleday, 1994), vol. 2, pp. 1213-32. Brown concludes that Joseph was probably not a disciple of Jesus when he requested the corpse from Pilate, but became one later (reflected in Matt. 27:57). At the same time, Brown acknowledges that Joseph risked being mistaken for one of Jesus' disciples when he requested the body for burial. If the reader of the story knows in retrospect that Joseph eventually did become a Christian, it is natural to interpret his actions as an example of disciple-like behavior.

12. In the book of John, no one emerges from the crowds that follow Jesus who truly resembles the minor-disciple characters in the Synoptics like Bartimaeus, although several candidates merit consideration. The royal official whose son is healed by Jesus in 4:46-54, for example, is said to have believed along with his whole house, but no indication is given that he began to follow Jesus or that he gave evidence of some other disciple-like behavior. Nicodemus (3:1-21) approached Jesus, recognizing him as a teacher come from God, and, at the end of this Gospel, he is credited with having assisted Joseph of Arimathea in the preparation of Jesus' body for burial. Serious defects in their commitment to Jesus, however, inhibit both of these figures from becoming fully realized models of discipleship. The faith of Nicodemus, for instance, never rises to the level of spiritual reality to which Jesus' enigmatic discourse points. Joseph's devotion is compromised by fear at the end of the story (19:38). Finally, the Greeks who seek out Jesus in John 12 are recognized as a kind of eschatological trigger with respect to Jesus' "hour," but they do not produce any confession or witness to Jesus and so cannot be taken as disciples.

The Johannine Jesus does call to himself at least one disciple directly. This is Philip, whose initial encounter with Jesus is told in the barest of terms in John 1:43-44. He is the only disciple in this Gospel whose relationship to Jesus is plainly established by a command to follow.[13] There is, however, no indication whatsoever in the story of Philip's call that he abandoned everything in obedience to this order, in contrast to the accounts of Jesus' call to the first disciples found in the Synoptics. Here, the reader has to assume solely on the basis of Philip's missionary activity (i.e., telling Nathanael about Jesus) that he had faithfully responded to Jesus' command. As we shall see, this way of portraying genuine discipleship is directly linked to the overall purpose of John's Gospel.

The healing of the man born blind, an extended narrative presented in John 9, represents a second instance of direct disciple-making by Jesus in the Fourth Gospel. Again, Jesus chooses to approach whom he will, rather than responding to some kind of entreaty. As the miracle story is told, no appeal is made to Jesus for healing. In fact, the man himself says nothing until *after* he gains his sight, speaking then in response to questions about the circumstances of his healing and what it might say about Jesus. Introductory remarks attributed to Jesus (9:3-5) establish that this incident is to be understood as another occasion on which the actions of Jesus make manifest the "works of God" by revealing his true identity as the "light of the world." The ensuing dialogue that involves the man, his parents, and a group of Pharisees allows other issues to surface, including Jesus' apparent violation of the Sabbath and, most important, the Pharisees' fatal pathology of spiritual blindness.

Nowhere in John 9 does Jesus command the man born blind to follow him, nor is the reader told explicitly that such is the result of this encounter, but one can reasonably surmise that the man healed of his congenital blindness in some sense became a disciple of Jesus. The narrator frames the forced choice before the man who had been born blind in these terms: "the Jews had already agreed that anyone who confessed Jesus to be the Messiah would be put out of the synagogue" (9:22).[14] To discourage the

13. The only other place in John's Gospel where this command is given occurs in chapter 21, where Jesus twice tells Peter, "Follow me." An intriguing but entirely undeveloped detail contained in the story of Philip's call mentions that he came from Bethsaida, "the city of Andrew and Peter" (John 1:44). The author of the Gospel casts no light on the role these two near neighbors might have had in Philip's journey to discipleship.

14. It is likely that many in the narrator's own community had faced or could antici-

man from confessing Jesus, the Pharisees offer counter-testimony to Jesus as a sinner (9:24). Mockingly, but ironically, they call the man a disciple of Jesus (9:28) and then expel him from the synagogue when he refuses to heed the correction they offer in the name of Moses. The man born blind confirms his allegiance to Jesus with a strongly worded confession ("Lord, I believe"), but even before this he had begun to act the part of a genuine disciple by witnessing repeatedly, with artless transparency, to the one who had opened his eyes.

An argument can be made that the Samaritan woman whose meeting with Jesus is portrayed in John 4:1-42 is a third individual called directly by Jesus in the Fourth Gospel to become his disciple. In many respects, her story resembles that of the man born blind. As on that occasion, Jesus is the one who initiates the conversation with her. After all, she had come to the well to draw water, not to see Jesus (4:7). Like the man born blind, the Samaritan woman is slow to recognize the full significance of who Jesus is. Her confession is also offered in several stages, the first of which focuses on Jesus as a prophet (4:19; cf. 9:17). In the course of the two narratives, each one's confession is seen to move toward an identification of Jesus as the Messiah. Certainly, it is easier to claim that the man born blind became an actual disciple of Jesus than to assert the same for the Samaritan woman. Her confession, for all its progress in the direction of faith in Jesus, never achieves the precision and fearless candor of the testimony offered by the man born blind in the presence of Jesus' enemies. In comparison, the Samaritan woman's faith — at least as she is able to articulate it verbally — remains ambiguous or tentative.[15]

The strongest grounds on which to suggest that the Samaritan woman became a disciple of Jesus are based on her actions, not her words.

---

pate having to make the same hard decision. Cf. Raymond E. Brown, *The Gospel according to John (1–12): Introduction, Translation, and Notes* (Garden City: Doubleday, 1966), pp. 379-80.

15. Commentators are divided with respect to the meaning of what the Samaritan woman says. Her strongest statement at John 4:29 ("He cannot be the Messiah, can he?") is variously interpreted as skeptical, hesitant, incomplete, hopeful, and/or faithful. Teresa Okure effectively summarizes the views of the commentators on this point in *The Johannine Approach to Mission: A Contextual Study of John 4:1-42*, WUNT 2/31 (Tübingen: J. C. B. Mohr [Paul Siebeck], 1988), pp. 169-70. It is certainly true that the Samaritan woman has nothing to offer by way of a verbal witness that could compare with the blind man's simple declaration of faith at 9:38 ("Lord, I believe") or even his earlier rhetorical affirmation of Jesus' relationship to God: "If this man were not from God, he could do nothing" (9:33).

The woman's first impulse, when it finally dawns on her that Jesus *might* be the expected Messiah, is to share this insight with her fellow Samaritans. We may recall that this is exactly what Philip did on the occasion of his own call to discipleship. And we may note that in spite of the Samaritan woman's less than ideal formulation of her witness to Jesus ("Come and see a man who told me everything that I have ever done! He cannot be the Messiah, can he?"), the outcome of her response to Jesus is far greater than what Philip was able to accomplish. In contrast to Nathanael's initially cautious reply to Philip's witness to him ("Can anything good come out of Nazareth?"), it is reported that "many Samaritans from that city believed in [Jesus] because of the woman's testimony" (4:39).

It is surely significant that even when Jesus takes the initiative to approach and call these three would-be disciples in the Gospel of John, the result is another kind of disciple-making that involves Jesus' followers giving witness to others. This is in keeping with a distinctive Johannine emphasis on testimony to Jesus as faith's most substantial foundation. The programmatic text in the Gospel for this idea is the reply of Jesus to Thomas: "Have you believed because you have seen me? Blessed are those who have not seen and yet have come to believe" (20:29). As Andreas Köstenberger has observed, a "widening" of the term μαθητής takes place in John, so that the difference between earlier and later followers of Jesus, those who responded to Jesus during his lifetime and those who come to faith subsequently, becomes meaningless. Seen from a Johannine perspective, as Köstenberger points out, following Jesus evolves "from a physical remaining with Jesus (cf. 1:37-43) to a spiritual remaining in Jesus' word (cf. 8:31) and a remaining 'in Jesus' beyond the time of his earthly ministry (cf. 15:4-7)."[16]

The way for this theological development to emerge is further prepared by the many stories presented in John's Gospel in which disciples of the historical Jesus are clearly shown to have come to him by means of the witness of someone else. According to the account given in the Fourth Gospel, this is the case even for the very first disciples of Jesus, who are pointed in his direction by John the Baptist. As related in 1:35-39, Andrew and another one of John's disciples hear the Baptist identify Jesus as the "Lamb of God," and, on the basis of John's testimony, they begin to follow

16. Andreas Köstenberger, *The Missions of Jesus and the Disciples according to the Fourth Gospel: With Implications for the Fourth Gospel's Purpose and the Mission of the Contemporary Church* (Grand Rapids: Eerdmans, 1998), p. 149.

Jesus. This leads to an invitation from Jesus to stay with him, which they accept. Next, the pattern is repeated when Andrew witnesses to his brother Simon ("we have found the Messiah") and then brings him to Jesus. Again a direct relationship is established as a second step of discipleship when Simon meets Jesus and is renamed Cephas/Peter (1:42).

Several other examples of disciples bringing friends and kin to Jesus are likewise highlighted in the Gospel of John. Thus, Philip seeks out his fellow Galilean, Nathanael, and tells him, "we have found him about whom Moses in the law and also the prophets wrote, Jesus son of Joseph from Nazareth" (1:45). Philip then issues to Nathanael the same invitation Jesus offered to Andrew and the other disciple of John: "Come and see." Jesus himself recognizes the role played by Philip in Nathanael's coming to him, but he relativizes it at the same time. Even before Philip spoke to Nathanael "under the fig tree," Jesus tells Nathanael, "I saw you" (1:48). Jesus' foreknowledge evokes an enthusiastic confession of faith from Nathanael: "Rabbi, you are the Son of God! You are the King of Israel!"

As noted above, the Samaritan woman also serves as a means by which Jesus becomes known to some who had never before heard of him. Her imperfect witness to Jesus in the city of the Samaritans induces a number of them to seek him out. "Many Samaritans" believe in Jesus, it is said, "because of the woman's testimony" (4:39). A short stay by Jesus among the Samaritans will result in "many more" coming to faith. At the end of the narrative, these latter believers in Jesus from Samaria will declare that their faith no longer rests on the woman's speech, but on Jesus' own word.

A hint of male chauvinism is certainly possible here, but another interpretation seems more likely. The Samaritans' robust confession of Jesus as the "Savior of the world" could hardly have resulted directly from the woman's testimony to Jesus as someone "who told me everything I have ever done." One does not have to discount her speech as a form of "idle chatter" in order to recognize the importance of Jesus' own testimony to himself. Rudolf Schnackenburg probably strikes the right balance when he observes that the Samaritan woman's report engendered an "initial faith," illustrated by a readiness to believe, which then became "more widespread (v. 41), firmer (42a) and deeper (42b) through Jesus' own work as revealer."[17] In any event, one must not overlook the obvious but crucial

17. Rudolf Schnackenburg, *The Gospel according to St. John,* trans. Kevin Smyth (New York: Crossroad, 1990), vol. 1, p. 455.

narrative fact that in this story the Samaritan woman was the critical evangelistic link between the inhabitants of her city and Jesus. The Samaritans' first contact with Jesus' word — and Jesus the Word — took place because the woman who met Jesus at the well of Jacob shared what she had experienced there with those closest to her.

A wonderful illustration of this story that not only treats the meeting of the Samaritan woman with Jesus but also the coming to faith of her neighbors is contained in an early-fourteenth-century Armenian illuminated manuscript now known as the Gladzor Gospels.[18] I include it here (fig. 12; plate 1) as a way to show how the witness of the Samaritan woman might be understood as an act of sharing Christ with friends. The miniature combines into one composite scene the several episodes in John 4 that involve the Samaritan woman. The Samaritan woman faces a seated Jesus with the well situated between them. Her jar rests on the ground while she uses some kind of rope to draw water from the well. In the background above the well are depicted three of the disciples, who have returned from a nearby village with a basket of food (cf. John 4:8). Behind the woman are four other figures. The one standing closest to her may be intended to represent her "husband" (4:16-18), or, perhaps, he is the spokesman for the group of neighbors who came out of their city to meet Jesus on the strength of her testimony.[19]

Two striking details included in this rendition of "Christ and the Samaritan Woman" beg for a missiological reading of the scene. The first appears in the distinctive form of dress worn by the man who stands just be-

18. This illustration is one of fifty-four magnificent paintings that grace the Gladzor Gospels. A recent study of the manuscript that includes a fine set of artistic reproductions is Thomas F. Mathews and Alice Taylor, *The Armenian Gospels of Gladzor: The Life of Christ Illuminated* (Los Angeles: J. Paul Getty Museum, 2001). *Christ and the Samaritan Woman* is reproduced as plate 54 in that book. The artist responsible for this miniature has been identified as T'oros (Theodore) of Taron, who was the most famous of the artists connected to the monastery at Gladzor in Armenia. On what is known about his background, see Mathews and Taylor, *Armenian Gospels of Gladzor*, p. 16.

19. Mathews and Taylor, *Armenian Gospels of Gladzor*, p. 45, interpret the standing figure as the woman's husband. Since his gestures appear to indicate that he is engaging Jesus in conversation, it seems more likely to me that he is acting as the villagers' spokesperson. If this is the case, he is either inviting Jesus to remain with them (4:40) or is articulating on their behalf the confession that concludes the story: "It is no longer because of what you said that we believe, for we have heard for ourselves, and we know that this is truly the Savior of the world" (4:42). The Samaritan woman's husband is referred to indirectly in the story but does not actually appear as a character.

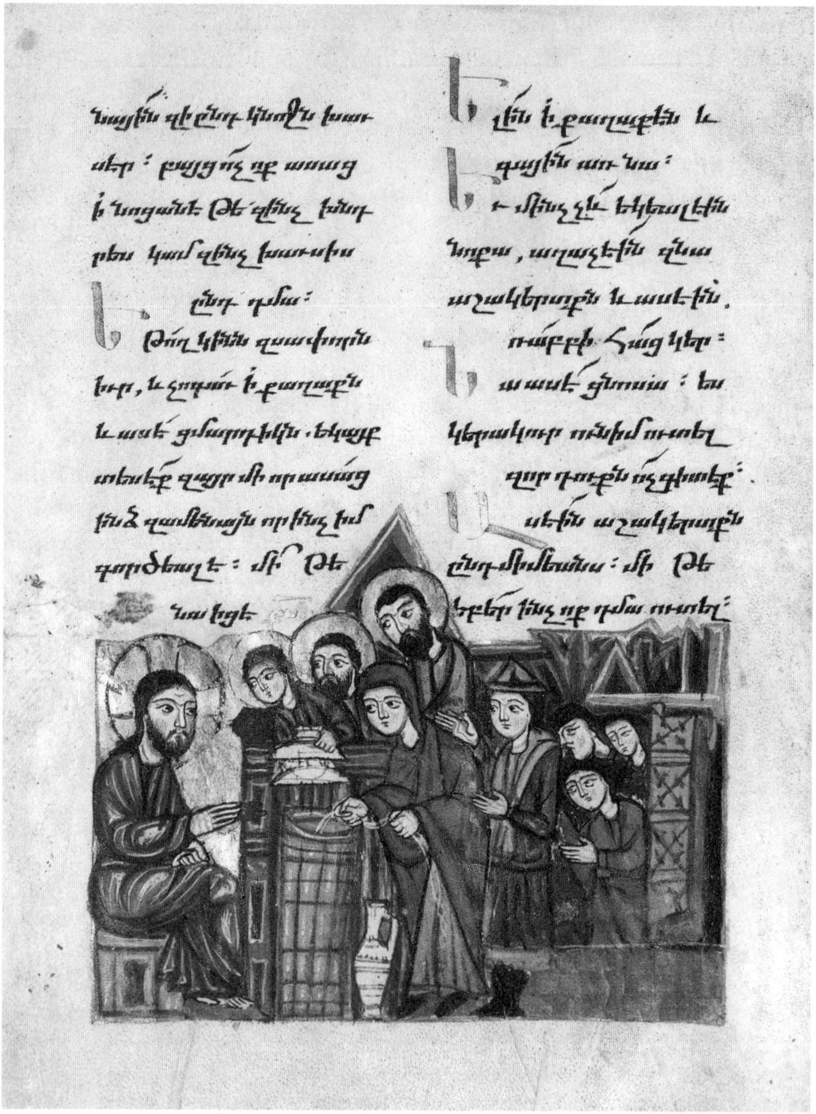

Fig. 12. *Christ and the Samaritan Woman,* by T'oros (Theodore) of Taron, a monk in the Armenian monastery at Gladzor (early fourteenth century)

hind the Samaritan woman. The style of his pointed cap and fur-lined coat has been identified as typical of the Mongols in this period, which would mean that a rather telling allusion to the artist's contemporary circumstances has been inserted into this visual account of Christ's story. In the thirteenth and fourteenth centuries, active efforts were underway to evangelize the Mongols, and the nation of Armenia in Central Asia was one of the first places where these nomads from the East would have come into contact with a region-wide social matrix dominated by Christianity.[20] If this reading of the painting is correct, then a rather extraordinary example of contextualization has taken place. By including a figure that would be instantly recognized as a non-Armenian from the East (and, therefore, most likely a non-Christian), the artist may be attempting, in the words of Thomas Mathews and Alice Taylor, to "express the universality of Christ's mission by extending it even to the Mongols."[21]

A second potentially significant detail is indicated by the way the other Samaritans are positioned in the painting and their posture. Even more than the Samaritan woman and the three disciples who appear in the tableau, these figures are shown leaning toward Jesus, as though listening intently. But because they are placed furthest away from Jesus in the picture, an impression is created that they are somehow listening in on the conversation taking place between Jesus and the Samaritan woman. In effect, when the woman reports to them a part of her interaction with Jesus, that is precisely what happens. By sharing what she knew about the man she had met at the well, the Samaritan woman gave her neighbors an opportunity to participate in a dialogue with Jesus that had begun with her. Something similar takes place when Christian believers share their experience of Christ with family, friends, and others living nearby.

20. At the turn of the fourteenth century, European efforts to evangelize the Mongols in China were achieving some success, which may have been known in Armenia. On these efforts, see James D. Ryan, "Conversion vs. Baptism? European Missionaries in Asia in the Thirteenth and Fourteenth Centuries," in *Varieties of Religious Conversion in the Middle Ages*, ed. James Muldoon (Gainesville: University Press of Florida, 1997), pp. 146-67. At the same time, outside of China, the Mongols were becoming increasingly Islamicized, with the result that they came to be perceived as a great threat to Christian interests. On this, see David Bundy, "The Syriac and Armenian Christian Responses to the Islamification of the Mongols," in *Medieval Christian Perceptions of Islam*, ed. John V. Tolan (New York: Garland, 1996), pp. 33-53.

21. Mathews and Taylor, *Armenian Gospels of Gladzor*, p. 45.

At this point, it might be useful to summarize briefly what has been learned so far about this image of mission. First, mission as "sharing Christ with friends" finds its firmest scriptural support in the Gospel of John. As noted above, the Fourth Gospel shows a special interest in the idea of Jesus' disciples taking the initiative to introduce others to him. Whereas the Synoptic accounts tend to highlight Jesus' own disciple-making activities and allow for the possibility of self-initiated enrollment, in John these routes to discipleship seem to give way to a third pattern in which Jesus' own followers play a key role as disciples who introduce others to the Christ.

From the meager evidence now available to us, it would be too much to say that this third pathway to a relationship with Jesus dominated quantitatively the historical Jesus' own practice of disciple-making, even within the narrative framework offered by John. Part of the difficulty here lies in the fact that very few call stories have survived in the traditions handed down from Jesus' day. Unfortunately, the calls of many important early followers of Jesus — characters in the Gospel of John like the Beloved Disciple, Lazarus and his sisters, and even a majority of Jesus' inner circle, the Twelve — are not recounted in the Fourth Gospel. The evidence of the Johannine traditions does seem strong enough, however, to support the claim that at least some of Jesus' own disciples were brought to him by other followers, who acted to introduce their friends and family to Jesus.

As a second observation, we are bound to notice that even when Jesus' followers contribute to the process of disciple-making, as they so obviously do in John's Gospel, Jesus is not thereby marginalized or rendered insignificant. Put most succinctly, the making of Christian disciples cannot take place without Jesus' participation. The disciples' primary motivation for mission appears to be an irresistible urge to introduce others to the Christ, which means that Jesus necessarily remains at the center of their evangelistic activity. The corporate metaphors offered in John reinforce the centrality of Jesus for Christian discipleship: he is the vine and his disciples the branches; he is the single shepherd of all his sheep, even those not of the original fold. Nor are the disciples left to act on their own after the resurrection of Jesus, because continuing guidance is offered to them through the Paraclete. Throughout, a divine initiative in mission is consistently asserted in the Gospels, but especially in John, so that purely autonomous action by the disciples as witnesses is inconceivable.[22] Thus, at John 6:70, Jesus refers to the Twelve and says he "chose" all of them, including presumably those brought to him by others (cf. John 15:16 — "You did not choose me but I chose you"). This accords with the more general statement made just before this that "no one can come to [Jesus] unless it is granted by the Father" (John 6:65).

Finally, taken together the passages from John discussed above provide a crucial indication for how to relate this form of the first disciples' mission to that of Jesus. There is no evidence to suggest that Jesus' disciples emulated his example of disciple-making by command. Thus, we may not say that they "converted" anyone to faith in Christ during his lifetime, even when they were giving testimony to him. Nor does it appear that their speech was powerful enough by itself to convince anyone that Jesus was the Christ. Rather, the witness of the disciples made possible, time after time, a direct encounter with Jesus, or with Jesus' word. Genuine, deeply rooted faith became conceivable in the aftermath of this initial interaction. This suggests that more than one step may be involved in the process of conversion. The story of the Samaritan woman illustrates the point most clearly. Her words (λαλιά) prepared the way for the λόγος of Jesus, which became available to the Samaritans when they invited him to stay for two days in their midst.[23] Only then were the Samaritans able to acknowledge Jesus as the Savior of the world.

What took place among the Samaritans merely repeated the pattern established near the beginning of the Gospel, when John the Baptist pointed the way to Jesus for two of his disciples by identifying him as the Lamb of God. The Baptist's witness prompted these two to address Jesus as "Rabbi" when they first met him (1:38). It was only after Andrew had stayed with Jesus for a day that he could announce to Simon, "We have found the Messiah" (1:41).[24] Similarly, Nathanael's strong confession of

22. Marinus de Jonge discusses the divine initiative assumed in the Fourth Gospel for Jesus in *Jesus, Stranger from Heaven and Son of God: Jesus Christ and the Christians in Johannine Perspective*, ed. and trans. John E. Steely (Missoula: Scholars, 1977), pp. 17-20.

23. Rudolf Bultmann, *The Gospel of John: A Commentary*, ed. R. W. N. Hoare and J. K. Riches, trans. G. R. Beasley-Murray (Philadelphia: Westminster, 1971), p. 201, characterized the testimony of the Samaritan woman as a form of "mediatory proclamation" or "mere words" that had no intrinsic value, even though it served to bring people to Jesus. Okure, *Johannine Approach to Mission*, pp. 171-72, argues convincingly for a more generous evaluation of the Samaritan woman's λαλιά as a genuine expression of μαρτυρία or "word of witness."

24. Indirect support for this idea of more than one stage in the missionary witness of

faith in Jesus as the Son of God was made subsequent to his own exchange with the one to whom Philip had given witness.

Of course, all these stories plucked from within the Johannine narrative are prefigured in the Gospel's prologue, where the witness of John the Baptist is characterized as a preparatory stage in the revelation of the light within the world (1:6-8). What cannot be overlooked is that however truthful and persuasive human speech might be, a disciple's discourse cannot be substituted for a living encounter with the Word that becomes flesh and dwells in the midst of humanity. Like a clue, such testimony points beyond itself to something greater. It exists not for its own sake, but to facilitate new opportunities for this eternal Word to be known and embraced. The witness of faithful disciples, whether offered during the lifetime of Jesus or sometime later, can aspire to no more glorious outcome than this.

Back to the Synoptics: Picturing the Image

While the Synoptic Gospels may not develop to the same degree as the Gospel of John the idea of Jesus' followers acting to share Christ with others, the notion is not entirely absent. Most often, when people were brought to Jesus in the first three Gospels, the issue was healing and the motivation of the intermediaries was to put the stricken one in the physical presence of an acknowledged thaumaturge in hopes that the person's sickness or disability might be overcome. At its theologically least significant level, this fits within a more general trend described earlier of loosely affiliated followers being drawn to Jesus as his reputation for wonder-working grew. The summary descriptions of Jesus' activities inserted here and there in the Synoptic narratives seem to indicate that this was an ordinary feature of Jesus' ministry in Galilee. Mark relates, for instance, that as soon as the people in Gennesaret recognized Jesus, they "rushed about that whole region and began to bring the sick on mats to wherever they heard he was. And wherever he went, into villages or cities or farms, they laid the

---

the church may also be detected in the difficult saying of Jesus at John 4:37-38, where Jesus talks about the disciples reaping what others have sown. The most vexing problem in this passage lies in the indistinct reference made to "others," the fruits of whose labors Jesus promises the disciples. See Okure, *Johannine Approach to Mission*, pp. 157-64, for a review of the interpretative options on this question.

sick in the marketplaces, and begged him that they might touch even the fringe of his cloak; and all who touched it were healed" (Mark 6:55-56).[25]

Even if invalids brought to Jesus could be healed simply by his touch, as the earliest Christians apparently accepted as a given, the phenomenon is not featured prominently in any of the Gospels, nor do the Evangelists report Jesus' mighty acts exclusively or even primarily as feats of power. There were good reasons, of which the Gospel writers themselves were obviously aware, to de-emphasize the marvelous aspect of the healings or to qualify its significance. At best, contrary-to-nature events in the life of Jesus could be understood as demonstrations of the power of an in-breaking reign of God, but the possibility also existed that when Jesus performed extraordinary deeds he was acting on behalf of a rival to God (like Beelzebul; cf. Mark 3:22-23). Less ambiguous and more revealing of Jesus' identity are the stories in which an articulated faith moves those with compassion to devise ways for the sick, the demon-possessed, and the dying to encounter Jesus, the source of life.

A prime example of this more complex approach to miracles is offered by Mark in the story of the synagogue leader named Jairus, whose appeal to Jesus on behalf of his dying daughter is interrupted by the desperate attempt of the woman with a twelve-year flow of blood to touch Jesus' garments. In both cases, the suppliants exhibit at the beginning of their stories quite naive expectations that some form of physical contact with Jesus would be enough to effect the healing they seek.[26] As the intertwined narratives develop, however, the magical element recedes and the importance of faith increases. This is done somewhat awkwardly with respect to the woman with the flow of blood, since it appears at first that just touching Jesus' clothes results in her immediate healing (5:29). The conclusion of the woman's story, however, teaches that ultimately her faith was the means by which she had been made well. To drive the point home, Jesus dismisses the woman by pronouncing her healed after the fact, as it were, while recognizing her faith and the new relationship that now bound them together: "Daughter, your faith has made you well; go in peace, and be healed of your disease" (5:34).

25. A similar impression is given at Mark 1:32-34, where it is said that the people of Capernaum "brought to him all who were sick or possessed with demons."

26. In Mark's account, Jairus asked Jesus to come and "lay your hands on [my daughter]" (5:23). The woman is reported to have said, "If I but touch his clothes, I will be made well" (5:28).

In the companion story of the synagogue leader and his daughter, circumstances require Jairus to go further than the woman to prove the depth of his trust in Jesus. When a discouraging report from home indicates that his daughter has already died (5:35), the decision to complete the journey has to rest completely on faith. Jesus tells him, "Do not fear, only believe" (5:36). Additional obstacles to faith, like the wrenching tumult of mourning and the mockery of skeptics who laugh at Jesus, will also have to be surmounted as they come nearer to Jairus's house, but the end result will be a happy one. When Jesus finally speaks directly to the little girl and she responds to his gentle command, the father's decision to rely on Jesus is sustained and the enduring lesson of this encounter for coming generations — persistent faith — is made clear.

Other stories in Mark in which the needy are brought to Jesus for him to touch show signs of a similar kind of development. Simple reports of physical healing are adapted by various means, with the result that more than one insight about Jesus and his mission is given expression. In the story of the deaf-mute brought to Jesus in the region of the Decapolis (7:31-37), for example, a straightforward and patently tactile account of miraculous healing is extended by linking it to broader theological issues, the most obvious of which is the messianic secret.[27] In a similar fashion, the brief but richly detailed story of Jesus healing a blind man brought to him in Bethsaida (8:22-26) concludes with Jesus telling the man after his cure, "Do not even go into the village." Both stories began with a request from others that Jesus "touch" or "lay his hand on" someone needing his help. Jesus does not disappoint, but in the course of recounting the incident the Evangelist has interwoven other themes into the story.

A similar kind of reorientation takes place in the familiar vignette of Jesus and the little children (Mark 10:13-16). Those who approach Jesus hope that he will touch the children. The disciples resist the idea and attempt to prevent this from happening, but no reason is given for their reluctance. Jesus will end up embracing the children and imparting a blessing by laying his hands upon them, but the communication of Jesus'

27. The remarkable details of Jesus' technique in this story ("He . . . put his fingers into his ears, and he spat and touched his tongue. Then looking up to heaven, he sighed and said to him, 'Ephphatha,' that is, 'Be opened.'") receive no further comment in the text. Instead, Mark focuses on the crowd's reaction and Jesus' instruction to them: "Then Jesus ordered them to tell no one; but the more he ordered them, the more zealously they proclaimed it" (Mark 7:36).

blessing by touch does not remain the primary concern of this story. The action of those who brought the children to Jesus prompts him to address an entirely different and more theologically significant question: how are followers of Jesus to receive the kingdom? (They are to receive it as children.) In this way, Mark passes on yet another story in which surprising things happen when friends and loved ones are brought into Christ's presence.

A final example of "sharing Christ with friends," also drawn from the Synoptic Gospels, will now be explored, with some attention given to how one might illustrate this image of mission. The particular text I have chosen to highlight, Mark 2:1-12 (cf. Matt. 9:1-8; Luke 5:17-26), is not commonly thought of as a story of disciples in mission, but a missiological reading along these lines is certainly possible, as we shall see. Depending on how one decides to picture the scene of the healing of the paralytic, Jesus' followers might be considered entirely incidental to the central message of the story. Two of the artistic renderings discussed below seem to assume precisely this. On the other hand, the four friends of the paralytic could be treated in quite another way, as active participants in Jesus' mission of healing and reconciliation. The last image examined below appears to be based on just such an understanding of Mark's story.

A high degree of interpretive flexibility is inherent in the text itself. Mark's account of Jesus healing the paralyzed man presents a complex narrative to the reader, through which swirl several thematic crosscurrents. At one level, the story is about healing, and, as such a story, it simply extends the series of miracles performed by Jesus in Galilee after the call of the first disciples. Seen in this way, the paralyzed man is like the raving demoniac in the synagogue (Mark 1:21-28) or the leper who begged Jesus to make him clean (Mark 1:40-45).[28] His healing will show that Jesus is more powerful than whatever caused these disabilities. The end of the story in Mark, where the crowd's strong reaction to the sight of the formerly paralyzed man carrying his bed is related, confirms the miraculous aspect of the account. An amazed audience recognizes Jesus' power by glorifying God and exclaiming, "we have never seen anything like this!"

---

28. In this sense, the man's paralysis resembles the possessed state of the man with an unclean spirit, the fever experienced by Peter's mother-in-law, and the disfigurement of the leper. As signs of dysfunction, these physical conditions all point to a created order under the influence of malevolent and destructive forces.

To illustrate any story, an artist has to decide on a point of view. For Mark's story of the paralytic, the key interpretive question is this: should the focus be on Jesus, the paralytic, the disapproving scribes, the astounded crowd, or the persistent friends of the disabled man? A Flemish painter of the sixteenth century, Jan Sanders van Hemessen, leaves the viewer in no doubt about the perspective he has chosen to adopt. Hemessen offers a dramatic rendering of the scene in which a single large-scale figure, the healed paralytic, is placed on its own in the foreground of a study entitled *Healing of the Paralytic* (fig. 13).[29] The reasons for Hemessen's approach seem at first to have little or nothing to do with the biblical text. The muscular physiognomy of the recovered paralytic, the natural flow of his clothing, and the fine rendering of the bedding carried on his back do not recall any specific details contained in Mark's narrative. The central figure is compelling, but strangely unconnected to any specific historical or literary setting, rather like a piece of freestanding sculpture. Considered on its own, then, the foreground image communicates an impression of dynamic power, which appears to issue from the tension the artist creates between the man's obvious strength in arm and leg and the weight of the burden he carries with him along the road.

Hemessen makes an explicit connection to Mark's account via the small-figure background scene that appears to the left of the central character (fig. 14, detail).[30] There one finds in a composite setting all of the particular narrative elements that define Mark's story: the friends on the roof, the crowd near the door, Jesus addressing the paralyzed man who lies on his bed, plus the different reactions of the witnesses (derision and praise) to what was taking place. Only when the foreground and background components of Hemessen's composition are put together is a coherent illustration of Mark's narrative finally produced. In the end, *Healing of the Paralytic* represents the healing of the paralytic as a miracle of Jesus, made

29. For biographical information on Hemessen, see Burr Wallen, *Jan van Hemessen: An Antwerp Painter between Reform and Counter-Reform* (Ann Arbor: UMI Research Press, 1983). A briefer but more recent treatment, also by Wallen, may be found in *DArt* 14:379-82.

30. At several points in his career, Hemessen favored the use of miniaturist backgrounds as a way to enlarge the context in which his genre studies of contemporary life in Antwerp could be situated. For some of these pictures, that expanded context was biblical. In addition to the *Healing of the Paralytic,* Hemessen's *Parable of the Prodigal Son* and *Parable of the Unmerciful Servant* both feature this technique. Wallen discusses the still-disputed identity of Hemessen's small-figure collaborator in *Jan van Hemessen,* pp. 89-95.

Fig. 13. *Healing of the Paralytic*, by Jan van Hemessen. Flemish (sixteenth century)

Fig. 14. Detail of
Healing of the Paralytic

all the more impressive by the robust vitality of the former invalid. Whether intentionally or not, Hemessen's artistic technique heightens the effect of this reading by separating the paralytic from all the other characters in the story. An alternative interpretation of the scene, based on some kind of interaction among the characters, is hardly possible in this case, given the isolation of the painting's main figure.

Fig. 15. *Healing the Paralytic,* The Andrews Diptych. Ivory (fifth century)

A second primary theme in Mark's story of the paralytic has to do with Jesus' authority to forgive sins. Not surprisingly, his assertion of this prerogative provokes an extreme reaction from the scribes in attendance, who hear an affront to God's sovereignty in Jesus' declaration that the sins of the paralytic are forgiven: "Why does this fellow speak in this way? It is blasphemy! Who can forgive sins but God alone?" (Mark 2:7). The scribes' challenge to Jesus is unvoiced ("the scribes were sitting there, questioning in their hearts") but apparently perceptible, and it initiates a series of confrontations extending beyond the limits of this pericope that eventuate in a decision by the Jewish authorities (the Pharisees and the Herodians) to destroy Jesus (Mark 3:6). Looked at from this angle, the story of the paralytic is much more than just another miracle tradition passed on by the Evangelists. Within the narrative structure of the Second Gospel, the healing of the paralytic may thus be recognized as a crucial moment of transition in the book's plot. This is a key turning point in Mark's story, where Jesus' human opponents emerge as major characters and the basis of their fierce antagonism to him is first revealed.

In figure 15, we encounter quite a different approach to the healing of the paralytic than that employed by Jan van Hemessen. In this version of the story, Jesus' authority to forgive sins is at least as important as his power to heal. The so-called Andrews Diptych is a set of late classical/early Byzantine ivory carvings of north Italian provenance, now owned by the Victoria and Albert Museum in London.[31] Six different miracles performed by Jesus in the Gospels are represented on the Andrews Diptych. Besides the healing of the paralytic, these include a scene in which the disciples present Jesus with two fish and five loaves of bread, the raising of Lazarus, the healing of a blind man, the changing of water to wine, and the healing of a leper. The various characters included in the different scenes are delicately rendered, with careful attention having been paid in each case to the details of the biblical story being illustrated.

The six scenes that comprise the two rectangular panels of the Andrews Diptych may all concern the miraculous exploits of Jesus, but the artist(s) who created them did not dwell solely on Jesus' exceptional power over nature. In several of the scenes, other narrative elements are introduced that broaden or modify the most obvious lesson of the images, which has to do with Jesus' ability to work miracles. Examples include the skepticism that appears on the faces of the disciples who bring the two fish and five loaves to Jesus (which raises questions about their faith) and the artist's integration into the Lazarus episode of a prostrate figure of a woman anointing the feet of Jesus with her hair.

31. John Beckwith, *The Andrews Diptych* (London: H. M. Stationery Office, 1958), is still the most complete study made of this work of art. Beckwith assigns a fifth-century date to the Andrews Diptych (p. 37).

The story of the paralytic told by the Andrews Diptych is similarly nuanced. In this rendition of the miracle story, three central figures are featured rather than the one who stands out in Jan van Hemessen's composition. The paralyzed man is there, of course, looking quite fit and ready to carry off his four-legged cot. On the right, Jesus stands facing in his direction and makes a sign of forgiveness with his right hand. In the middle of the group is a third figure, whose grim expression seems to mark him out as a scribe.[32] Jesus' gesture and the brooding presence of the scribe would indicate that more than an ability to work wonders is on display in this splendid ivory carving. A second and more fundamental theme appears to inform this portrayal of the paralytic's healing: Jesus' authority to forgive sins.

A third perspective on Mark 2:1-12, one that admits of a specifically missiological reading, emerges in figure 16. Unfortunately, few biographical details are available to describe the East African artist whose rendition of *Christ Heals the Paralytic* is reproduced here. All we know for sure is that Napawesa was one of a group of African Christian students from Kenya, Tanganyika, and Uganda who were enrolled in the School of Art established in 1937 at the Makarere University in Kampala, Uganda. An instructor at the university, K. Margaret Trowell, gathered together a sampling of the students' work in 1956 and published the collection in pamphlet form as an African life of Christ.[33] Trowell's aim was to contextualize the gospel

32. It is also possible that the middle figure is meant to be one of the apostles. Writing as an art historian, Beckwith draws this conclusion, *Andrews Diptych*, pp. 13, 21. It is important to note, however, that the Twelve are not mentioned by any of the Evangelists as participants in this story. Indeed, from a narrative point of view, the apostles recede to the background in this part of Mark (1:40–3:6), while the Pharisees and their supporters become more sharply defined as Jesus' most dangerous antagonists, who vow to oppose him utterly. A similar approach may be observed in the story of the lame man's healing at the pool of Bethzatha (or Bethesda), told in John 5:1-18. As in Mark 2:1-12, the apostles do not figure in John's story, not even as observers of what happened at the pool by the Sheep Gate, while "the Jews" emerge from this incident unambiguously characterized as Jesus' mortal foes. Thus, I take the roll or scroll carried by the middle figure in this scene portrayed on the Andrews Diptych to be a symbol of the scribal office rather than an indicator of apostleship. This is in keeping with the basic meaning assigned to the scroll in Greco-Roman art, where it served to identify men of learning (usually philosophers) rather than religious functionaries. On this point, see Thomas F. Mathews, *The Clash of Gods: A Reinterpretation of Early Christian Art* (Princeton, N.J.: Princeton University Press, 1993), esp. pp. 38-39.

33. K. M. Trowell, *And Was Made Man: The Life of Our Lord in Pictures* (London: SPCK, 1956). Several of these illustrations, including the one created by Napawesa, were subsequently reproduced in Arno Lehmann, *Christian Art in Africa and Asia*, trans. Erich Hopka

Fig. 16. *Christ Heals the Paralytic,* by Napawesa, a student at Makarere University, Kampala, Uganda (mid-twentieth century)

for an East African audience. As she noted in the introduction to her booklet, she hoped in this way to contribute to a larger effort to preach Christianity in Africa by portraying Christ "as a man among men as we know them here" rather than in "foreign dress."

Napawesa's picture exhibits several graphic elements that immedi-

---

et al. (St. Louis: Concordia Publishing House, 1969). Both Trowell and Lehmann were seeking through their publications to promote an awareness of and appreciation for emerging indigenous expressions of Christian art in nations outside the North Atlantic region. Lehmann's interest in non-Western art extended to a wide variety of forms besides painting, including music, dance, poetry, drama, sculpture, and architecture. See also Arno Lehmann, *Die Kunst der Jungen Kirchen,* second ed. (Berlin: Evangelische Verlagsanstalt, 1957).

ately connect it to an African context, from the open style of the house to the clothing and physical features of the people. The rough-hewn simplicity of the paralytic's pallet is in all probability a closer fit to Jesus' first-century Palestinian milieu than the piece of furniture featured in the Andrews Diptych. From a compositional point of view, one notices also how a majority of those in the room with Jesus are seated on the floor.

With respect to the plot of Mark's story, what the artist offers in this picture is a snapshot of the scene inside the house, taken just before the episode reaches its narrative climax. Neither Jesus' power to heal nor his contested authority to forgive sins has yet emerged as a discernable theme within the plot of the story. The artist focuses our attention rather on the precipitating action of the men who had struggled to bring the paralyzed person into Jesus' presence. Nearly everyone gathered together in the room, including the tall figure slightly to the right of center that represents Jesus, watches with rapt attention as the operation unfolds from above. A small child on the left side of the picture points to the descending pallet, thus reinforcing the impression that the focal center of the composition is defined by the triangle of figures comprised of the paralyzed man and those working to lower him safely into the room.

Napawesa's painting vividly portrays a key aspect of Mark's story that both Jan van Hemessen and the Andrews Diptych fail to develop. In this picture, followers of Jesus are shown to have taken the initiative to bring a friend in need to the Christ. The crowdedness of the room forces the friends of the paralyzed man to devise an unusual mode of entry. Their inventiveness is a sign of persistence, which is an aspect of faith praised by Jesus elsewhere in the Gospels.[34] By highlighting the intense focus of Jesus and the others already with him in the room on what the figures on the roof were doing, Napawesa directs our particular attention to the small but decisive role the friends of the paralyzed man play in the story. This appears to be true to Mark's narrative purpose, since he seems to intend for us to see the action of the pallet-bearers as the crucial hinge on which the story's plot turns.[35] It is, after all, when Jesus sees "their faith" that he decides to an-

34. The importunate widow, who finally wore down the unjust judge (Luke 18:1-8), is a striking example of this behavior. In Luke, Jesus also suggested in answer to a question from the disciples about how to pray that they should not hesitate to direct their petitions to God, in the same way that friends are apt to knock insistently on each other's doors when they need something desperately (Luke 11:5-13; cf. Matt. 7:7-11).

35. A comparison with the other Synoptic accounts is illuminating on this point. Luke

nounce to the paralyzed man that his sins have been forgiven (Mark 2:5). A demonstration of Jesus' power to heal, plus the ensuing conflict with the scribes, will follow on from this dramatic development. The friends of the paralytic have not themselves cured the invalid, nor have they presumed on their own to pardon his sins, but they have participated in Jesus' life-giving mission. His was a ministry that consistently astounded the multitudes while also threatening the religious authorities, precisely because it was marked by these signs of an in-breaking reign of God.

Focusing on the Friends

With Napawesa's visual representation of "sharing Christ with friends" in mind, it is now possible to move, finally, to an evaluation of this image. The reflections to follow will draw on the exegetical work presented above from the Gospels. Also instructive is the contrast created when this image of mission is compared to the one examined in the previous chapter: heralds of Christ "announcing Good News." Clearly, both images are biblical, but each one has something distinctive to say about the character of mission and the range of possible forms that Christian outreach might take. It may be useful to organize these concluding reflections by using the five headings below.

Identity of the Missioners

In the stories examined earlier in which certain followers of Jesus took the initiative to share Christ with friends, a common feature that invites comment is found in the very low profile struck by all the missioners involved.

---

enhances the presence of the authorities by adding to Mark's simple description of a crowd with "some of the scribes sitting there" an assertion that Pharisees and teachers of the law were in attendance, "[who] had come from every village of Galilee and Judea and from Jerusalem." Luke also makes a point of drawing attention to Jesus' power to heal (5:17). For his part, Matthew compresses together his introduction to the scene so much that hardly any basis is left to sustain Jesus' acknowledgement of the pallet-bearers' faith. Only Mark allows the action in the first part of the story to develop fully without obvious reference to Jesus' authority and power to heal, a narrative approach that enables the faith of those who bring the paralyzed man to Jesus to play a critical role in the story.

In the case of the four pallet-bearers mentioned in Mark 2, for example, no personal details of any kind are provided. These friends of the paralytic are completely anonymous. Similarly, the Samaritan woman is given no name, although we do learn something about her background in the course of her dialogue with Jesus. Likewise, the people who brought the sick and disabled to Jesus for healing (or the children in Mark 10, for his touch) are rarely described with individual characteristics. In the few instances where a named disciple close to Jesus shares his experience of the Messiah with a family member or friend, that disciple tends not to figure prominently within the inner circle of Jesus' followers. Thus, it is Andrew who brings the better known Peter to meet the Lamb of God in John 1, and Philip, rather than one of the "pillar" apostles, who ends up approaching Nathanael with an invitation to meet the one who had called him earlier to discipleship.

The commonness of these anonymous missionaries and relatively unknown evangelizers points to an important feature of this image of Christian outreach. Unlike the first image of mission discussed earlier in this study, "sharing Christ with friends" assumes no special set of leadership skills on the part of those who participate in this kind of missionary activity. Thus, one does not have to be a master of rhetoric and the arts of persuasion in order to share Christ in this way. No commanding public presence is required. In this image of mission, we are reminded that anyone can function as a witness who believes sincerely that faith in Jesus Christ is something worth sharing with those closest and most dear to oneself. Seen from this perspective, mission issues directly out of discipleship, rather than needing a special situation of commissioning. It is not reserved for just a few of those who follow Jesus, as though limited to a restricted cadre of specially chosen experts. The picture of mission that emerges out of these biblical data is decidedly inclusive and expansive.

Scale of Mission

The idea of sharing Christ with friends further suggests something crucial about the scope of mission. While it is true that evangelism can happen in the context of large gatherings of people mostly unknown to each other, in which case broadband announcements of Good News may be the most appropriate way to make Christ known, this pattern of witnessing to the gospel need not always obtain. Indeed, the New Testament stories examined in this chapter all call attention to a different kind of social interaction, one in which the sharing of faith takes place by means of small-scale forms of interpersonal communication and action.

Here mission is more likely to be undertaken as an act of sitting beside rather than standing in front of those to whom one hopes to pass on the experience of Christian faith. This kind of faith sharing could, for example, be a matter of one individual conversing privately with another, as spouses, intimate friends, or close siblings are apt to do when life-changing events or profound insights break into and upset the givens and routines of daily life. Just as easy to imagine are scenarios in which an experience of conversion leads to a radically redefined self-understanding that one naturally wants to share within the larger family circle or the extended clan of the village or neighborhood. Without assuming that most Christians operate in missionary mode all of the time, one may rightly presume, on the basis of what has been learned already about these New Testament–era followers of Jesus, a variety of social settings in addition to the mass meeting in which new faith commitments might be revealed and communicated to ever-wider spheres of acquaintance and association. To the extent that these personal exchanges are essentially *informal* in nature, they are appropriately encompassed by the image of mission described in this chapter.

The "official" record of early Christianity, if that is what we have preserved in the Acts of the Apostles, tends to pay scant attention to forms of Christian witness that take place along the lines of kinship and friendship. As a result, the reader of Luke's history is conditioned to expect dramatic public confrontations and great speeches to mark the progress of the gospel at every stage. Yet, one suspects that the stories of the Samaritan woman and the friends of the paralytic are, perhaps, more representative of the Christian experience of mission than what is recounted about the heroes and giant figures of faith who dominate the action in Acts.[36] In any

36. On the importance of interpersonal networks to sustained high rates of conversion to any new religious movement, see Rodney Stark, *The Rise of Christianity: A Sociologist Reconsiders History* (Princeton, N.J.: Princeton University Press, 1996), esp. pp. 13-27. Lending further support to this perspective, Reidar Hvalvik carefully examines the different ways ordinary Christians may have participated in the mission of the early church and likewise concludes that families and other social networks were a primary means by which growth and expansion took place. See Hvalvik, "In Word and Deed: The Expansion of the Church in the pre-Constantinian Era," in *The Mission of the Early Church to Jews and*

event, neither the mass baptisms performed by Peter nor the prodigious journeys of the itinerant Paul, by themselves or even together, can account for the spectacular growth exhibited by the early church. Thus, we are prompted to look in the shadows around the edges of the New Testament narratives where hints of other evangelizers, considerably less well known, may lie waiting to be discovered. The *institutional* future of the Christian church may have been shaped more directly by Paul's apologetic strategies than by the witness of the man born blind, but the fact that the gospel spread as far and as widely as it did in the first century owes something to each of them. Our understanding of mission in the New Testament period cannot hope to be complete unless provision is made to honor the contributions of these subordinate characters, who quietly operated out of sight on a small rather than large scale, even as the apostles performed their more spectacular exploits of outreach and witness.

Motivation of the Missioners

It is certainly significant that all of the missionary activity recounted in this chapter from John and the Synoptics took place *before* the risen Christ announced the Great Commission to the eleven at the mountain in Galilee. As important as that event may have been with respect to the start of an explicitly Gentile mission on the part of the church, it was hardly the point of origin for all Christian witness in the first century. In fact, on the basis of the material examined in this chapter, it appears that some followers of Jesus began to share their new perceptions with others almost as soon as they became acquainted with the Christ. For these disciples, no command or commissioning event was needed to trigger their intention to give witness, which came to them already embedded in the experience of discipleship itself.

Gentiles, ed. Jostein Ådna and Hans Kvalbein, WUNT 127 (Tübingen: Mohr Siebeck, 2000), pp. 265-87. We have every reason to believe that these patterns continued well beyond the apostolic era. As historian Ian Wood has observed with respect to the process of evangelization that transformed early medieval Europe, "The work of saints is only one element in the Christianisation of Europe." Small-time, anonymous priests, he notes, were the real "workers at the coalface," whose impact could be significant even when their competence as interpreters of the faith was less than perfect. See Wood, *The Missionary Life: Saints and the Evangelisation of Europe, 400-1050* (Harlow, England: Longman, 2001), pp. 265-66.

Thus, in no case do these disciples share Christ with friends out of a sense of duty or as though under orders. Compulsion from without does not power this form of mission. Questions of authority do not arise. These missioners do not require a legal mandate in the same way that heralds and other commissioned agents might. They are moved to act primarily out of joy, excitement, or deep feelings of compassion. Their motivation to give witness resembles the spilling over of an enthusiasm that wants to share its source in much the same way that the Word by its very nature wants to be known.[37] Sharing Christ with friends is, therefore, a spontaneous act, far removed from the intellectual processes of calculation and planning.

Mission in Action

Mission does not always have to be a matter of speeches and palaver. As many of the stories related in this chapter plainly show, verbal declarations and announcements of gospel truth simply do not exhaust all the possibilities of Christian witness. Sometimes, action augments testimony, as in the case of the disciple Andrew, who not only tells his brother Peter about having found the Messiah but also decides to do something in order to bring the two together in one place (John 1:42 — "he brought Simon to Jesus"). In a similar fashion, Philip informs Nathanael about having met the successor of Moses promised in the Scriptures and then bids him to "come and see" for himself. For the man born blind, the physical evidence of his healing effectively dwarfs the impact of his words. The religious authorities are shown brushing aside his attempts at explanation quite easily, but they could not refute the obvious fact that he had been physically changed after having encountered Jesus. The transformed presence of the man born blind, standing in the midst of the community that had known him since birth, constituted the most vivid and compelling aspect of his testimony to Jesus. Then we have the example of the four friends of the paralyzed man.

---

37. Roland Allen has described something of the same phenomenon in his classic study, *The Spontaneous Expansion of the Church and the Causes Which Hinder It*, second ed. (London: World Dominion, 1949), p. 14: "[The speaker] speaks from the heart because he is too eager to be able to refrain from speaking. His subject has gripped him. He speaks of what he knows, and he knows by experience. The truth which he imparts is his own truth. . . . Inevitably, [the hearer] is moved by it. Before he has experienced the truth himself he has shared the speaker's experience."

So far as the contemporary reader of Mark's story can tell, their witness to the power of Jesus to heal was expressed entirely without words, discernible only in a set of actions that refused to yield to initial discouragement.

Whether in the Synoptics or John, we have seen that the idea of sharing Christ with friends is often connected to incidents of physical healing. I take this to be another indicator pointing to the comprehensiveness of this image of mission. Mission conceived in terms of teaching or debate might be satisfied with efforts to pass on vital information about Christianity, thinking it enough to enhance the hearers' intellectual grasp of Jesus and his cause; yet that would be a shallow imitation of Jesus' own missionary example, in which we find instruction, exhortation, healing, and care for the physical needs of the crowds that followed after him among the matters of concern he addressed directly. If the purpose of mission as sharing Christ with friends is somehow to make Christ present for others, then the fullness of a Christian's experience of Jesus needs to be expressed in ways that respect his obvious solicitude for the whole person. Here I see a place for Christian ministries of service and compassion, especially when these efforts are directed to those most broken in body and spirit. A desire to share Christ with family, friends, and community properly aims to incarnate the gospel at every possible level of human existence.

A Means to Encounter Christ

Considered together, the different artistic renderings featured above that treat Mark's story of Jesus healing the paralyzed man can tell us one more thing about the idea of disciples in mission sharing Christ with friends. As noted already, Napawesa's treatment highlights the role of the paralytic's friends. Their unusual activity on the roof of the building attracted the attention of all the other characters in the scene, including Jesus. In the interpretations offered by Jan van Hemessen and the Andrews Diptych, on the other hand, the persistent and faithful stretcher-bearers have been relegated to the margins of the picture or are nowhere to be seen.

In large part, these three portrayals of Mark 2:1-12 diverge from each other because the artists involved chose to focus on different moments in the story. Early in the narrative, the friends of the paralytic are crucial to the plot, because they are the means by which direct contact is made between the paralyzed man and Jesus. What happens next, however, does not depend on them, and so, appropriately, they move to the edge of the composition. Having been introduced, Jesus will speak directly to the man on the bed. That individual then has to decide whether or not to respond to Jesus' command to get up. What happened in Mark 2 is not unlike what the Samaritan villagers in John 4 reported about their own experience of evangelization. Their neighbor, the Samaritan woman, shared with them what she had learned about Jesus. Her testimony triggered a face-to-face encounter that resulted in the making of new disciples. In that context, too, by the time the story ended the Samaritan woman was no longer at the center of the action. Andrew, likewise, facilitates Peter's meeting with Jesus. But he has to get out of the way in order for the special relationship between Jesus and Peter, acknowledged in all four Gospels, to develop.

A rather vivid example of the same concept is provided by E. Stanley Jones, whose searching analysis of Christian mission in early-twentieth-century India, *The Christ of the Indian Road,* has long been considered a classic expression of mission theology. In this book, Jones argued for a fundamental shift in thinking about the role of the Christian missionary in India, from an authoritative teacher who demands always to have the last word to a learner and friend of Indians, whose special task it is to introduce others to the Christ. Jones chose to conclude his study with a cultural anecdote that beautifully illustrates once more the temporary, instrumental nature of Christian witness, when it is practiced as an expression of deep caring for the happiness of one's dearest companions and kin:

> There is a beautiful Indian marriage custom that dimly illustrates our task in India, and where it ends. At the wedding ceremony the women friends of the bride accompany her with music to the home of the bridegroom. They usher her into the presence of the bridegroom — that is as far as they can go, then they retire and leave her with her husband. That is our joyous task in India: to know Him, to introduce Him, to retire — not necessarily geographically, but to trust India with the Christ and trust Christ with India. We can only go so far — he and India must go the rest of the way.[38]

38. E. Stanley Jones, *The Christ of the Indian Road* (New York: Abingdon, 1925), pp. 212-13. For more on the remarkable missionary career of Jones, see Richard W. Taylor, "E. Stanley Jones, 1884-1973: Following the Christ of the Indian Road," in *Mission Legacies: Biographical Studies of Leaders of the Modern Missionary Movement,* ed. Gerald H. Anderson et al. (Maryknoll, N.Y.: Orbis, 1994), pp. 339-47.

In just this way, "sharing Christ with friends" is not a matter of standing in as a replacement for Jesus. It is a temporary role by which disciples in mission hope to introduce Jesus to family and friends. As such, this image of mission is about how to be an *instrument* of encounter and conversion, rather than a way for muscular actors to effect Christianization by converting, convincing, transforming, or curing others. Followers of Jesus who engage in this kind of mission do not presume to control the outcome of these encounters. They aspire, rather, to be a means by which God may decide to act through the power and guidance of the Holy Spirit.

chapter 4

Interpreting the Gospel

Communicating Good News across Cultures

In the two images of mission examined thus far, the cross-cultural dimensions of the enterprise are obscured. This is especially so with respect to mission as an act of sharing Christ with friends and family. Almost by definition, those with whom we are most intimate participate together with us in a common cultural framework and a mutual language. In this situation the gospel does not come from a foreign source, even when it arrives as a new idea. There is little need to adapt the message to the circumstances and social background of the new hearer, because this has already happened. Within the tight bonds of kinship and the warm embrace of friendship, cultural resistance to the message of the gospel ebbs to its lowest level.

An announcer of Good News may likewise be imagined without direct reference to the troublesome fissures of cultural difference. Assuming a common idiom for the exchange of ideas, an authorized speaker like the king's herald may be thought to need only boldness, born of confidence. Were one to base a theology of mission on the Great Commission alone, this might well be the result. Surprisingly, in the Gospels, the last words of the resurrected Jesus betray no awareness whatsoever of the cultural challenges that were soon to confront his chosen emissaries. Peremptory instructions to preach and teach seem to assume that communication will be easy, even though "all nations" (Matt. 28:19) and the "whole creation" (Mark 16:15) are proposed as the apostles' prospective mission field.

At other points in their portrayals of Jesus and his earthly ministry, the Evangelists' accounts anticipate more closely the gospel's impending cultural breakout. Jesus in Mark, for example, journeys beyond the Galilee and appears to welcome demonstrations of faith from believing Gentiles, while continuing to affirm the salvation of the Jews as his primary concern. Significantly, the decisive turn in Mark's narrative structure takes place at its northernmost point, outside of Jewish territory. There, at Caesarea Philippi, Peter makes his famous confession and Jesus reveals in clear terms his coming destiny (8:27-33).

For his part, Matthew is able to signal early on a universal intention behind the whole of God's activity in Jesus by including at the scene of the nativity strangers "from the East" who come to worship the child at Bethlehem. Similarly, in Luke, Jesus' first sermon (4:16-30) dramatically highlights two unexpected examples of faith from the history of Israel, a widow at Zarephath in the region of Sidon in the days of Elijah, and Naaman the Syrian. By implication, it was the foreignness of these two exemplars that so vexed the hometown congregation at Nazareth, causing them to reject Jesus outright and to threaten him with violence.

As we have already seen in the previous chapter, the Johannine Jesus is shown to be active among the Samaritans to a degree not evident in the Synoptic Gospels. Their ready response to him is taken to be evidence that the "fields are ripe for harvesting" (John 4:35). John is also the Evangelist who provides the most intriguing detail regarding the inscription on the cross, said to be written by Pilate himself (19:19-22). The trilingual form of the announcement indicated there — in Hebrew, Latin, and Greek — implicitly foreshadows the church's intercultural missionary task in the post-resurrection era to come.[1]

In the Acts of the Apostles, the capacity of the gospel to cross formidable barriers of geography and culture is demonstrated repeatedly. That is, in fact, one of the primary themes of the book, set out in programmatic terms for the apostles by Jesus on the occasion of his ascension: "you will be my witnesses in Jerusalem, in all Judea and Samaria, and to the ends of the earth" (Acts 1:8). Under the power of the Holy Spirit, the early leaders of the church would indeed present the gospel to Jews "from every nation

---

1. Of course, some would argue later in the history of the church that Pilate's inscription described the *upper* limit of languages qualified to receive the gospel. For more on this, see below (p. 151).

under heaven" (2:5), as well as to Samaritans and a variety of pagans scattered across the Roman Empire. In this way, the cross-cultural implications of Jesus' example and message were given explicit expression through the story of the newly formed Christian community.

The special concern of this chapter is to construct an image of mission as interpretation. The book of Acts is a good place to start because Luke's historical narrative not only traces out a sharp arc of geographical expansion for the church but also sheds light on how the earliest evangelists responded to a succession of unexpected opportunities for disciplemaking among culturally diverse groups of people. At the Spirit's leading, the apostles were thrust into circumstances they could not have foreseen. A sectarian movement within first-century Palestinian Judaism developed into something else. There were still occasions on which the gospel could simply be announced, but at other times novel contexts and unfamiliar frames of reference invited more creative approaches to witnessing and new postures for mission. In just this kind of situation, outside of established relationships and ingrained cultural patterns, the missioner as interpreter aims to facilitate meaningful contact between the gospel and new sets of hearers in terms that do not seem strange to them. After examining a selection of key texts from the Acts of the Apostles, we will explore further with the help of several illustrations this way of envisioning mission, after which I will describe and analyze its most important features.

Pentecost: Inaugurating the Church's Mission across Social Boundaries

Questions of culture lie embedded in the book of Acts, only here and there poking through the surface of Luke's narrative in ways that might betray conscious reflection on their importance. Overtly theological interests, on the other hand, are everywhere apparent, so much so that Luke's own claim at the beginning of his great work, in the literary preface to his Gospel (1:1-4), simply to be writing an "orderly" historical account based on eyewitness reports is not easily taken at face value.[2] Quite naturally, Luke's

2. Joseph A. Fitzmyer offers a concise but detailed appraisal of Lukan theology in the introduction to the first volume of his commentary on Luke, which also guides his approach

theological convictions shaped the structure of the story presented in Acts and influenced the selection and weighting of the different episodes in it. Luke is clearly eager, for example, to show how the Holy Spirit became an instrument of guidance for the early church, a crucial means by which God's ongoing salvific intentions became known to the apostles. Another need was to connect the earthly activities and distinctive message of Jesus to the story of a faith community devoted to the memory of the resurrected Christ. Luke's handling of the two narratives together as a double work (Luke-Acts) suggests a strong parallel based, in particular, on a common history of rejection and persecution. A closely linked issue was the status of an expanding Christian movement within the common public space created by the Roman Empire. Acts may not be a formal apologetic treatise written in order to persuade Roman officials to recognize a misunderstood religious sect, but Luke's careful description of the church's origins and early development could and did enhance Christianity's claim to legitimacy as a respectable and law-abiding cultic society.[3]

A major theme of Acts that does bear directly on intercultural issues concerns the emergence of Gentile Christianity. Luke shares with the letter-writer Paul a desire to explain how a faction within Judaism came to take on an unmistakably Gentile face. For Paul, this is, above all, a theological problem. In nearly every epistle from his undoubted oeuvre, Paul is seen to wrestle with the difficult implications of this surprising twist in the biblical history of salvation. Paul's experience in mission prompts him to reflect in the most profound way on the Jewish foundation of the Christian movement and the continuing relevance of the old dispensation (as in Romans 9–11). In light of God's gracious turn to the Gentiles, are God's exclusive promises to Israel now void? What place, if any, is there for the Mosaic Law in the life of this new covenant community? On what basis could Jew and Gentile hope to be reconciled in Christ, if not through a common set of cultic norms?

Luke does not ignore such questions, but in the course of telling the story of the church's first generation he adds an invaluable perspective on what was both a theological shift and a cultural transition. The multiple

---

to Acts; see Fitzmyer, *The Gospel according to Luke (1-9): Introduction, Translation, and Notes* (Garden City, N.Y.: Doubleday, 1981), pp. 143-270.

3. On Acts as a form of apologetic literature, see F. F. Bruce, "Paul's Apologetic and the Purpose of Acts," *BJRL* 69 (1987): 379-93.

layers of Luke's finely nuanced approach to his subject are already evident in the way he presents the story of Pentecost. At one level, this first major episode in the life of the newly reconstituted community (Judas's defection having been remedied by the election of Matthias) is about the fulfillment of God's promises, a patently theological concern. The dramatic arrival of the Spirit validates Jesus' assurances to the disciples that they would "be baptized with the Holy Spirit" (Acts 1:5) and so receive "power from on high" (Luke 24:49; cf. Acts 1:8).

Moreover, Peter's speech to the bewildered multitude of pilgrims in Jerusalem serves to extend the significance of the event to an earlier layer of prophetic expectation. Those drawn to the enormous sound produced by the Spirit's sudden appearance were witnessing nothing less than the realization of an ancient hope for the last days, articulated in wonderfully graphic terms by the prophet Joel. The curious behavior of Jesus' disciples, Peter tells the crowd, is not the result of drunkenness but an apocalyptic sign. The pouring out of God's Spirit had initiated a new era of extraordinary prophesying, dreaming, and visions. Additional wonders could be expected, as the culmination of the "great and glorious" day of the Lord drew nearer (Acts 2:20). Peter would have the "entire house of Israel know with certainty" that the source of this power was Jesus, descended from David and praised by him in the Psalms, lately crucified in Jerusalem, who now sat exalted at God's right hand as "Lord and Messiah" (2:36).

Where is the cultural dimension at Pentecost? It appears most obviously in the ethnic diversity of the festival crowd that thronged Jerusalem that year during the Feast of Weeks. The fifteen countries and peoples enumerated by Luke are said to comprise "every nation under heaven" (Acts 2:5). Luke's hyperbole allows him to represent the gathering of Jews and devout proselytes addressed by Peter as the whole nation of Israel, whether resident in Palestine or scattered abroad in the diaspora. By extension, these also stood more generally for their respective local cultures. When each hearer in the crowd perceived the disciples to be speaking in his own native language, it was as if, by proxy, the entire *oikoumene* had been made privy to "God's deeds of power" (2:11). Such is the opinion of Huub van de Sandt, who concludes, "In [the Jews of the dispersion present at Pentecost] all the inhabitants of the world are potentially present."[4]

4. Huub van de Sandt, "The Fate of the Gentiles in Joel and Acts 2: An Intertextual Study," *ETL* 66 (1990): 68. Much the same conclusion is reached by James M. Scott, "Acts 2:9-

Subtle details sprinkled throughout the narrative reinforce the notion that Pentecost was more than just a matter of one group of Jewish believers fighting with another in intramural fashion over the future of their joint theological patrimony. Even here, at the outset of the book of Acts, when Peter appears to be addressing only his fellow Israelites, the choice of words attributed to him points to a broader audience just beginning to assemble offstage. Most striking is the way in which Luke has handled the material quoted from Joel (Acts 2:17-21).[5] In their original context, these words about the Spirit's arrival hold no comfort for the Gentiles. In the prophet's vision the nations can expect only an awful destruction on the last day, because they have opposed Judah. Stripped of this conclusion (Luke does not allude in any way to the last, grim chapter of Joel), Peter's re-announcement that the Spirit is to be poured out on "all flesh" (Acts 2:17) easily admits of a more inclusive interpretation. So does his open-ended promise to the multicultural gathering in Jerusalem that "*everyone who calls on the name of the Lord shall be saved*" (2:21). At the conclusion of his remarks, Peter offers a third ambiguous declaration that again fits both the immediate circumstances of the scene in Jerusalem and the Gentile mission to come. Peter urges the crowd, "Repent, and be baptized every one of you. . . . For the promise is for you, for your children, and for all who are far away, everyone whom the Lord our God calls to him" (2:38-39). In the context of the long story Luke is about to relate, "those far away" at the time of Pentecost may, with justification, be construed to include non-Jews native to the lands from which these faithful pilgrims to Jerusalem have come.[6]

---

11 As an Anticipation of the Mission to the Gentiles," in *The Mission of the Early Church to Jews and Gentiles*, ed. Jostein Ådna and Hans Kvalbein, WUNT 127 (Tübingen: Mohr Siebeck, 2000): "the Pentecost event is an anticipation of the whole mission to the nations which unfolds in the rest of the book of Acts" (p. 122).

5. For what follows in this paragraph, I am indebted to the analysis of van de Sandt, "Fate of the Gentiles."

6. Ernst Haenchen's carefully worded comment on Acts 2:39 in *The Acts of the Apostles: A Commentary*, trans. Bernard Noble et al. (Oxford: Basil Blackwell, 1971), p. 184, reflects well the ambiguous nature of Peter's closing remarks: "The listeners cannot take [his mention of "those far off"] as a reference to the Gentile mission, though there is nothing in the text to preclude this idea." Joseph A. Fitzmyer, *The Acts of the Apostles: A New Translation with Introduction and Commentary* (New York: Doubleday, 1998), p. 267, has drawn attention to Luke's choice of tense here (literally, "everyone whom the Lord our God *will call* to himself"). Cf. "whom the Lord *has called* to himself" at Joel 3:5 (LXX). If these words are

Less ambiguously, the Pentecost episode shows how the social habits of Christian mission had been redefined by its first-century practitioners in at least two crucial ways. With respect to language, Peter's speech in Hellenistic Greek served notice of the disciples' fateful decision to embrace a dialect other than the one Jesus customarily used in order to announce to the world the good news of his death and resurrection. It is not necessary here to resolve the problem of whether the precise terms of Peter's oration quoted in Acts were of his own formulation or a composition put into his mouth by Luke.[7] In either case, the situation required Greek, because that was the only language this diverse group of Jews from Palestine and the diaspora could possibly all have understood. That Peter and others from Jesus' original band of disciples were capable of expressing themselves in Greek is not seriously to be doubted.[8]

One cannot overestimate the significance of the disciples' choice of idiom. As Lamin Sanneh has shrewdly observed, when the church crossed the linguistic frontier that lay between Aramaic and Hebrew, on the one hand, and Greek, on the other, the effect was to relativize Christianity's Judaic roots, while destigmatizing Gentile culture.[9] Language, in this case, was the leading edge of the gospel's move from a separatist, culturally idiosyncratic point of origin into an unknown but wide-open future. This had enormous implications for what came next in the history of Christian mis-

---

meant to recall Joel's prophetic word, then a small but significant pointer toward the future has been introduced into the text.

7. As was noted in Chapter 2, the problem of authorship regarding the speeches in Acts is concisely reviewed in Marion L. Soards, *The Speeches in Acts: Their Content, Context, and Concerns* (Louisville: Westminster/John Knox, 1994), pp. 1-17.

8. J. N. Sevenster, *Do You Know Greek? How Much Greek Could the First Jewish Christians Have Known?* trans. J. de Bruin, NovTSup 19 (Leiden: Brill, 1968), called it an "established fact that, as a rule, the Jews outside Palestine spoke and wrote Greek and almost always thought in that language, particularly in the centuries around the beginning of the Christian era" (p. 82). Joseph A. Fitzmyer agrees and argues, in addition, for the widespread use of Greek by Jews living *within* Palestine, especially among those living in more thoroughly Hellenized areas like the "Galilee of the Gentiles" (Matt. 4:15). See Fitzmyer, "The Languages of Palestine in the First Century A.D.," in *A Wandering Aramean: Collected Aramaic Essays*, ed. Joseph A. Fitzmyer (Missoula: Scholars, 1979), pp. 29-56. Gerard Mussies, "Greek As the Vehicle of Early Christianity," *NTS* 29 (1983): 359, likewise concludes that "Greek was the second language of many people if not of a majority of the population" living in the environs of Nazareth.

9. Lamin Sanneh, *Translating the Message: The Missionary Impact on Culture* (Maryknoll, N.Y.: Orbis, 1989), p. 1.

sion, as the work of Sanneh, Andrew F. Walls, and Kwame Bediako has made clear.[10] If no single language or cultural point of view could claim ultimate privilege with respect to the revelation of God in Jesus Christ, then all the world's vernaculars stood by equally ready to receive the gospel. Once the linguistic seal of cultural isolation had been broken, the infinite capacity of the gospel to be translated made possible an astonishing variety of indigenized forms, each of which implies an interpretative task. Seen from this perspective, we are bound to insist that Pentecost did not reverse Babel's curse by holding out the prospect of a single language of salvation. Instead, when each one in the crowd heard about the mighty deeds of God in his own native language, the fact of a multilingual and multicultural world had been decisively blessed.[11]

A second shift in cultural orientation, no less significant for the future of the church and its mission than the adoption of Hellenistic Greek, is also prefigured at Pentecost. This is the transformation of Christianity from a rural movement into a predominantly urban phenomenon. In the first chapter of Acts, a dedicated but tiny Christian community takes form in Jerusalem and then at Pentecost began its efforts at outreach within the cosmopolitan environs of the city.[12] Consistent with this starting point, the new centers of the movement highlighted in Acts also tend to be located in the great cities of the Empire or to spring up at the principal stops along the most important trade routes that crisscrossed the Eastern Mediterranean. The contrast with Jesus' missionary methods is obvious and striking. Except for Philip's interception of the Ethiopian eunuch by the side of the Gaza road and one other reference in passing to the evangeli-

---

10. Two of Walls's most important contributions on this subject are "The Gospel As Prisoner and Liberator of Culture" and "The Translation Principle in Christian History." Both essays are reprinted in Andrew F. Walls, *The Missionary Movement in Christian History: Studies in the Transmission of Faith* (Maryknoll, N.Y.: Orbis, 1996), pp. 3-15 and 26-42. For Kwame Bediako's views, see especially chapter 7 ("Translatability and the Cultural Incarnations of the Faith") of his *Christianity in Africa: The Renewal of a Non-Western Religion* (Edinburgh: Edinburgh University Press, 1995), pp. 109-25.

11. This aspect of the miracle is remarked on by the crowd no less than three times (Acts 2:6, 8, 11).

12. Luke's exclusive focus on Jerusalem and its environs after the resurrection puts him somewhat at odds with Matthew and Mark, both of whom appear to see Galilee as the starting point of the apostolic era (cf. Matt. 28:16-20 and Mark 16:7). John 20 supports the Lukan tradition of Jerusalem resurrection appearances, but the final scenes reported in the last chapter of the Fourth Gospel are set in Galilee.

zation of rural Samaria (Acts 8:25), Luke focuses exclusively on the apostles' efforts to give witness to the risen Christ in the cities of the Roman Empire.

The development of urban Christianity cannot be attributed solely to Paul's prodigious travels and influence. Even before such a thing as "Pauline" Christianity began to emerge after the middle of the first century of the Common Era, major congregations of Christian believers had already been established outside of Palestine in Damascus, Antioch, Rome, and, perhaps, Alexandria. In many respects, diaspora Judaism both prepared the way and offered a proven model of expansion for first-century Christianity. Quite soon after Pentecost, devoted adherents of the new sect ventured out from Jerusalem along the trail blazed earlier by a Jewish community in exile that had already come to terms with its Hellenistic, urban environment. We learn from Acts that some of these early Christians were compelled to relocate in times of persecution (cf. Acts 8:1-4). Presumably, many more migrated or traveled for reasons of commerce. A few, like Paul, are known to have itinerated for the express purpose of propagating their faith. Whatever the particular circumstances may have been in each case, the overall pattern of expansion suggested in Acts and confirmed by Paul in his letters assumes an urban bias. That meant growth in the cities, but an apparent lack of continued missionary activity in the first heartland of the Christian movement led to the loss of a demographically meaningful presence in countryside areas by the end of the first century, even in those places where Jesus himself had been active.

Wayne A. Meeks has evaluated the sociological importance of this shift from the village to the city in these terms:

In those early years, then, within a decade of the crucifixion of Jesus, the village culture of Palestine had been left behind, and the Greco-Roman city became the dominant environment of the Christian movement. So it remained, from the dispersion of the "Hellenists" from Jerusalem until well after the time of Constantine. The movement had crossed the most fundamental division in the society of the Roman Empire, that between rural people and city dwellers, and the results were to prove momentous.[13]

13. Wayne A. Meeks, *The First Urban Christians: The Social World of the Apostle Paul* (New Haven: Yale University Press, 1983), p. 11.

A socially dynamic, culturally diverse urban context in which a variety of religious cults competed for the allegiance of great and small was quite unlike the environment in which Jesus had tutored his first disciples. The agricultural metaphors preferred by the master teacher had to make way for the language of the merchant, the philosopher, the soldier, the athlete, and the Roman jurist.[14] Ideas of the church as a form of voluntary society began to modify the covenantal identity of God's people inherited from ancient Israel, whose membership had traditionally been determined by birth. Even the principle of territoriality was sacrificed as a new religious identity was framed for a mobile and increasingly far-flung constituency. Missiologically speaking, this transition from rustic to urban ways of thinking implied a major first-century feat of translation that was plainly more than linguistic.

Pushing the Cultural Envelope in Acts

Following Pentecost, four episodes within the Acts narrative stand out as illustrations of the gospel crossing significant cultural barriers. One is the incident Luke himself highlights by virtue of its placement within the overall structure of the book and the number of verses he devotes to it. This is the pivotal story of Peter and the conversion of the Roman centurion Cornelius (10:1–11:18). Two other episodes depict Paul interacting with Gentile pagans, first in the company of Barnabas at Lystra (14:8-18) and then on his own in Athens (17:16-34). A fourth vignette features Philip and tells of his encounter with the Ethiopian eunuch alongside the Gaza road (8:26-40). Each of these stories has something to contribute to our understanding of the missioner as an interpreter of the gospel.

Luke leaves the reader in no doubt that the conversion of Cornelius was an epoch-making event in the history of early Christianity. What Pentecost had only implied about the future — the participation of non-Jews in God's plan of salvation — is shown in this story to be taking place already in the life of the church's first generation. Cornelius is introduced as

14. Lucien Legrand, *The Bible on Culture: Belonging or Dissenting?* (Maryknoll, N.Y.: Orbis, 2000), pp. 131-32, discusses Paul's move from Jesus' system of metaphors to an entirely new "symbolic field" and offers a succinct but highly illustrative list of examples to demonstrate the point.

480

Plate 1. *Christ and the Samaritan Woman,* by T'oros of Taron,
Gladzor Gospels (early fourteenth century)

Plate 2.   Illustration for Acts 8:31, by Kees de Kort, watercolor (late twentieth century)

Plate 3.   Illustration for Acts 8:35, by Kees de Kort, watercolor (late twentieth century)

Plate 4. *Red Rice Planting Women*, Nepal, photo by Jacob Holdt (late twentieth century)

Plate 5. *The Preaching of St. Peter,* by Masolino, with Masaccio, Brancacci Chapel, Florence (1425)

Plate 6. *Baptizing the Neophytes,* by Masaccio, with Masolino,
Brancacci Chapel, Florence (1425)

Plate 7.   *St. Peter Healing with His Shadow,* by Masaccio, Brancacci Chapel, Florence (1425)

Plate 8. *The Distribution of Goods and the Death of Ananias,* by Masaccio,
Brancacci Chapel, Florence (1425)

a Roman soldier whom the Jews of Caesarea Maritima hold in extremely high esteem.[15] He is credited with having offered alms and constant prayers to the God of Israel (10:2), actions acknowledged by an angel that appears to Cornelius in a dream (10:4) to have been acceptable demonstrations of faith in God's sight. Cornelius is not circumcised and so cannot qualify as a Jew or even a proselyte to Judaism.[16] Nevertheless, the faith of the centurion is sympathetically described. He is a "devout man who feared God" (10:2), a man who is also reckoned to be "upright" (10:22). Cornelius is thus identified for the reader as a righteous Gentile believer in God, a Greek "God-fearer" who follows the ethical teachings of the Torah and attends at least some of the religious services held at the synagogue.[17]

The primary function of the Cornelius story within the broader narrative of Acts is to demonstrate the basis on which Gentiles were first accepted into the Christian community. Luke is concerned both to indicate God's approbation of Peter's actions and to show how the early church as a body came to embrace this fateful change in mission strategy. The dreams of Cornelius and Peter are offered as evidence of God's initial leading in the matter. Peter's subsequent decision to mix with Gentiles and to bear witness to the gospel in their midst receives further divine confirmation when the Holy Spirit falls on Cornelius and his household. The incident will conclude with Peter convincing skeptical elements within the Jerusalem church that he was compelled by divine necessity to baptize these Gentile believers. The heart of his argument is summed up in a single rhetorical question: "Can anyone withhold the water for baptizing these people who have received the Holy Spirit just as we have?" (10:47).[18]

15. The delegation sent to fetch Peter testify to him that Cornelius was a man "well spoken of by the whole Jewish nation" (Acts 10:22).

16. This circumstance, along with a report of Peter having eaten with non-circumcised Gentiles, is the basis of the complaint lodged by some Jewish Christians in Jerusalem against Peter's actions: "Why did you go to uncircumcised men and eat with them?" (Acts 11:3).

17. An extensive and still expanding literature treats in detail the technical terms associated with Gentile adherents to Judaism, including "proselyte," "God-fearer," and "God-worshipper." See the summary list of published resources offered in Fitzmyer, *Acts of the Apostles,* p. 450.

18. Stepping back from the details of the story, one can begin to appreciate the thoroughness with which Luke has built his case for a church composed of both Jews and Gentiles. In contrast to the picture of dissension given in Galatians 2, both Peter and Paul are shown in Acts to be ardent advocates of this development. Even James, the third of the three

Enough narrative detail is given in the Cornelius story for us to construct a coherent picture of Peter's missionary role. While he does give a speech to those gathered at the house of the centurion in the manner of an announcer of Good News, hints given in the description of the action leading up to Peter's declaration suggest that something else besides mere sermonizing is taking place. Two features stand out. First, one notices that it is not Peter but Cornelius who takes the initiative to invite the apostle to visit him (at God's prompting, to be sure). This stands in contrast to what one would expect from a herald figure. An already authorized announcer of the gospel does not require an invitation from his or her audience to speak. Certainly, none is assumed to be necessary within the purview of the Great Commission ("Go therefore and make disciples . . ."). If one understands the messengers of Cornelius to be more than a literary device or a convenient means by which the narrator brings his two principal characters into direct contact with each other, then the active participation of Cornelius himself in the shaping of this missionary encounter needs to be acknowledged.

Second, in the account of Cornelius's conversion we find that he is not the only one to have gained a new insight into God's purposes in the course of the narrative. Both Cornelius *and* Peter are groping toward understanding in this story. Each has had a dream, the full meaning of which becomes clear only when considered in combination with the experience of the other. Robert C. Tannehill is on the right track, I believe, when he detects in Luke's complex narrative structure an attempt to show God at work on both sides of what is, above all, a cross-cultural missionary encounter. "Indeed," he writes, "the visions in question here have the specific purpose of opening a relationship between persons of different cultures," so that mu-

---

most important figures in the community and, according to Paul, the reputed leader of the "circumcision faction" (Gal. 2:12), is portrayed in Acts 15 as having endorsed the decision not to impose the whole of the Mosaic law on Gentile converts, albeit while suggesting a short list of restrictions to which they ought to submit nevertheless. Luke also forestalls the possibility that what happened in Caesarea will be characterized later as a rogue operation or the result of an individual having misinterpreted God's intentions. Circumcised believers from the church in Joppa are said to accompany Peter when he travels to meet Cornelius, and so they stand ready to corroborate Peter's story of a second Pentecost. Most important, the church in Jerusalem is shown to have affirmed Peter's course of action (Acts 11:18) when they hear his reasons for acting as he did. The Jerusalem "council" meeting described in Acts 15 reviews and upholds this initial decision and then applies its logic to other situations of Gentile evangelization.

tual sharing can take place.[19] The evangelizer Peter, who finally perceived "that God shows no partiality, but in every nation anyone who fears him and does what is right is acceptable to him" (10:34-35), has had to develop in understanding since being "greatly puzzled" by the vision God gave to him initially (10:17). Thus, the most surprising aspect of Cornelius's story may be the fact that his evangelization became the context in which another conversion could take place — that of the apostle Peter.[20]

We turn now to consider Paul's activities in Lystra and Athens. The two accounts are often considered in relation to each other, because they are the only two places in Acts where groups of Gentile pagans are engaged directly with the gospel. Clearly, a new phase in the history of Christian mission begins at Lystra. These were the first recorded steps taken by the early church beyond the social world of Hellenized Judaism.[21] Previously, witnesses to Jesus the Messiah could approach those affiliated with the synagogue in one capacity or another, confident that their worldviews would overlap each other to a significant degree. In such circumstances, even Gentile adherents to Judaism like Cornelius could be reached with a Christian message expressed in essentially Jewish categories, as John Kilgallen has pointed out.[22] In Lystra and Athens, on the other hand, followers of the Christ encountered new frames of reference completely outside the orbit of the Torah. A rethinking of missionary technique and kerygmatic focus was in order.

---

19. Robert C. Tannehill, *The Narrative Unity of Luke-Acts: A Literary Interpretation*, vol. 2: *The Acts of the Apostles* (Minneapolis: Fortress, 1990), p. 131.

20. Cf. Beverly Roberts Gaventa, "'You Will Be My Witnesses': Aspects of Mission in the Acts of the Apostles," *Missiology* 10 (1982): 421.

21. Luke glosses over the interpretive challenges that faced the first evangelists working among the Samaritans. At Acts 8:5 Philip is said simply to have "proclaimed the Messiah" to them. This begs the question of what sense the Samaritans might have made of such a message, since they had no expectation of a Messiah. On this, see Fitzmyer, *Acts of the Apostles*, p. 402. If the mission to Samaria led to any serious effort to contextualize the gospel there or elsewhere, Luke does not allow the reader to see it.

22. John J. Kilgallen, "Acts 17,22-31: An Example of Interreligious Dialogue," *Studia Missionalia* 43 (1994): 43-44. Kilgallen goes on to suggest a brief list of the most fundamental ideas held in common by Jews and their Gentile converts: "Covenant, the Son of David, the Son of Man, the Suffering Servant, the Messiah, the Kingdom of God, the Creation, the Final Judgment, the Providence of Yahweh — these and the morality and historical figures and prophets of Israel remained meaningful tools by which to interpret Jesus, anywhere in the Mediterranean Basin."

In the Lystra episode, the action begins with Paul healing a man who had been crippled from birth. The narrator credits the man's faith as the cause of his healing ("And Paul, looking at him intently and seeing that he had faith to be healed . . ." [Acts 14:9]), but the witnessing crowds appear to understand what had just happened as the work of divinities already known to them by the names of Zeus and Hermes. Moved by the immensity of the miracle and/or by the prospect of further interaction with these two divine figures, they prepared to honor Paul and Barnabas with an appropriate sacrifice.[23] Far from welcoming their impending deification, the two apostles indicated by their actions ("they tore their clothes and rushed out into the crowd, shouting . . .") that they could not participate in the ritual about to begin. A short speech attributed to Paul lays out an alternative point of view: turn from vain things to worship the living God. The story of Barnabas and Paul in Lystra then concludes with the narrator reporting the appearance of some Jews from Antioch and Iconium, who are said to instigate the stoning of Paul and the removal of his nearly lifeless body to a place outside the city. In spite of this dramatic act of rejection, the missionaries do manage to leave behind a viable group of disciples in Lystra that a recovered Paul will visit in the course of his subsequent travels through the region (cf. Acts 14:21 and 16:1).

Luke uses Paul's visit to Athens as a way to develop further his portrayal of the gospel's encounter with Greek paganism. This time around, the reader is made privy to a fuller version of Paul's preaching than at Lystra and then has the chance to see how his pagan audience will react without the distraction of outside Jewish agitators. Paul's theological appeal to the Athenians begins with a definition of common ground, which is their mutual interest in matters of piety ("I see how extremely religious you are in every way"; Acts 17:22).[24] By referring to an altar in the city dedi-

---

23. Repetitions in the text (three terms are used to describe the man's condition: he was a man "who could not use his feet and had never walked, for he had been crippled from birth") may be a way to emphasize the magnitude of the healing. Cf. Haenchen, *Acts of the Apostles*, p. 430. Luther H. Martin, "Gods or Ambassadors of God? Barnabas and Paul in Lystra," *NTS* 41 (1995): 152-56, discusses the Hellenistic background to local Lycaonian expectations that divinities or their representatives might appear in the midst of common society disguised as human beings.

24. A preliminary scene (17:16-18) shows Paul in daily conversation with mixed crowds in the marketplace of Athens. Other debates took place in the synagogue. Paul's great address in Athens, however, seems to be crafted especially for a pagan audience. Luke takes

cated "to an unknown god," Paul creates a rhetorical bridge to the real subject of his address. What the sincere pagans of Athens sought in ignorance to honor with their worship, Paul tells them, is none other than the Creator of this world and everything in it, the source of all life, who is also responsible for the natural ordering of human society (17:24-26).[25] This God can be known ("he is not far from each one of us") and wills to be found, but Paul cautions the Athenians not to reduce the Lord of heaven and earth to a manufactured object that can be placed in a shrine, like "an image formed by the art and imagination of mortals" (17:29). Paul's Areopagus speech concludes with a call to repentance issued in the light of a coming judgment, the existence of which is no longer a matter of ignorance for his audience. Indirectly, Jesus is named as the one who will judge the world on the appointed day (17:31). Upon hearing a second time about the resurrection of the dead, the crowd neatly divides into those who scoff, a second group that wants to discuss the matter further, and a few pagan hearers who believe and so join with Paul.

A substantial literature has attached itself to the story of Paul in Athens. To a large degree, these studies have tended to look backward from the text to its supposed roots. New Testament scholars have long scrutinized the structure and content of Paul's speech, for example, in order to establish its historical authenticity. In particular, they have wanted to know whether the address was an invention of Luke or could be attributed with any confidence to Paul.[26] A related question, also discussed at length, asks how closely the theological approach of the speech matches what Paul had

---

care to establish that the philosophers and Paul separated themselves physically from the usual assembly of Jews, their proselytes, and Gentile worshippers at the synagogue: "they took him and brought him to the Areopagus" (17:19). In this paragraph, I intend only to summarize the contents of the address. In what follows, further analysis of the Lystra and Athens episodes together will consider other aspects of Paul's missionary performance in Athens besides his rhetoric.

25. These remarks parallel the reference made at Lystra to "the living God, who made the heaven and the earth and the sea and all that is in them" (Acts 14:15). On the other hand, Paul's claim at Athens that the "Lord of heaven and earth . . . [f]rom one ancestor he made all nations to inhabit the whole earth, and he allotted the times of their existence and the boundaries of the places where they would live" (17:24, 26) has no counterpart at Lystra.

26. The work of Martin Dibelius was a milestone in the history of these investigations. Several of Dibelius's most important essays on the speeches of Paul in Acts are collected together in Dibelius, *Studies in the Acts of the Apostles*, ed. Heinrich Greeven, trans. Mary Ling (London: SCM, 1956).

to say about Greek paganism in his own letters, written well before Luke finished his composition.[27] Others have striven to uncover the precise classical antecedents of Paul's discourse in Athens.[28] All these inquiries are important, but none of them defines our primary interest here. Instead, with the theologians of religion, we will approach the accounts of Paul (and Barnabas) in Lystra and Athens with an eye on their apologetic future, which, it must be admitted, has all along been the chief reason for believing Christians to return to these texts. This requires that particular attention be paid to how Luke treats the intercultural dynamics that attended the gospel's first contacts with groups of pagan hearers.

The stories set in Lystra and Athens show unmistakable signs of contextual sensitivity. A brief but vivid description of the place and people, for example, serves to highlight the new circumstances Paul faced as a cross-cultural missionary in Athens.[29] A decisive interest in matters contextual may be detected, too, in the shaping of the evangelistic message Paul delivers in these two locations. The content of the speech at Lystra is quite unlike the several addresses that precede it in Acts, including one attributed to Paul in connection with his visit to Antioch of Pisidia (13:16-41). To earlier audiences of Jews, proselytes, and God-fearers, the apostles consistently chose to highlight the peculiar messianic expectations of Israel and then hammered home with simple direct strokes the idea that these were fulfilled in Christ.

In contrast, at Lystra and Athens, familiarity with the Old Testament does not seem to be assumed and specifically christological assertions give way to appeals based more on general revelation or extra-scriptural evidence of God's existence and character. Paul proclaims at Lystra, for exam-

27. On this set of questions, see especially Leander E. Keck and J. Louis Martyn, eds., *Studies in Luke-Acts: Essays Presented in Honor of Paul Schubert* (Nashville: Abingdon, 1966). Key passages in Paul's letters include 1 Corinthians 1:18–2:13 and Romans 1:18-32.

28. See, for example, E. Earle Ellis, "Midrashic Features in the Speeches of Acts," *Mélanges bibliques en hommage au R. P. Béda Rigaux,* ed. Albert Descamps and André de Halleux (Gembloux: Duculot, 1970), pp. 303-12; Bertil E. Gärtner, *The Areopagus Speech and Natural Revelation,* trans. Carolyn Hannay King, ASNU 21 (Uppsala: C. W. K. Gleerup, 1955); and, again, Dibelius, *Studies in the Acts of the Apostles,* esp. pp. 26-83 and 138-85.

29. Haenchen, *Acts of the Apostles,* p. 527, provides a handy summary of the most important features of the story that connect it to life in first-century Athens: "the many temples and images, the special religiosity of the Athenians, their philosophical schools, the Areopagus (hill and court!), the Socratic dialogues in the market place, the introduction of new gods, the Athenian curiosity."

ple, that the blessings of nature give witness to God in the midst of every people (14:17), so that no one is left completely without knowledge of the Creator. Correspondingly, the Paul we meet in Athens draws attention to the order of the universe as a reasonable basis for proper religious behavior. Paul declares that God set the nations in their places and fixed the rhythms of time (17:26), in order to induce an inquisitive humanity (inquisitiveness being a quality of which the Athenians were a renowned exemplar; cf. 17:21) to seek after its Author.[30] This premise allows Paul to interpret the public displays of piety he discovers in the city as expressions of a genuine desire to know God. The role of the Christian evangelist in this situation then becomes twofold. As a friendly start, encouragement can be given that no quest for ultimate reality is futile, because the God whom Christians worship "is not far from each one of us" (17:27). Further, more specific forms of revelation can be shared, which, if accepted, will enable these fellow seekers after God to know more fully the one whom they are already attempting to honor.

An awareness of context may also be discerned in the subtle portraits of pagan religiosity one discovers in these two brief stories. It is remarkable that in just a few verses, Luke manages to allude to at least three different levels of pagan religious culture. The Stoics and Epicureans, who are singled out for mention from among the crowd in Athens (17:18), represent sophisticated expressions of a pagan ethos that focused on moral discourse and other forms of elite philosophical activity. One meets another kind of religious experience in the figure of the priest at Lystra. His role was cultic, not intellectual or literary. At the local temple dedicated to Zeus, he concerned himself with the sacrificing of animals and the weaving of garlands, two very physical means at his disposal to meet the immediate ritual needs of his neighbors. This, too, was a part, if not actually the heart of, popular religious practice in countless villages, towns, and cities located within the Roman Empire.

In the identification of Barnabas and Paul as Zeus and Hermes come to earth in disguise, we see a third aspect of pagan religious life. The crowd's exclamation may have spilled out in their mother-tongue of Lycaonian, but

---

30. The cause and effect reasoning set out in 17:26-27 by means of an infinitive of purpose (ζητεῖν) is significant but easily missed: "From one ancestor [God] made all nations to inhabit the whole earth, and he allotted the times of their existence and the boundaries of the places where they would live, *so that* they would search for God and perhaps grope for him and find him — though indeed he is not far from each one of us" (emphasis added).

the invocation of this mythic conceptual framework to make sense out of their experience served to tie an isolated event into a much broader network of shared assumptions about this world and its relationship to other realms. By applying the names of Zeus and Hermes to these visiting wonder-workers, the populace of Lystra was tapping into a well-stocked storehouse of meta-narratives that they shared in common with a host of other communities spread throughout the Eastern Mediterranean world of the first century. The work of Robin Lane Fox has demonstrated how widespread pagan expectations were of a visit from the gods, whether for good or ill.[31]

Luke was a theologian of mission, and it is to his credit that he did not create a stick-figure of crude polytheism and/or cultic debauchery to stand in for the religious worldview of the pagans Paul and Barnabas met in Lystra and Athens. On the contrary, Luke's heroes appear to take the religious attitudes and practices of their pagan interlocutors seriously, even when they are constrained to disagree. In this "yes and no" response to a purely Gentile form of religiosity, Luke defined a path into the future for a church ready to move conceptually beyond its early preoccupation with the synagogue. It remains now at the end of this section to characterize the trajectory for cross-cultural mission plotted out by Luke in these two stories and to indicate in a preliminary way how this approach contributes to the image of the missioner as an interpreter of the gospel.

Jacques Dupuis sees in Paul's Areopagus speech the inauguration of "a missionary strategy based on a positive approach to the religiosity of the Greeks."[32] In his view, this and other key passages from the Old and New Testaments constitute a solid biblical basis on which Christians can and, indeed, should affirm the worth of other religious traditions. Dupuis recognizes that more pessimistic views on the religions also exist in Scripture, but he maintains that these should not be allowed to obscure the warrant provided by Luke's Paul and the Logos-theology of John to approach other religious communities expecting to find theological and cultural values that can be embraced. Certainly, it is beyond question that many second-century apologists and evangelists ventured willingly after Luke into the midst of what might otherwise have been seen as an entirely alien Helle-

---

31. See especially his chapter on "Seeing the Gods" in *Pagans and Christians* (New York: Knopf, 1987), pp. 102-67.

32. Jacques Dupuis, *Toward a Christian Theology of Religious Pluralism* (Maryknoll, N.Y.: Orbis, 1997), p. 50. Many other scholarly sources could be cited to support or further explicate this reading of the Areopagus speech.

nistic environment, confident that points of contact between pagan cultures and Christian belief could be found.

Dupuis's analysis correctly underlines the critical role played by the Areopagus speech in the history of theology to follow, but it is not an adequate representation of the missionary stance assumed by Paul and Barnabas in Lystra and Athens. As we have seen, alongside an openness to pagan piety in these two episodes one also finds a critique of the same that resonates with other parts of the New Testament, including the epistles of Paul. At Lystra, for example, the evangelizers resist unconditionally the crowd's suggestion that they were the principal actors in a pagan religious drama of the gods come to earth. Similarly, Paul at Athens is forthright about certain aspects of pagan worship that he cannot reconcile with faith in Christ (for example, the idea that God is housed in a temple or can be represented by material objects), even as he affirms God's life-sustaining connection to all of humanity.[33] In both of these stories Paul invites his hearers to conversion, imploring them to leave behind the empty promises of idolatry by turning to the living God (14:15; cf. 17:30). For their part, a majority of the philosophers Paul addressed apparently found his notion of a bodily resurrection completely unacceptable, if not altogether ridiculous. This is enough to demonstrate that even at Lystra and Athens no smooth path is laid out over which thoroughly pagan religious sensibilities and the church's witness to Christ could travel side by side without serious tension.

Some time ago, Lucien Legrand wrote, "It is Kerygma and Sophia that meet on Mars' Hill."[34] By this expression, he meant to summarize his argument for a dialogical understanding of Paul's Areopagus speech and the discourse at Lystra. Taking up this subject again in a recent series of lectures on the Bible, mission, and culture, Legrand has elaborated and refined his approach, which I believe gets us very close to Luke's vision for mission among Gentiles not related to Judaism. In Luke's figure of Paul, an apologetic position is portrayed that lies somewhere between two ex-

---

33. Neither Luke nor Paul can be faulted here for bias against specifically pagan forms of idolatry. Paul's sharply worded declaration that "God . . . does not live in shrines made by human hands" (Acts 17:24) essentially repeats Stephen's earlier assertion, delivered to an audience of Jews devoted to the temple, that "the Most High does not dwell in houses made with human hands" (7:48).

34. Lucien Legrand, "The Areopagus Speech: Its Theological Kerygma and Its Missionary Significance," in *La Notion Biblique de Dieu: Le Dieu de la Bible et le Dieu des philosophes,* ed. J. Coppens (Leuven: University Press, 1975), p. 349.

tremes, which Legrand identifies as "Maccabean rejection" and "Alexandrian harmonization." The first is a flat refusal to engage an unbelieving culture at any level for fear of contamination. At the other extreme, one risks infidelity on both sides of the encounter of religions by simply ignoring all meaningful distinctions between them.[35] Paul in Athens, Legrand suggests, exemplifies a dialogical stance that is responsibly critical: "As dialogue, this stance reflects the Lukan sympathetic approach to the surrounding world; as critical, it maintains the call to conversion that cannot be dissociated from the Christ-event."[36]

Two final observations may be offered on Luke's handling of the Lystra and Athens episodes, which may help to fill out Legrand's picture of mission as critical dialogue. First, we should recognize that some of the most negative statements in these stories are narrative comments offered up to the reader privately, as it were, rather than taking the form of direct speech among the characters. Thus, Paul's great annoyance (even anger) in Athens at the sight of so many idols in the city (17:16) remains an interior feeling, unexpressed in his exchange of views with the philosophers. Instead, when Paul makes reference to the religious practices of the Athenians (17:22), he will use an ambiguous term (δεισιδαιμονεστέρους) that could indicate either praise for well-meant devotional practices or mild disdain of superstitious behavior.[37]

35. Jewish apologists in Alexandria like Artapanus and Aristobulus represent the far edges of irresponsible acculturation in Legrand's analysis of pre-Christian Jewish wisdom literature. The former was zealous to recognize the heroes of Israel's faith as the real architects of Egypt's greatest cultural achievements, while the latter too easily imagined Israel's covenant partner in evidence at the mention of Greek divinities. See Legrand, *The Bible on Culture*, pp. 52-60.

36. Legrand, *The Bible on Culture*, p. 150. Legrand's conclusions find additional support in the analysis of Eckhard J. Schnabel, *Early Christian Mission* (Downers Grove, Ill.: InterVarsity, 2004), pp. 1392-1404. As Schnabel puts it, "We find both in Paul's Areopagus speech: points of contact or agreement *(Anknüpfung)* and points of contradiction *(Widerspruch)*. Paul distinguishes between religion and revelation as on a razor's edge, referring to the common notions and rejecting the elements that are contradicted by the revelation of Scripture" (p. 1396).

37. The commentators all discuss the ironic possibilities of this word. Cf. Fitzmyer, *Acts of the Apostles*, pp. 606-7. In Mark D. Given, "Not Either/Or but Both/And in Paul's Areopagus Speech," *BibInt* 3 (1995): 356-72, the whole of the discourse is examined for other examples of ambiguous language that may well have meant different things to Paul's Athenian audience, on the one hand, and Christian insiders like Theophilus, on the other. See also Mark D. Given, *Paul's True Rhetoric: Ambiguity, Cunning, and Deception in Greece and Rome* (Harrisburg, Pa.: Trinity Press International, 2001), esp. pp. 39-82.

In a similar spirit, Paul's comment on the Athenians' ignorance of God is made indirectly, by way of reference to a monument in the city that presumably would be quite well known already to his audience.[38]

On their side, the philosophers also have some sharp things to say about Paul. Amongst themselves, Paul is called a "babbler" and a "proclaimer of foreign divinities" (17:18). The first term points toward intellectual shallowness — a serious deficiency, one would expect, in the eyes of this audience! The other term hints at seditious intentions, especially if the example of Socrates is being recalled.[39] When the philosophers address Paul directly, however, they do so using relatively bland language: "May we know what this new teaching is that you are presenting? It sounds rather strange to us, so we would like to know what it means" (17:19-20). The one place where Luke's Paul goes beyond neutral description or a positive declaration of Christian belief is in Lystra, where he characterizes the people's intention to offer homage to himself and Barnabas as a vain, empty, or worthless gesture. The bluntness of Paul's reaction in this case may be attributed to his surprise at what the Lystrans were contemplating. In any event, no indication is given that the crowd took offense. Indeed, Luke reports that they still wished to carry through with their pagan sacrifice to the two visitors but that Paul's remarks somehow restrained them from doing so.

Courtesy, then, is one dimension of the cross-cultural pattern of mission Luke brings to life in Acts. In the Athens scene especially, the reader discovers a rich variety of people with strong opinions about ultimate concerns, who moderate their speech for the sake of candid but sensitive communication. Critical dialogue in Acts is marked, second of all, by the open nature of the interaction begun at Lystra and Athens between the gospel and these new sets of hearers. In neither location is a single instance of contact the end of

---

38. Some time ago Martin Dibelius analyzed Luke's portrayal of Paul from a related angle. In his opinion, Luke essentially compromised the "true Paul" by suppressing the "coarse story of a Savior on the gallows" that lay at the heart of his primary message of Christ crucified. Instead, Luke's Paul preached "in the way that he thought the Greeks ought to be preached to at that time: with philosophical proofs, with comparative acknowledgements to Greek monotheism, and pressing into service the words of wisdom spoken by Greek poets." Dibelius endorsed Luke's apologetic strategy, founded as he thought it was on a wise assessment of what was most likely to work in Hellenistic culture. The quoted material may be found in Dibelius, *Studies in the Acts of the Apostles,* pp. 76-77. My comments here are not about the eventual outcome or usefulness of the methodology used by Paul in Acts, but the tone of his approach.

39. On both terms, see Haenchen, *Acts of the Apostles,* pp. 517-18.

the matter. With respect to Lystra, we know that Paul returned to the city at least twice afterward (14:21; 16:1-2). This means that despite being rudely ejected from the town during his first visit, Paul was not ready to capitulate to those who opposed the gospel by knocking the town's dust off his feet as he and Barnabas had done in Antioch of Pisidia (13:51). Unfortunately, Luke too briefly summarizes the later visits to Lystra and so fails to provide the reader with any information about subsequent discussions Paul may have held with the non-Jewish population there. For Athens, the situation is reversed. No return to the symbolic center of Greek paganism is recorded in Acts, but the scene of Paul's first visit there ends with an explicit appeal by part of the audience to resume their exchange of views later.[40]

Of course, we know that whatever may have happened in Athens itself, many gifted interpreters of the gospel, scattered widely across the Roman Empire, eventually did dedicate themselves to the creative challenge of witnessing to Christian faith in a thoroughly Hellenized cultural environment little affected by the Jewish salvation narrative. Clement of Rome, Irenaeus, Justin Martyr, and an entire school of apologists centered in Alexandria are just the best known of those in the early church who would turn their missiological attention from the synagogue to the Greek pagan temple and so effect on a larger scale the monumental cultural transition Luke seems to have anticipated even in his Gospel. Through the experience of Paul and Barnabas in Lystra and then Paul in Athens, Luke was beckoning the church to engage the rest of humanity with the claims of the gospel. In this way, Luke initiated a conversation that continues to be conducted today in a growing number of languages and dialects all over the world.

The Vanishing Translator

In the passages from Acts examined thus far in this chapter, Luke seems to be communicating with his audience on two different levels with respect to his idea of mission. The result is somewhat confusing, because the dual

---

40. The commentators do not agree about the precise meaning of the philosophers' final words to Paul: "We will hear you again about this" (Acts 17:32). If a polite put-down, then these words point to a tone of respectful disagreement, which still stands in contrast to the derisive "scoffing" of those who vehemently rejected Paul's arguments. On the other hand, if the language is understood to signal a more neutral position, then this group of hearers may be issuing Paul a genuine invitation to resume their conversation later.

messages being transmitted resist easy harmonization. Conceptually, Luke represents the cross-cultural mission of the early church as a boundary-breaking venture, a spirit-led leap into a still evolving future not yet fully grasped by Jesus' followers. The ideal missionary in this situation must be alert to God's guidance and ready to adapt quickly to new contexts and un-expected situations. As we have seen, it may even happen that the mission-ary discovers new things about the gospel, when God's activity outside the tightly circumscribed circle of Christian fellowship becomes better known. But Luke imparts a different impression of the church's mission at the vi-sual level of his storytelling. The many long speeches of Acts, in particular, suggest a picture of apostolic activity in which formal pronouncements delivered by static lecturers invariably dominate the climactic scenes of missionary engagement.[41] This leads almost inevitably back to an under-standing of mission as the task of announcement, a job best performed by skilled orators and public figures whose postures and refined styles accen-tuate their command over the circumstances of their evangelistic exploits, even when they are faced by hostile audiences.[42] In each of the missionary situations in Acts considered so far, the confident self-control of the speak-ers tends to belie the unpredictable and surprising nature of the revolu-tionary message they were preaching.

Happily, the incongruities of Luke's approach elsewhere in Acts are decisively overcome at least once in the book. The crucial exception occurs in the story of Philip and the Ethiopian eunuch. In this episode, the style of mission Luke depicts visually complements rather than offsets the theo-logical substance of his missiological stance. A consistent and distinctive image of mission emerges that lends itself equally well to verbal descrip-

41. The apostles' high profile in Acts also serves to reinforce an impression of tight, top-down control over the early church by highlighting the leadership role played by a small inner circle of apostles headquartered in Jerusalem. From time to time, it appears that this key fellowship grouping acted to monitor and regulate developments taking place else-where. Thus we read about the supervisory visit of Peter and John to Samaria after its initial evangelization by Philip (8:14-17) and the dispatch of Barnabas by the mother church when reports reach Jerusalem about a great number of Greeks in Antioch turning to the Lord (11:21). Luke's account of the conclave that meets after the Cornelius incident (15:1-35) is an-other example of oversight, which also serves to illustrate the importance of Peter and James within the Jerusalem church.

42. In Acts, the apostles' serenity in the presence of danger is matched by their forti-tude when confronted with rejection. Both qualities, of course, recall Jesus' model of faithful witnessing presented in the Gospel of Luke.

tion and graphic illustration. This is the missioner as an interpreter of the gospel. In what follows, an attempt will be made both to analyze the most important features of the Ethiopian eunuch's conversion story and to consider how this image of mission might be portrayed.

Philip "the evangelist," as he is called late in Acts (21:8), was one of seven leaders chosen by the church in Jerusalem and appointed by the Twelve to look after the physical needs of the Greek-speaking part of the early Christian community (6:1-6).[43] Oddly enough, Luke provides no examples of the Seven actually performing the "table service" ministry to which they ostensibly had been called. Two members of the group, however, do figure prominently in Luke's account of the early church. Stephen is remembered as a wonder-worker (6:8), whose eloquent and powerful defense of Jesus before the Sanhedrin (7:2-53) indicts the Jews for their betrayal of the Law and accuses them of misusing the benefits previously bestowed on them by God, like the tabernacle. Stephen's death gave the church its first martyr. Afterward, a period of persecution ensued that propelled Philip and other witnesses to the gospel beyond the narrow world of Jewish Christianity centered in Jerusalem. It is at just this point that Luke inserts two separate stories about Philip's evangelistic activities and so integrates them into the larger narrative framework he is constructing, which is concerned, above all, to show how the gospel was carried to Samaria and thence to "the ends of the earth."

In the first of these stories, Philip is credited with the introduction of the gospel into Samaria (Acts 8:4-8). This is a significant development with respect to the progress of the Christian message across major cultural barriers, since the Jews considered the Samaritans to be a separate people, outside of the covenant community. Unfortunately, Luke provides so few details in his summary account of Philip's work among the Samaritans that a distinctive approach to evangelization fails to come into focus. We do learn something about the general content of Philip's preaching in Samaria.[44] Luke also alludes to an impressive set of miracles that had no

---

43. These are the "Hellenists" of Acts 6:1, whose poor widows were being overlooked in the church's daily distribution of food aid. The "Hebrews" appear to be those within the community who customarily used Aramaic or Hebrew as their first language, although most of these also probably understood Greek. On these identities, see Fitzmyer, *Acts of the Apostles*, pp. 347-48.

44. Luke reports that Philip referred to the Messiah (Acts 8:5), as well as the kingdom of God and the name of Jesus Christ (8:12), in the course of his preaching.

small part in moving many of the local population toward baptism. Philip's leading role in Samaria ends as soon as the apostles sent from Jerusalem arrive on the scene (8:14).

In many ways, the story of Philip and the Ethiopian eunuch smoothly correlates with the Samaritan phase of Philip's ministry, by showing how the influence of the gospel radiated in a new direction out from Jerusalem, to the south. This time, the location specified is far from any area of settlement (cf. the "city of Samaria" indicated in 8:5) and the missionary encounter is a highly personal one that features just a single individual and the evangelist Philip.

A host of interpretive issues present themselves in connection with the identity of the Ethiopian eunuch.[45] As a highly placed functionary in the court of the Nubian kingdom of Meroe, the Ethiopian hails from a region considered very near the edge of the known world, from a Mediterranean-centered point of view. Does this make him a Gentile? On the other hand, he has just been to Jerusalem to offer worship and is in possession of a scroll of Isaiah, which together might indicate that he is either a proselyte to Judaism or, much more likely, a God-fearer like Cornelius.[46] Then one must consider the question of his social status. In the first-century setting of Luke's audience, being rendered a eunuch meant that one would suffer permanent stigmatization in the eyes of both Jews and Greeks. As such, the Ethiopian is, without question, a marginalized figure. Yet Luke describes the figure of the eunuch in terms that signal tremendous social power. He is a royal official with responsibility for the treasury of the Candace (as the Queen of the Ethiopians was called). He also has the means to travel in high style on a religious pilgrimage of extraordinary distance, which was then — as now — an opportunity usually restricted to the wealthiest from among the elite of one's society.

Because Luke declines to describe the Ethiopian eunuch using any of

---

45. F. Scott Spencer, *The Portrait of Philip in Acts: A Study of Roles and Relations,* JSNTSup 67 (Sheffield: Sheffield Academic, 1992), pp. 158-73, presents a full discussion of the problems associated with the identity of the Ethiopian eunuch.

46. Pilgrimage to Jerusalem, however, does not necessarily indicate formal adherence to Judaism. In the often-quoted view of Emil Schürer, "real" Gentiles (i.e., other than proselytes or God-fearers) routinely participated in the sacrificial system connected to the Jerusalem temple. Schürer summarizes his argument in an appendix to his classic work, *The History of the Jewish People in the Age of Jesus Christ (175 B.C.–A.D. 135),* ed. Geza Vermes et al., rev. ed. (Edinburgh: T&T Clark, 1979), vol. 2, pp. 309-13.

the technical terms of religious status he employs elsewhere (Jew, proselyte, God-fearer/God-worshipper, or Gentile, for example), we are left with a conversion story the full meaning of which cannot be fixed on the basis of the eunuch's identity. Perhaps the most that can be said in this regard with total confidence is that this African pilgrim to Jerusalem shares with the Samaritans a correspondingly obscure status with respect to official Judaism, notwithstanding in both cases a genuine desire to worship the God of Abraham, Isaac, and Jacob. The overall narrative intention behind the two stories in Acts 8 connected to Philip may thus be to signal a half-step of the gospel toward the Gentiles, as the witness of the Christian community begins to move north and south, away from Jerusalem. As we have seen, the next and decisive stage will soon unfold by way of the Roman centurion Cornelius, an unambiguously identified Gentile God-fearer whose baptism triggers a full-scale crisis of institutional identity within the early church.

However suggestive the identity of the Ethiopian eunuch may be, the kerygmatic power of his conversion story derives more, I believe, from its careful plotting and dialogue than from the nebulous background of this exotic character. In order to appreciate this, we must look at the way in which the principal figures in the story interact with each other. Philip, of course, is an important character. He performs the active roles of preaching and baptizing, but the most remarkable feature of his dramatic persona may be the alacrity with which he submits to God's promptings. Philip's movements throughout are attributed to God's initiative. The story opens, for example, with an "angel of the Lord" telling Philip to position himself beside the Jerusalem to Gaza desert road (Acts 8:26). Then, when the Ethiopian appears on the scene, reading to himself from Isaiah while riding in his carriage or chariot, it is "the Spirit" that instructs Philip to approach the returning traveler (8:29). The Divine will is further in evidence at the end of the story, since Philip's exit is said to have been effected by the "Spirit of the Lord," which snatches him out of the water immediately after the eunuch's baptism and then transports him to Azotus/Ashdod, a well-known city also located on the coastal plain (8:39-40).

In the view of Beverly R. Gaventa, the Ethiopian eunuch is the "real protagonist" in this story.[47] Philip may comply with God's instructions, but the eunuch takes eager steps to appropriate new knowledge about God

---

47. Beverly R. Gaventa, *From Darkness to Light: Aspects of Conversion in the New Testament* (Philadelphia: Fortress, 1986), p. 102.

and is quick to act on what he learns. "Indeed," Gaventa points out, "the Ethiopian does not merely receive the gospel but reaches out to grasp it."[48] It is certainly significant that at each critical juncture in the story, the Ethiopian eunuch — not Philip the evangelist — decides what happens next. Thus, Philip runs to intercept the traveling party, but the eunuch must extend an invitation to him to mount the chariot before their dialogue can begin. After this, the eunuch will ask Philip to interpret the Scripture he is reading, a request that constitutes an explicit appeal to be evangelized with the gospel. The eunuch will also be the one to suggest that Philip baptize him. One might even go so far as to say that the eunuch essentially commands his baptism to be performed, since he himself gives the order for their vehicle to be halted for just this reason. The eunuch understood the appearance of water in the desert to be a sign of God's blessing that ought not to be ignored. In any event, the form of the eunuch's final question to Philip (v. 36) implies that the burden is on the latter to produce a good reason *not* to perform the baptism ("What is to prevent me from being baptized?").[49] In the end, Philip the evangelist appears to have little or no personal discretion in the matter of the Ethiopian eunuch's baptism, surely an unexpected twist in the story of a conversion!

Viewed from the perspective of literary analysis, it thus appears that Luke has created space in the narrative for the eunuch to emerge as a more fully fledged character than he might otherwise have been by minimizing the heroic features of Philip's role. This runs counter to the usual way Luke portrays the apostles and other evangelizers in Acts. As we have seen, dramatic interactions among the characters often seem to function as mere preludes for the apostolic declarations that follow. Rather like arias, the speeches function as the emotional heart of Luke's opera, into which he pours his most impassioned testimony to the gospel for the benefit of Theophilus and the rest of his audience.[50] Those about to be evangelized in

48. Gaventa, *From Darkness to Light*, p. 123.

49. The same locution is used at Acts 10:47 and 11:17 in connection with the decision to baptize Cornelius. C. K. Barrett carefully considers the possibility that the eunuch's question has specific liturgical significance, but decides against it. See his discussion in *A Critical and Exegetical Commentary on the Acts of the Apostles* (Edinburgh: T&T Clark, 1994), vol. 1, pp. 432-33. Only very weak textual support can be mustered to support the inclusion of verse 8:37, which represents Philip's supposed response to the eunuch's question.

50. I am assuming with a large majority of the commentators on Acts that the speeches were, for the most part, creations of Luke's literary imagination. Certainly, none is

Acts tend to lapse into passivity or virtually disappear once they have posed a question to which the apostles' orations and actions are a bold response. Philip, on the other hand, delivers no formal address in this passage, although it is said in summary fashion that he proclaimed to the eunuch the good news about Jesus (8:35). Remarkably, Philip has but one line of direct speech in the whole scene, a rather neutrally phrased question he puts to the eunuch at the beginning of their encounter: "Do you understand what you are reading?" (v. 30). Thus, while Philip has a crucial part to play in the conversion of the Ethiopian eunuch, his evangelistic stance does not fit the typical pattern in Acts. This is why the familiar template of announcing Good News does not fit the social dynamics of this missionary encounter.

Another approach is suggested in a fine series of illustrations developed for the story of Philip and the Ethiopian eunuch by the Dutch artist Kees de Kort.[51] On the surface, his style may appear to be simple, but a rather profound understanding of the story shines through the pictures he has rendered of this episode in Acts for a children's Bible story booklet. Two of these are reproduced here (figs. 17, 18; plates 2, 3). In the first picture, three figures appear. One is an attendant who restrains the horse that had been pulling the carriage of the Ethiopian official. The eunuch is shown wearing a brightly colored set of outer garments, the fine quality of which obviously contrasts with the plainer attire of Philip and the attendant alike. The Ethiopian reaches down to help Philip up into the carriage, an expression of some eagerness appearing on his face. For a time, Philip and the Ethiopian eunuch will be fellow travelers on the road that snakes southward from Jerusalem, passing through Gaza on its way to the continent of Africa.

In the second picture, Philip and the Ethiopian are together in the carriage. Philip is speaking, but at the same time pointing to a book, presumably the passage from Isaiah that had so mystified the Ethiopian court official. What is particularly insightful about this portrayal of the scene is

---

long enough as reported to stand as a formal address. At the most, these are synopses of actual remarks, in which case the editorial judgment exercised by Luke still reflects his particular theological interests.

51. The watercolor paintings of Kees de Kort appear as illustrations in a church curriculum resource series originally published in the Netherlands. My copy of the Ethiopian eunuch conversion story is part of the same set of materials published in German as *Ein Afrikaner wird getauft* (Stuttgart: Deutsche Bibelgesellschaft, 1983). I am exceedingly grateful to the Reverend Michael and Jane Klatt of Hannover, Germany, for their suggestion that I look at these materials and then for their gracious assistance in obtaining for me a copy of this book.

Fig. 17. Illustration for Acts 8:31, by Kees de Kort.
Watercolor (late twentieth century)

the way the artist has positioned the principal actors in it. Philip and the
Ethiopian eunuch sit side by side, with their full attention focused on the
biblical text in front of them. This does justice to the place the Isaiah quotation occupies in the literary structure of the Ethiopian eunuch's conversion story.[52] The central question of the Acts passage has very little to do

52. By and large, the literary critics agree that a chiastic pattern governs Luke's presentation of the story, with the quotation from Isaiah 53 placed deliberately at the center of
the structure. Spencer, *Portrait of Philip in Acts*, pp. 131-35, reviews the earlier literature and
makes some additional proposals of his own.

Fig. 18. Illustration for Acts 8:35, by Kees de Kort.
Watercolor (late twentieth century)

with the identity of the Ethiopian eunuch or the authority of Philip the evangelist; it asks, rather, "Who is Jesus?"

In this situation, Philip shares what he knows from his own experience of the Christian life, guided by the Holy Spirit as he was throughout the encounter. He does not attempt to interpose himself between the Ethiopian and the Word that the Ethiopian is attempting to understand. He does not confront the Ethiopian eunuch, face to face, as a herald would be expected to do. Instead, Philip interprets, which in this situation means attempting to facilitate meaningful communication between the gospel and this new hearer. The Ethiopian eunuch does not become an object of mission, because he remains actively engaged throughout the story. As noted above, he chooses the point of contact from within his own religious experience. By virtue of his position and social power, he retains the initiative to invite Philip into his thought-world and then can decide what to do with Philip's insights concerning the Suffering Servant of Isaiah 53.

Philip, for his part, cannot be said to have imposed himself on the Ethiopian. Nor does he control the outcome of his meeting with the eunuch. Philip's missionary role is temporary, subservient, even self-effacing. Not surprisingly then, once contact has been made between the gospel and the Ethiopian, it is the evangelizer, rather than the evangelized, who vanishes from the scene. Philip does not linger as a guardian of the sacred text or permanent guide for this new Christian. His extraordinary disappearance leaves a joyful pilgrim free to resume his journey, transformed and marked as one of Christ's own. The now invisible translator is not even allowed to know the ultimate result of what took place alongside the desert road that connects Jerusalem and Gaza.

Mission As Interpretation after Acts

Looking back over the history of Christian mission, one soon learns how fundamental to the future of the enterprise the task of interpretation became in the post-apostolic period. The apostles themselves, led by the Spirit, had shown the way forward by demolishing the Judaic ramparts that initially threatened to hold the gospel captive. By the second century of the Common Era, an expansive church began to apply itself to the challenge of contextualizing the gospel among the various cultures that subsisted within the Roman Empire, and then pushed beyond the geographical limits set by the extent of imperial power. The universal implications of what God had done through Jesus Christ gave urgent warrant to their efforts. The commonality of human experience that lay behind the awesome diversity of the world's languages and cultures provided a sure basis of hope for their success.

Many examples could be produced from the historical record to demonstrate the importance of mission as interpretation to the future of the church following the age of the apostles. We will confine ourselves to just one, which ought to be enough to show the durability of this pattern for mission, which had been made manifest first in the post-Pentecost story of Philip and the Ethiopian eunuch. Our illustration comes from the justly famous missionary achievements of saints Cyril and Methodius, who are widely recognized as the premier evangelizers of the Slavs. The Byzantine Emperor Michael III sent the brothers to Moravia in 863. At the time, Frankish rulers in the West contended with Byzantium for geopolitical hegemony over this part of central Europe, and so, inevitably, issues of culture, language, and religion became intertwined with political and military objectives. For our purposes, the essential facts of the story are as follows.

First, the brothers' mission commenced when the local ruler over Moravia, Prince Ratislav, invited the Emperor Michael to send an ecclesiastical embassy to teach his people the true way of Christianity. Ratislav's appeal alluded to the presence of other Christian missionaries in the area: "many Christian teachers have come to us from among the Italians, Greeks and Germans, teaching us in various ways."[53] According to Ratislav's testimony, Catholic missionaries directed by Rome had succeeded in their initial efforts to evangelize the Slavs, who had already renounced paganism and begun to follow "Christian law."[54] No hint is given that the Slavs resisted evangelization, but Ratislav apparently feared the prospect of his people being fully Christianized in the manner of the Germanic tribes to the north, whose culture had been brutally suppressed as a condition of their subjugation by the zealously Christian Emperor of the Franks, Charlemagne. His request, then, had political overtones, but what he and the princes of Moravia asked for was an interpreter of the Christian faith. Ratislav wanted a teacher, someone who could "explain to us in our language the true Christian faith; so that other countries which look to us might emulate us."[55]

Second, Prince Ratislav's request was well aimed. Because Cyril and Methodius operated from within a Byzantine frame of reference, they were prepared to proceed on the assumption that the local language and at least some of the customs of the Moravian Slavs could be incorporated into any native church that came into being as a result of their work. This was a nor-

53. The Vitae of Constantine and Methodius are published in Marvin Kantor and Richard S. White, trans. and eds., *The Vita of Constantine and the Vita of Methodius* (Ann Arbor: Department of Slavic Languages and Literature, University of Michigan, 1976). This quotation is drawn from chapter 5 of the *Vita of Methodius* (*VM* 5), p. 75 in Kantor and White.

54. Kantor and White, *Vita of Constantine*, p. 43 (*VC* 14).

55. Kantor and White, *Vita of Constantine*, pp. 43-45.

mal expectation outside the Latin West, since Eastern Christians had long grown used to the idea of practicing ecclesiastical unity amidst wide-ranging cultural diversity. Within the Byzantine sphere of influence, no official Vulgate had been allowed to supplant rival translations of Scripture already rendered into Coptic, Armenian, Syriac, Ge'ez, and other languages. By extension, later missionaries who embraced the principle of translatability could turn any number of additional languages into potential media of evangelization. Such was the intention of Cyril and Methodius, it appears, but first they had to confront a substantial hurdle in the way of their missionary work. The Slavs of Moravia lacked a tradition of letters, having no written form of their vernacular tongue. As a remedy, Cyril devised the Glagolitic alphabet for them and then used it as the orthographic basis of an entirely new literary language, which came to be known as Old Church Slavonic. The first texts to be translated into Slavonic were liturgical, but these, of course, contained portions of Scripture. Eventually, the brothers would produce a Slavonic translation of nearly the whole Bible, if the testimony of Methodius's biographer can be accepted as factual.[56]

Third, the commitment of Cyril and Methodius to indigenize the witness of Scripture by enabling Slavs to hear it in their own language would be sorely tested by the rapidly shifting circumstances of their politically charged mission field. More purely theological objections were also voiced. Some opposed the very premise of entrusting the gospel to any but the three heavenly languages of Hebrew, Greek, and Latin. Others dreaded the possibility that liturgical novelties might be introduced (wittingly or unwittingly) in the process of transferring meaning from one language to another. A third set of concerns revolved around the potential demand for independent governance that might be unleashed if the Slavs had their own means for self-theologizing. As ecclesiastics, Cyril and Methodius could do little to shape

56. According to *VM* 15, Methodius "took two priests from among his disciples, who were excellent scribes, and translated quickly from Greek into Slavic — in six months, beginning with the month of March to the twenty-sixth day of the month of October — all the Scriptures in full, save Maccabees." See Kantor and White, *Vita of Constantine,* p. 89. Not surprisingly, some scholars find the miraculous quality of Methodius's feat unbelievable. An example is Henry R. Cooper Jr., "The Origins of the Church Slavonic Version of the Bible: An Alternative Hypothesis," in *Interpretation of the Bible,* ed. Jože Krašovec (Sheffield: Sheffield Academic, 1998), pp. 959-74. Writing in support of the *Vita's* claim is Francis Dvornik, *Byzantine Missions among the Slavs: SS. Constantine-Cyril and Methodius* (New Brunswick: Rutgers University Press, 1970), pp. 174-76.

the geopolitical realities of their situation. They showed themselves quite able and willing, however, to engage the theological challenges posed by their critics. Evidence of success materialized when the papacy lent its blessing to the Slavonic liturgy used in Moravia by the missionaries. A trip to Rome in 867 was decisive in this regard but also tragic, as Cyril died while visiting the city. Methodius returned to the region in 869, having been ordained Archbishop of Pannonia and Moravia by Pope Hadrian II.[57]

A set of carved wooden panels added in 1929 to Prague's medieval Cathedral of St. Vitus commemorates the missionary labors of Cyril and Methodius among the Slavic peoples. The two scenes shown here (figs. 19, 20) depict the missioners engaged in the kind of work that may be thought to characterize the concept of mission as interpretation. In the first panel, one of the brothers stands next to a tonsured figure, who holds a pen in one hand and a tablet in the other. In all probability, the missionary is Methodius and the seated person is one of the scribes who helped him to translate the Scriptures into Slavonic. We may assume that the scribe is a native speaker of the target language; this would have been the normal qualification expected of an assistant translator. If so, the tender gesture of Methodius, whose hand rests gently on the shoulder of the scribe, may imply something important about the spirit of his missionary technique. At least as significant is the way in which the two individuals are posed in relationship to each other and to the book displayed on a reading stand in front of them. We seem to have a triangular relationship depicted here similar to what Kees de Kort created for the story of Philip and the Ethiopian eunuch. Methodius stands back slightly, in order to avoid disrupting the scribe's line of sight to the reading stand. At the same time, his left hand directs the attention of the scribe to the text, which thereby becomes the focal point of the tableau.

Both brothers appear in the second panel, which has the date of 868 inscribed at its base. A third person is shown kneeling in front of an open book, which he seems to be reading. The hat and robe of the kneeling figure, quite unlike the clothes of the missionaries, mark him out to be a native Slav. Again, the positioning of the actors is crucial to the missiological message that underlies the artist's rendering of the scene. This time, the missionaries stand *slightly behind* the one in whose hands they have literally placed the Word by

57. Dvornik, *Byzantine Missions,* pp. 131-51, discusses the arguments offered by those in opposition to Cyril and Methodius and treats in some detail Rome's role in the crucial period of intrigue that unfolded between 867 and 869.

Fig. 19.
St. Methodius and a scribe,
door of the choir chapel,
Cathedral of St. Vitus, Prague.
Wood relief (1929)

Fig. 20.
St. Cyril and St. Methodius
and a kneeling Slav, door of
the choir chapel, Cathedral
of St. Vitus, Prague.
Wood relief (1929)

virtue of their pioneering work in linguistics. Contact has been made: it is the Scripture that confronts the person and occupies his attention, not the missionaries. The evangelized have been given an opportunity to hear and respond to the gospel in their own language, just as Prince Ratislav had initially hoped. The missionaries, withdrawing into the background, pray together for a happy outcome. The next step depends on the Spirit.

The example of Cyril and Methodius confirms and illustrates once again what we have already learned from the Acts of the Apostles about mission as interpretation. Ratislav's invitation resembles the earnest appeals and questions that earlier had prompted Philip, Peter, and Paul to cut fresh pathways of understanding through the xenophobic thickets that too often impede communication across cultures. The brothers' perseverance attested to the deep-seated respect with which they approached a culture not their own, while the quality of their translation work bore witness to the readiness of yet one more form of the vernacular to receive the gospel. They could hardly have imagined the rich harvest of cross-cultural missionary sowing that would, in time, be reaped in Eastern Europe. Eventually, success in Moravia would be followed by the evangelization of many other Slavic peoples, from the nearby Serbs and Bulgars to the Poles and the Rus, who lived further to the north.[58] Cyril and Methodius thus practiced a hopeful dedication to God's mission, even as they labored under the same foreshortened historical horizon that had also kept their apostolic forebears from being able to observe all of the fateful consequences of their own decisions and actions.

There are still places in the world where the Christian faith has yet to realize a truly indigenized presence. In these circumstances, a sharing of Christ among family and friends may not yet be possible and a simple announcement of the Good News might not be intelligible. Enter the missioner as interpreter, a linking figure who attempts to establish meaningful contact across cultures and languages between Christ and those who do not yet know him. In this way, missionary interpreters at work today also push toward the consummation of a culturally unlimited future for the gospel and the church. Christian witness that would be truly global — "to the ends of the earth" — is bound to embrace the cross-cultural dimension of the missionary enterprise.

---

58. Nearly a third of Dvornik's great work on the missions of Cyril and Methodius (pp. 194-282) is devoted to the subsequent working out among the Slavs of what he calls the "Cyrilo-Methodian heritage."

chapter 5

Shepherding

Disciples As Shepherds

The Gospel of John presents two leading images of disciples engaged in mission. The first of these was featured above in Chapter Three, where we considered the idea of Jesus' followers "sharing Christ with friends," in the manner of Andrew, the Samaritan woman, and the man born blind. The second, which will be developed in this chapter, is founded on the concept of shepherding.

It is something of a surprise to discover that the image of the commissioned herald who announces Good News is not highlighted in the Gospel of John. In fact, despite the obvious importance of "testimony" to the theology of the Fourth Gospel, the principal disciples of Jesus are scarcely shown exercising this ministry function in John.[1] Other figures,

---

1. Passing references to the disciples as witnesses do occur, as at John 15:27, 17:20, and 19:35. What's missing in the Gospel of John is an attempt to help the reader visualize the form of this ministry. In particular, the omission of the disciples' preaching tour reported in the Synoptics (Mark 6:7-13 and parallels) weakens the presence of the herald image in the Fourth Gospel. Additionally, the Baptist's energetic confrontation with the priests and Levites sent from Jerusalem by the Pharisees (John 1:19-28) stands in marked contrast to the disciples' relatively low level of activity throughout the time of Jesus' earthly ministry. In *The Johannine Approach to Mission: A Contextual Study of John 4:1-42*, WUNT 2/31 (Tübingen: J. C. B. Mohr [Paul Siebeck], 1988), p. 222, Teresa Okure points out that the disciples in John actively participate in Jesus' ministry only in the feeding scene recorded in 6:1-14 and then

outside the ranks of those who will lead the early church as apostles, most notably John the Baptist and the Paraclete, are featured instead as explicit examples of public witness to God's truth in the context of the world.[2] The expressive language used to describe the missionary qualities of the Spirit is especially noteworthy. In his last discourse, Jesus promises that the Father will send the Spirit to "teach" the disciples (14:26), to "bear witness" to Jesus (15:26 RSV), and to "convict" the world concerning sin, righteousness, and judgment (16:7-11 NKJV).

In comparison, the twelve (or eleven) disciples tend to remain witnesses in the abstract in John. This is true even at the time of their commissioning as apostles, told in John 20:19-23. Using terminology that reflects closely the book's distinctive phrasing and thematic perspective, the risen Jesus defines the apostles' mission on that occasion not by designating any particular kind of action (such as preaching, teaching, healing, or baptizing), but by identifying its ultimate source: "As the Father has sent me, so I send you." As John Stott has observed, the character of Jesus' final command to his disciples in John is incarnational, rather than verbal.[3] The key factor is their relationship to Jesus. Their prime directive is to abide in him (15:1-11) by loving one another (15:12-17).

In John, the inchoate features of the formally commissioned disciple come into sharp focus only in the Gospel's last chapter. The crowning image is that of the shepherd. The position I will take here is that the shepherd's role has an inherent missionary aspect, of which Jesus seems to have

---

without full comprehension (she takes the indirect reference to the disciples baptizing at 4:2 to be proleptic). Significantly, it is the crowd rather than the disciples who proclaim at the conclusion of the miraculous feast, "This is indeed the prophet who is to come into the world" (6:14).

2. To these two figures should be added the ironically true and very public testimonies of the High Priest (John 11:50) and Pilate (19:19). In contrast, when individual members of the twelve disciples give unambiguous witness to their faith in Jesus, as at John 6:69 (Peter: "You are the Holy One of God") and John 20:28 (Thomas: "My Lord and my God!"), the crowds and authorities are well out of earshot. I consider "the disciple whom Jesus loved," John's premier model of faithful witnessing by a disciple of Jesus (19:35, 21:24), to be an internal figure whose testimony is meant to strengthen the faith of those already in the community.

3. John R. W. Stott, *Christian Mission in the Modern World* (Downers Grove, Ill.: InterVarsity, 1975), pp. 22-25. Cf. Mortimer Arias and Alan Johnson, *The Great Commission: Biblical Models for Evangelism* (Nashville: Abingdon, 1992), pp. 78-97, on the "Johannine incarnational model for mission."

been well aware but which the church has often neglected in favor of other features of the pastoral office (especially the privilege of governance). The rest of this chapter will attempt to interpret the figure of the shepherd as a particular kind of missionary agent. The Gospel of John will have much to contribute to this discussion, not only because of the commands given to Peter in John 21 to feed and tend Jesus' sheep, but also with respect to what Jesus had to say about himself as the Good Shepherd in John 10. Other New Testament materials will also be surveyed, as will a selection of key texts from the Old Testament that quite likely informed first-century understandings of the shepherd image. Regrettably, limitations of space will restrict the number of pictorial representations that can be incorporated here out of the huge trove of Christian and secular art devoted to the theme of shepherding.[4] With regard to the selection of illustrations presented below, my primary aim will be to show how the image of the shepherd has been variously perceived within the church over time.

According to John 21, Jesus himself established the link that first connected the image of the shepherd with his disciples. The heart of the matter is contained in a remarkable dialogue that takes place between Jesus and Peter, reported in John 21:15-17. Three times, Peter is asked about his devotion to Jesus: "Do you love me?" Peter answers in the affirmative each time, after which Jesus addresses him with a command. The terms of Jesus' charge to Peter are variously phrased ("feed my lambs," "tend my sheep," "feed my sheep"), but its overall character is unmistakable. Peter is to become a shepherd, with responsibility for the care of Jesus' sheep.

Elsewhere in the New Testament, it is established beyond question that the duty of shepherding was not to be restricted to the person of Peter. Other leaders of the early Christian community were soon called to the same vocation. In Acts 20, for example, in the midst of his farewell speech given at Miletus, Paul takes up the situation of those who will watch over the congregation at Ephesus after his departure for Jerusalem. In his description of their task, the image of shepherding predominates. The people for whom the Holy Spirit has made these leaders responsible are called a "flock" (20:28-29). They will soon face danger in the form of "wolves," who

---

4. For a brief review of several biblical, classical, and secular treatments of pastoral themes in art, see Sarah S. Gibson, "Shepherds/Shepherdesses," in *Encyclopedia of Comparative Iconography: Themes Depicted in Works of Art,* ed. Helene E. Roberts (Chicago: Fitzroy Dearborn, 1998), pp. 819-25.

will attempt to disrupt the unity of the congregation as soon as Paul has been removed from the scene. The assembled elders, Paul tells them, are to "shepherd" the church of God, as they keep watch over it.[5] This is the purpose for which they have been given a ministry of oversight at Ephesus.

The language of shepherding also crops up in 1 Peter 5:1-4. Elders associated with a variety of congregations scattered across Asia Minor are addressed here in the name of the apostle Peter. As a "fellow elder" (RSV), Peter exhorts them to "tend the flock of God." This they must do without abusing their authority or seeking after their own gain. To shepherd responsibly means to lead by example, they are advised, rather than to dominate the flock. An intriguing detail in this passage adds depth to the overall context in which the elders are expected to fulfill their pastoral charge. We learn that shepherd-disciples are not meant to replace Jesus as Shepherd. From the perspective of this passage, Jesus remains the "chief Shepherd," who will one day be revealed (1 Peter 5:4). At that time, faithful shepherding by disciples will be recompensed accordingly, with a "crown of glory." In the meantime, the tenders of Jesus' sheep are urged to exercise their leadership responsibilities in continuing subordination to his ultimate authority.[6]

We find shepherds (that is, pastors) included in the brief catalog of ministries presented in Ephesians 4:11, alongside apostles, prophets, evangelists, and teachers. Of course, a bare register like this does not reveal much about the functional capacities or limits of each office included in the group, but the mention of pastors here does show that the category of shepherding was used to designate a certain kind of congregational leader in the sub-apostolic era. This is the only place in the New Testament where the office of pastor is included in such a list.[7] It could be that a separate position of shepherd/pastor became superfluous for a time, as other offices (i.e., bishops, elders, and deacons) continued to develop until they dominated the more permanent administrative structures of the post-apostolic

---

5. The verb used here — ποιμαίνω — also occurs in John 21:16.

6. The idea that Jesus remained the preeminent shepherd of the whole community, even after calling Peter and others to exercise a similar kind of ministry on his behalf, is reinforced at 1 Peter 2:25. The same idea lies behind the reference to Christ as the "great shepherd of the sheep" in Hebrews 13:20.

7. For example, Paul does not include pastors among the offices he lists in 1 Corinthians 12:27-31. Nor does Paul mention any particular quality directly associated with shepherding as one of the spiritual gifts he lists in Romans 12:4-8 or 1 Corinthians 12:4-11.

church. This does not mean that the metaphor of shepherding was abandoned after the close of the New Testament period. To the contrary, early Christian artists vigorously perpetuated the image of the Good Shepherd, who is usually shown in the catacombs as a rescuer of wayward sheep or a nurturer of the flock.[8] At the same time, a kind of conceptual fusion was taking place that eventually knit together the increasingly institutionalized office of bishop and the symbolism of shepherding. The fourth-century writings of Gregory of Nazianzus provide the earliest written reference to the shepherd's staff as an accouterment of the bishop's office.[9] One suspects, however, that the association was formed well before then. The now commonplace result is that the crosier has become a nearly universal emblem of the bishop's authority within the church. In the figure of the bishop, at least, disciples in the patristic era and beyond could claim to be fulfilling Jesus' command to Peter to feed and tend his sheep. The degree to which their shepherding would be an act of mission, however, remains to be discussed further below.

The Old Testament Background

We turn now to consider more precisely the meaning of shepherding. My purpose is to determine the kinds of activities that might be involved in pastoral leadership, in order to understand the possible missionary dimension(s) of this vocation. A complication to be faced lies in the fact that the image of shepherding leads us into a complex symbolic world, with a rich history extending far back into time and across many cultures. Within the

8. Robin M. Jensen, *Understanding Early Christian Art* (London: Routledge, 2000), p. 38, draws attention to the widespread use of the Good Shepherd image in primitive Christianity, noting that over 120 different representations of this figure can be identified among the extant Roman catacomb frescoes alone. Boniface Ramsey, "A Note on the Disappearance of the Good Shepherd from Early Christian Art," *HTR* 76 (1983): 375-78, goes so far as to say that the image of the Good Shepherd "was by far the most popular representation of Christ in the Church's first four centuries." Ramsey believes that interest in this figure began to drop in the fifth century as Christ was reconceived in royal terms, becoming "the king of the sheep, rather than their shepherd." Jaroslav Pelikan addresses some of the broader theological and cultural issues implied by this shift in *Jesus through the Centuries: His Place in the History of Culture* (New Haven: Yale University Press, 1985), especially pp. 46-56.

9. Pippin Michelli offers this historical judgment in an article on "Crosier" in *DArt* 8:193-95.

Bible itself, pastoral metaphors abound. This is not surprising, since many of the greatest figures out of Israel's past at one time or another earned their livings as shepherds (Jacob, Moses, and David, for example). In addition, animal husbandry formed a significant part of Israel's economy throughout the period of the Old Testament. For his part, Jesus was not a herder in the literal sense, but he evidently preached and taught knowing full well that many in his various audiences would be quite familiar with the vocabulary and life patterns practiced by those who tended sheep and other animals. For this reason, Jesus often used imagery drawn directly from the milieu of shepherding.

Adequate surveys of the biblical data already exist.[10] Here I want to summarize and describe the primary features of this material, paying particular attention to the symbolic meanings or extended analogies that became attached to the physical work of shepherding. In the Old Testament, at least four distinctive functions can be identified that together define the occupation of shepherd. The first of these is *guiding*. The shepherd is responsible for leading the flock from place to place. Without guidance, the flock tends to wander aimlessly and break apart, with the result that many of the basic needs of the individual sheep are not met. The shepherd might lead from the front, calling or whistling for the flock to follow, or drive the sheep forward from the rear. Either way, conscious thought on the part of the shepherd defines a route for each stage of the day's journey, and a strategy for long-term existence (with implications both for the sheep and for the shepherd) is formulated and carried out.

A deeply held conviction that God guided Israel in the manner of a shepherd surfaces again and again in the literature of the Old Testament. This was a joyous fact to be celebrated in times of plenty (for example, Psalm 100) and a surety of faith to be invoked when danger threatened: "Give ear, O Shepherd of Israel, you who lead Joseph like a flock! . . . Stir up your might, and come to save us!" (Ps. 80:1-2). The piety of Israel admitted the possibility that others could lead the community on God's behalf, as vicars or instruments of divine pastoral care: "You led your people like a flock by the hand of Moses and Aaron" (Ps. 77:20). Following the establish-

10. See, for example, Joachim Jeremias's article on "ποιμήν" in the *TDNT* 6:485-502, and, more recently, Nicholas Cachia, *The Image of the Good Shepherd As a Source for the Spirituality of the Ministerial Priesthood* (Rome: Editrice Pontificia Università Gregoriana, 1997), pp. 37-225.

ment of the monarchy, the figurative language of shepherding was applied to the kings of Israel. The positive potential of this identification was realized most fully with respect to David (2 Sam. 5:2; Ezek. 34:23-24). Many other kings were castigated for being poor shepherds of God's people (Jer. 23:1-4; Ezek. 34:1-10) because they led their charges astray or in some other way failed to maintain the integrity of the flock.

The shepherd not only guides but also *provides* for the sheep under his or her care. Sheep need to eat, and so it is the responsibility of the shepherd to lead them to places where proper nourishment can be found. Of course, when this aspect of the shepherd metaphor is applied to Israel in Scripture, much more than physical hunger or thirst is at stake. By implication, the shepherd's work involves the whole of the flock's existence, since a lack of food or water imperils life itself. Through the language of shepherding, Israel's poets challenged the offspring of Jacob not only to acknowledge their state of dependence in a marginal physical environment but also to probe the depth of their confidence in God's providence. The results were often profound, as in Psalm 23, where Israel's trust in God to provide for all their essential needs is affirmed with quiet certainty: "The LORD is my shepherd, I shall not want. . . ."

A third function of the shepherd is to *protect* the sheep. The rod of the shepherd was an effective symbol of this role (Ps. 23:4). The sheep were likely to be set upon by predators, against which they had no natural defense. With the rod, a kind of stave or club, the shepherd could defend the flock from its most rapacious enemies, including the wolf, the lion, and the bear (1 Sam. 17:34-35). Here again, Israel found deeper meanings suggested in the physical reality of the world of actual shepherds. Because Israel was a small nation set in a vulnerable geopolitical setting, the aspirations and actions of its more powerful neighbors constantly threatened it. In this situation, fear was the ever-present demon to be faced. The Israelites were encouraged to draw comfort from the thought that God was near to them, just like the shepherd in the midst of the flock. A complete sense of serenity would be indicated when the sheep felt secure enough to lie down, stretching themselves out: "Then they will pasture and lie down, and no one shall make them afraid" (Zeph. 3:13).

Finally, Old Testament shepherds are also shown having to *gather* sheep. When disoriented lambs wander off or become separated from the flock for some other reason, the shepherd is responsible for bringing them back into the gathered community. The actions associated with this shep-

herding function include "seeking after" lost sheep, "finding" the strag-
glers, and "restoring" them to the fold.[11] This part of the shepherd image
touches on a primal fear of Israel, which was the prospect that the corporate identity of the covenant community might somehow be destroyed, either by geographical separation (as occurred during the Exile) or by assim-
ilation into the surrounding cultures of the ancient Near East (or by a
combination of both). The ultimate danger was that Israel would find itself alone, dispersed like "sheep without a shepherd," vulnerable and scattered far away from their usual grazing land. This part of the shepherd
analogy received its fullest application in the Old Testament through the
prophets Jeremiah and Ezekiel. Each saw bad shepherding as a primary
cause of Israel's exilic crisis.[12] God pledged through these prophets to seek,
find, and restore the remnant of Israel to their accustomed pasture. The
prophets declared that God, in doing so, would be acting the part of the
shepherd who gathers lost sheep:

> For thus says the LORD God: I myself will search for my sheep, and will
> seek them out. As shepherds seek out their flocks when they are among
> their scattered sheep, so I will seek out my sheep. I will rescue them
> from all the places to which they have been scattered on a day of clouds
> and thick darkness. I will bring them out from the peoples and gather
> them from the countries, and will bring them into their own land; and
> I will feed them on the mountains of Israel, by the watercourses, and in
> all the inhabited parts of the land. (Ezek. 34:11-13)

But Is It Mission?

When the shepherd and sheep metaphor is used in the Old Testament to
describe the relationship of Israel's kings to their subjects, little or no missionary intent is evident. Kings govern. They administrate. Kings wield au-

11. See Cachia, *Image of the Good Shepherd,* pp. 51-58, for a more detailed discussion of
the Hebrew vocabulary involved in this set of shepherding actions.
12. The whole of Ezekiel 34 is relevant. Jeremiah indicts not only the rulers of Israel as
poor shepherds but also the false prophets who led the people and their leaders astray (Jer.
23:1-2, 13). Somewhat incongruously here, but fully in accord with the fundamental assumptions of Israel's theology concerning God's role in history, Jeremiah asserts, in addition, that
God was responsible for the flock having been driven out of the land (Jer. 23:3).

thority over the citizens in their realms and inevitably resort to coercion in the exercise of their power (1 Sam. 8:10-18). As leaders of the nation, Israel's kings could be good shepherds to the extent that they faithfully guided, protected, and provided for their own people. The analogy breaks down, however, with respect to gathering. Kings reign and rule. Generally speaking, they do not concern themselves with lost lambs or wandering citizens that have strayed beyond the boundaries of their political control. In any event, when exilic promises were made to return the people to their land, those who had governed Israel and Judah as monarchs were given no part to play. They were in total disgrace for having failed as shepherds, because their misrule had resulted in the dispersal of the nation. No one looked to them to restore the integrity of God's flock by making it whole again. Significantly, when it came time at the end of the Exile to gather the far-flung remnant of Israel, it was a non-Israelite royal figure, the Persian king Cyrus, who was chosen to be God's shepherd (Isa. 44:28).

In the Old Testament, when Israel describes God using shepherd language, does a missionary figure emerge? By and large, the answer here must also be no. The key fact is Israel's self-perception as the chosen people of God. According to this way of thinking, the covenant concluded at Sinai defined a relationship of particularity, uniting God and a people that considered itself to be separate from all the other nations of the earth. So long as an exclusive understanding of this bond obtained, God's role as a shepherd could refer to only a very small part of humanity. When the hostility of the surrounding nations to Israel and her sovereign Lord is further assumed, then the missionary edge of God's role as shepherd becomes even duller. Against this background, the first responsibility of the divine shepherd would be to preserve the safety and well-being of a sectarian group that regarded itself as an alien presence in the midst of the nations. Viewed from this perspective, God is reduced to Israel's powerful patron, and even the act of gathering becomes no more than an operation to reassemble an already circumscribed entity with more or less impermeable social boundaries.

The ideology of election is so strong in the Old Testament outside of Genesis 1–11 that universal counter-themes only here and there are allowed to poke through the dominant narrative line. When they do appear, however, it is as though a bright new light is cast on the concept of shepherding, which then can be appreciated as a truly missionary vocation even in the Old Testament. Faint hints of this possibility may be detected, for example, in the accounts of the Exodus. Scholars have long recognized that the people led by God through the wilderness were not a homogeneous group. Those who fled from Pharaoh's tyranny probably came from a variety of ethnic backgrounds. The tantalizingly imprecise term "Hebrew," used by Pharaoh to describe the identity of the escaping host (Exod. 1:15, 22), certainly encompassed more than the blood descendents of Jacob, whose extended family had come to Egypt centuries earlier seeking refuge.[13]

With the inclusion of this fact, a highly suggestive picture of shepherding emerges out of the Exodus narrative, a more fully rounded portrait that encompasses all of the pastoral actions discussed above. By means of a pillar of cloud by day and a pillar of fire by night, God guided a motley assemblage of former slaves, outsiders, and exiles through the desert to the Promised Land. When their safety was imperiled, God acted to protect them. At the prospect of hunger and thirst in the wilderness, God provided miraculous springs of water and an abundance of food. Most significantly, the journey from Egypt to Sinai, as a whole, can be understood as an act of gathering. Indeed, it may be argued that, on the way to the mountain, the people of God were not yet a fully defined entity. They were caught up in a process of formation, as participants in a movement of becoming that found its culmination only in the covenant-making ceremony at Sinai. Later, in retrospect, a claim of ethnic separation would be advanced, as Israel expressed its ardent hope that later generations would continue to honor the strict terms of the covenant made with God by their ancestors. In the midst of the journey, however, the primary requirement for inclusion in the sacred company was not pure descent but trust in God the Shepherd, who was acting to gather Egypt's outcasts into one body, while guiding, providing, and protecting those willing to set out in faith.

The missionary horizon of shepherding in the Old Testament is further tested in two passages of late exilic prophecy included in the book of Isaiah. These come at the beginning and end of a major section within the book (chapters 56–66) that modern scholarship has designated "Trito-

---

13. A pair of articles by Niels P. Lemche in *ABD* discuss the relationship of the term "Hebrew" (vol. 3, p. 95) to the broader phenomenon of population migration in the second millennium covered by the designation "Habiru, Hapiru" (vol. 3, pp. 6-10). The important point to note here is that a status of marginal foreigner (from the perspective of the Egyptians) was the likely common denominator shared by the totality of "the Hebrews" referred to in the Exodus narrative.

Isaiah."[14] The historical situation behind this block of material seems to assume that the Babylonian exile had come to an end. God had already acted through a chosen instrument, Cyrus, in order to bring to a conclusion Israel's long sojourn abroad. Yet the joy of restoration was dimmed by slow progress in the rebuilding of Jerusalem and its temple. It seems that the end of captivity did not automatically result in the fulfillment of every promise articulated by the prophets before and during the Exile, which led to widespread feelings of disappointment.

The crisis of the community lay in how to interpret the meaning of these circumstances. Some continued to blame outside powers for Israel's troubles. Their point of view is reflected in the many sharply worded oracles that foresaw the nations submitting abjectly to Zion, with dire consequences predicted for those that refused: "For the nation and kingdom that will not serve you shall perish; those nations shall be utterly laid waste" (60:12; cf. 45:14). Others argued for redoubled efforts to purify their society, particularly by honoring the sabbath (58:13-14) and practicing righteousness (57:1-13; 58:1-7). A third voice speaking through Isaiah 56–66 opened up the possibility that Israel's present situation was but a prelude to the next stage in the history of salvation. The prophet declared that God was not yet finished with the work of bringing together a people that would be the special possession of Israel's Lord.

We find a guiding principle for the new dispensation in Isaiah 56:6b-7: "all who keep the sabbath, and do not profane it, and hold fast my covenant — these I will bring to my holy mountain, and make them joyful in my house of prayer." The revolutionary aspect of this commitment is made clear earlier in the passage. Even pious foreigners and faithful eunuchs were to be welcomed into the sacred assembly (56:3-6a) — this despite the probability that lineal descendents of the twelve tribes would object, protesting that the Law of Moses stood in the way of such a development.[15]

14. On the integrity of Isaiah 56–66 as a distinctive subset of chapters within the canonical book of Isaiah, see Joseph Blenkinsopp, *Isaiah 56–66: A New Translation with Introduction and Commentary* (New York: Doubleday, 2003), pp. 27-91.

15. Certain provisions in the Torah seem to preclude altogether the possibility of adding eunuchs and foreigners to the covenant community: "No one whose testicles are crushed or whose penis is cut off shall be admitted to the assembly of the LORD. . . . No Ammonite or Moabite shall be admitted to the assembly of the LORD. Even to the tenth generation, none of their descendents shall be admitted to the assembly of the LORD, because

As a daring counterproposal to traditional attitudes, the prophet offered up a marvelous vision of the not yet rebuilt temple, which he announced was about to become "a house of prayer for all peoples" (Isa. 56:7). This is a step well beyond the expectation that "all people" will see God's glory from afar, when they observe Israel's exiles returning to the land (40:5; cf. 62:2: "The nations shall see your vindication, and all the kings your glory."); it also goes beyond the earlier claim that the Israelites will erect altars to God in foreign lands and practice their religion as a people set apart in the midst of the nations (19:18-25). We have here also a significant modification to the more familiar messianic hope that somehow, at the end of time, the nations will be drawn centripetally to Jerusalem to offer worship in the house of the Lord (for example, 2:2-4; 66:23). Instead, Israel is told that God does not intend to stand by passively, waiting for the nations to come to Israel. Like a shepherd, God is preparing to set forth, in order to gather new sheep (including foreigners and eunuchs!) into the fold of those already delivered from oppression: "Thus says the Lord God, who gathers the outcasts of Israel, I will gather others to them besides those already gathered" (56:8).[16]

The final lines of Isaiah 66 recall one last time in the Old Testament the image of God the Shepherd, whose vision of salvation for "the new heavens and the new earth" still under formation is decidedly universal: "From new moon to new moon, and from sabbath to sabbath, all flesh shall come to worship before me, says the Lord" (66:23). Not only that, but the day is foreseen when priests and Levites will come from the nations (66:21). How will this come to pass? The prophet speaks of a bi-directional flow of people and ideas between Zion and the nations. Exiles will continue to be brought back to the land like cereal offerings intended for the temple, until "all your kindred from all the nations" have returned (66:20). At the same time, God proposes to go to the nations, by setting up a sign and sending witnesses to those living in the remote places where no news of God's fame and glory has yet been heard or seen.[17]

---

they did not meet you with food and water on your journey out of Egypt. . . . You shall never promote their welfare or their prosperity as long as you live" (Deut. 23:1, 3-4, 6).

16. The vocabulary at Isaiah 56:7 ("these I will bring to my holy mountain") does not necessarily suggest the shepherd image, but the piling up of words derived from the verb "to gather" in 56:8 certainly does. Cachia, *Image of the Good Shepherd*, p. 53, asserts correctly, in my view, that gathering is "one of the main features of God as Shepherd" in the prophetic corpus of the Old Testament.

17. The unusual grouping of locations listed in Isaiah 66:19 brings to mind the regis-

Shepherding provides the framework within which all this activity will take place. The movement of God's messengers outward and the streaming of Israelites back to the land are two parts of a single divine plan, which is "to gather all nations and tongues" (66:18). This is bold thinking and an astonishing turn in the theology of the Old Testament. It is also as close as one gets in Israel's Scripture to an apostolic understanding of mission, such as one might encounter in the Gospels and Acts.[18]

New Testament Approaches to Shepherding

Within the literature of the New Testament, the further one moves beyond the ambit of Jesus' own ministry into the world of the church, the more likely it becomes that the shepherd will be portrayed as a custodial figure. That is to say, a missionary understanding of shepherding is more likely to derive from Jesus' example and precept than from the experience of Christians in the sub-apostolic era and beyond. The so-called "Pastoral Epistles" of Paul are a clear case in point. If we accept the current scholarly consensus that these letters were written in the name of Paul but reflect the historical conditions of a later time, then the corpus illustrates well a developmental curve for shepherding that heads in the direction of supervision and maintenance.[19]

In the view of the Pastorals, the ideal shepherd tends his flock by pre-

---

ter of nations that appears in Acts 2, at least in its apparent randomness: "to Tarshish, Put, and Lud — which draw the bow — to Tubal and Javan, to the coastlands far away that have not heard of my fame or seen my glory." Besides being rather obscure, the places named are similar in that they tend to suggest the edges of the known world, if one looks due west, southwest, and northwest from Jerusalem.

18. The conclusion of Claus Westermann, *Isaiah 40–66, A Commentary,* trans. David M. G. Stalker (Philadelphia: Westminster, 1969), p. 425, reflects well the path-breaking spirit of the prophet, but may be stretching the point with respect to the degree to which his Old Testament vision approximated the historical situation of first-century Christianity: "This [Isa. 66:19] is the first sure and certain mention of mission as we today employ the term — the sending of individuals to distant peoples in order to proclaim God's glory among them. This completely corresponds to the mission of the apostles when the church first began."

19. In his introduction to *The First and Second Letters to Timothy: A New Translation with Introduction and Commentary* (New York: Doubleday, 2001), pp. 20-99, Luke Timothy Johnson describes the historical process of interpretation by which this consensus was realized, even as he attempts to put anew the case for Pauline authorship.

serving it. This means protecting the faithful from false teaching, while building up the institutional structures of a settled church life and promoting establishment virtues like dignified leadership, social order, doctrinal consistency, and respect for authority. The letters to Timothy and Titus attributed to Paul are full of advice for those who would lead inward-oriented faith communities beset by threats from without: "guard the good treasure entrusted to you" (2 Tim. 1:14); "guard what has been entrusted to you" (1 Tim. 6:20); "continue in what you have learned and firmly believed" (2 Tim. 3:14); "these are the things you must insist on and teach" (1 Tim. 4:11); "a bishop . . [must] be able both to preach with sound doctrine and to refute those who contradict it" (Titus 1:7-9). In my view, the problem with this approach to shepherding lies in its assumption that the church is a static entity that has to be ruled with a firm hand, lest it disintegrate or mutate into an impure form. If such fears become the preoccupation of the pastor/shepherd, the figure ceases to be a useful model for missionary leadership.

An incipient conservatism also seems to mark the view of shepherding found in Acts 20 and 1 Peter 5, two other places in the New Testament outside the Gospels in which direct references to disciples as shepherds occur, as noted above. In each case, a scene is sketched in which a member of the apostolic generation offers advice to his successors about how to lead the congregation(s) entrusted to their care. In Paul's speech delivered at Miletus to the elders of Ephesus, he tells them, "The Holy Spirit has made you overseers [ἐπισκόπους], to shepherd [ποιμαίνειν] the church of God that he obtained with the blood of his own Son" (Acts 20:28). Similar vocabulary occurs in 1 Peter 5, where the author writes to those who would follow him in leadership over the church in Pontus, Galatia, Cappadocia, Asia, and Bithynia: "tend [ποιμάνατε] the flock of God that is in your charge, exercising the oversight [ἐπισκοποῦντες] . . . as God would have you do it" (5:2).[20]

The joining together of the shepherd metaphor with the language of an emerging episcopate in these two passages is significant and, perhaps, marks a preparatory stage on the way to the historical circumstances implied in the Pastoral Epistles.[21] In any event, the confluence of these two ideas

20. A third example of a word derived from the verb "ποιμαίνω" being used in conjunction with a word based on the root "ἐπισκοπ-" occurs at 1 Peter 2:25, where Jesus is referred to as "the shepherd and guardian" of believing slaves' lives.

21. It is impossible to be certain about the precise dating of 1 Peter, Acts, and the Pastoral Epistles, but the ecclesiastical structures implied in 1 Peter and Acts seem, on the whole, to be less developed than the group of offices (bishops, elders, and deacons) described in the

shows where the post-apostolic church will eventually take the image of the shepherd. Governing rather than gathering is going to become the primary pastoral function exercised with respect to the flock of God. Far too often, shepherding will be conceived as an act of defense, whereby order within the community is maintained and threats to its unity are countered by appeals to authority vested in the person of the bishop. Such a development was probably inevitable, given the needs of an evolving human institution that had to respond to the imminent passing of its founding generation.

All three of the Synoptic Gospels provide support for the claim that Jesus saw himself as a shepherd, whose mission it was to save the lost and to gather a community of disciples. From this perspective, Jesus expressed compassion for the crowds that were drawn to him "like sheep without a shepherd" (Matt. 9:36; Mark 6:34). Jesus told stories about lost sheep and the joyful shepherds who risked much in order to find them (Matt. 18:12-14; Luke 15:3-7). By his actions, too, the Synoptic Jesus reinforced the impression that he was fulfilling the role of a shepherd. The calling together of his closest disciples, for example, modeled on a small scale the larger aim of gathering to himself a redeemed community of people dedicated to the worship and service of God. Further, as a provider for his larger flock, he fed the great crowds that thronged to him during the period of his teaching ministry. The eager willingness of the twelve disciples to follow the one who called them to his side affirmed Jesus in this leadership role, although the disciples proved incapable of persevering to the end. Their failure, however, would not extinguish the identity of Jesus as a shepherd. On the basis of Old Testament prophecy, Jesus in Mark explains to the disciples just before his arrest that even their faithlessness and eventual dispersion will bear witness to his pastoral character. Thereupon, his coming resurrection will begin a new act of assembly, made possible by the fact that, once again, he will show the way by going before them:

> And Jesus said to them, "You will all become deserters; for it is written, 'I will strike the shepherd, and the sheep will be scattered.' But after I am raised up, I will go before you to Galilee." (Mark 14:27-28)[22]

Pastorals. See Paul J. Achtemeier, *1 Peter: A Commentary on First Peter* (Minneapolis: Fortress, 1996), pp. 321-22, for a summary of the evidence on this point.

22. The Old Testament passage Jesus quotes in Mark 14 is Zechariah 13:7. A less direct allusion to the same passage may lie behind John 16:32: "The hour is coming, indeed it has

Finally, Jesus the eschatological shepherd is described in Matthew 25:31-46. In this scene, reminiscent of Ezekiel 34:17-22, Jesus sits as a royal figure on a throne, performing an action attributed to shepherding. Those gathered before him (called here "all the nations") are a mixed company of two kinds. Jesus the shepherd judges between them, deciding on the basis of their actions in life which ones deserve to remain as part of his flock: "he will separate people one from another as a shepherd separates the sheep from the goats" (Matt. 25:32).

What is most striking about Jesus' approach to shepherding, based on the Synoptic evidence, is the emphasis placed in this material on *gathering* at the expense of the shepherd's function as a *protector* of the flock. This is graphically portrayed in the parable of the lost sheep. What could possibly possess the shepherd to abandon the greater part of the flock to chase after a missing animal? Only the joy that follows upon the recovery of the one that had been lost.

Luke's version of the story (15:3-7) is particularly vivid in this respect. The single sheep is truly "lost," not merely "gone astray," as in Matthew.[23] Considerable effort has to be expended in the search ("*until* he finds it") and to bring the sheep back to the fold.[24] Kenneth Bailey has drawn attention to some of the ways the figure of the shepherd has been depicted in art.[25] The piece of sculpture reproduced here (fig. 21) is notable for the relatively large size of the animal borne on the shoulders of the shepherd. Other depictions may be better known (for example, the third-century fresco in the Roman catacomb of Priscilla, seen in fig. 22), but none communicates more effectively the idea that good shepherding im-

---

come, when you will be scattered, each one to his home, and you will leave me alone. Yet I am not alone because the Father is with me." There is some disagreement about whether "going before" constitutes a *terminus technicus* of shepherding. Regardless of where one stands on that detail, the meaning of the action foreseen in Mark 14:28 and 16:7 is clear: Jesus leads the way to Galilee. For a discussion of the interpretive options, see Lucien Legrand, "The Good Shepherd in the Gospel of Mark," *Indian Theological Studies* 29 (1992): 240-46.

23. As Ulrich Luz notes in *Matthew 8–20: A Commentary*, trans. Wilhelm C. Linss (Minneapolis: Fortress, 2001), p. 443, this difference in vocabulary is crucial. In biblical and Jewish literature, to "go astray" usually means to exhibit "fundamentally flawed behavior before God," which can be corrected with discipline. The shepherd as tutor is alien to Luke's approach, but does fit well into the "church discourse" of Matthew 18.

24. Matthew softens the resolve of the shepherd: "*if* he finds it" (18:13).

25. Kenneth E. Bailey, *Finding the Lost: Cultural Keys to Luke 15* (St. Louis: Concordia, 1992), p. 76.

Fig. 21. *A Shepherd Carrying a Lamb*, marble statue found in the vicinity of Gaza (fourth-fifth century)

plies hard work, which does not end once the lost sheep is located. The Gospel of John will have more to say about the sacrifices expected of those who tend God's flock on behalf of Jesus. In the meantime, I will simply note that Bailey's decision to characterize the shepherd's efforts in Luke's parable of the lost sheep as "the burden of restoration" is both evocative and fitting.[26]

The shepherd's joy finds expression in both Matthew (18:13) and Luke (15:5). Luke (but not Matthew) goes on to show the whole commu-

26. Kenneth E. Bailey, *Poet and Peasant: A Literary-Cultural Approach to the Parables in Luke* (Grand Rapids: Eerdmans, 1976), p. 148.

Fig. 22.
The Good Shepherd, vault of Capella Greco, Catacomb of Priscilla, Rome (c. 250)

nity joining in the celebration that ensues when the shepherd returns with the once-missing sheep. This is not an incidental motif, but an aspect of the story Luke pointedly emphasizes by repeating certain details from the parable of the lost sheep nearly word for word in the following story about the lost coin (15:8-10).[27] In that parable, a diligent woman sweeps her house *until she finds* the coin she had lost. When it is found, she calls her *friends and neighbors* together (into community) and invites them to share her joy: "*Rejoice with me, for I have found* the coin that I had lost."

The conclusion of Luke's parable of the lost sheep is also telling. Departing again from Matthew's approach, Luke completes the story by lik-

27. In the next few sentences, italicized words indicate expressions that are common to both parables.

ening the fate of the found sheep to that of a sinner who repents.[28] This move profoundly affects the final impression left on the reader, in at least two ways. One is that the story is thereby connected directly to its immediate literary context, where the Pharisees are seen murmuring about Jesus' practice of eating with tax collectors and sinners (15:1-2).[29] A second effect of Luke's treatment is that the focus of divine concern is shown to move from those living within the customary boundaries that define the flock of God to those standing outside the protective enclosure. Of course, the logic of the Good News points in precisely this direction. Jesus Christ came to save the lost, those most in danger because of their separation from God. When shepherding is placed within this interpretive frame of reference, defensive ways of thinking have to give way to more dynamic approaches to pastoral care in which guiding, providing, and even protecting will continue to be important, but finding and gathering will be essential.

Jesus' discourse on the Good Shepherd in John 10 complements and deepens the overall picture of dominical shepherding gained through the Synoptics. As the most extensive treatment of the image in the New Testament, it deserves our fullest attention. What is learned about shepherding from John 10? First, what Jesus has to say about himself as the Good Shepherd is offered in the context of his ongoing confrontation with the Pharisees. As the text now stands, the same audience, with a group of Pharisees included in it, is presupposed for chapters 9 and 10. This is a circumstance of setting that naturally prompts the reader to ask about the relationship between the two blocks of material. In addition, a reference back to the story of the man born blind (John 9:1-41) seems to occur in 10:21.

The result of this juxtaposition and interweaving is that the Pharisees opposing Jesus are cast into the role of false shepherds, whose attitudes and behavior contrast absolutely with the motives and practice of the Good Shepherd. By implication, they are the ones Jesus has in mind when he talks about the "thieves and bandits" (10:1, 8, 10) or "hired hands" (10:12-13), who have made themselves strangers to God's flock. The sheep,

---

28. The parable of the lost coin finishes on the same note: "Just so, I tell you, there is joy in the presence of the angels of God over one sinner who repents" (Luke 15:10).

29. Jesus' critique of the Pharisees is dramatically reinforced in the story of the prodigal son presented in Luke 15:11-32. The younger son's return to life from death provokes his elder brother to anger rather than joy.

like the man born blind, do not recognize the voice of these shepherds, but they do listen to Jesus. Tacitly, Jesus seems also to be comparing the Pharisees to the duplicitous leaders of ancient Israel, whom the prophet Ezekiel excoriated for having abused the authority given to them, causing the people of God to become scattered in exile "with no one to search or seek for them" (Ezek. 34:6). In sum, Jesus in John 10 uses the example of the Pharisees as bad shepherds, in order to present himself in high relief as the Good Shepherd. He is their anti-type.

Second, the positive qualities of the Good Shepherd combine to describe an attractive figure that continued to be cherished within the church. From the point of view of the sheep, the physical attribute that distinguishes the Good Shepherd from all others is his voice or special call. The sheep follow the shepherd because "they know his voice" (10:4).[30] But more than simple obedience is indicated here. The shepherd's voice is the medium by which a relationship of trust is established and then renewed at the beginning of each day, when the shepherd enters the gate of the sheepfold and calls out to the sheep (10:1-3). The sheep not only recognize the voice of their true shepherd, but they "know" him in the same way that Jesus and the Father know each other: "I am the good shepherd. I know my own and my own know me, just as the Father knows me and I know the Father" (10:14-15a).

For his part, Jesus the shepherd demonstrates an intimate knowledge of the sheep when he calls them "by name" (10:3). The depth of the shepherd's devotion to the sheep goes much further than this, however. Jesus pledges, as the Good Shepherd, to lay down his life for the sheep (10:11, 15b, 17-18). This promise has no parallel in the shepherding literature of the ancient Near East. From time to time, shepherds that worked in rugged conditions might find themselves at risk, but it was not commonly expected that they would feel obligated to sacrifice their lives when the flock was threatened.[31]

The intimate bond that knits together the sheep and the shepherd defines a special and unusual relationship between them, which necessarily entails boundaries that differentiate the flock in some discernible way

30. The voice of the shepherd is referred to four times in this chapter (John 10:3, 4, 16, 27). An additional reference is made to the unheeded voice of strangers (10:5).

31. Bailey, *Finding the Lost*, p. 72, uses the Mishnah tractate Baba Metsi'a to discuss the practical and moral limits of a shepherd's responsibility in first-century Palestine, when confronted by dangerous natural predators of the sheep or brigands.

from its surrounding social context. On this basis, Jesus speaks of sheep that belong to him, while also acknowledging that there are others who exist outside of the flock. Some of these others are the Pharisees, about whom Jesus says, "you do not believe, because you do not belong to my sheep" (10:26). This kind of statement, taken on its own, might suggest a division of humanity into two inflexible categories, completely and, perhaps, forever separate.[32] Yet a simple dualism cannot account for the whole of Jesus' worldview in John 10. A third category is also posited, which encompasses those sheep belonging to Jesus that are *not yet* part of the flock. John 10:16 is the key verse on this point: "I have other sheep that do not belong to this fold. I must bring them also, and they will listen to my voice. So there will be one flock, one shepherd."

The idea of another "fold" within a united flock is the third distinctive mark of the shepherd discourse in John 10. Whether or not this concept was meant in the first instance to refer to a Gentile mission is debatable, but it is surely consistent with such a development. The future tense verbs in verse 16 seem to point in this direction, by anticipating a yet-to-be-realized factor of ethnic diversity within the unity of the flock. There is also the fact that Jesus introduces the notion of multiple folds within a single flock immediately after reiterating his intention to sacrifice himself for the sheep. In the context of the Fourth Gospel, the universal implications of such a statement would naturally occur to the reader. After all, God sends the Son in order that the whole world might be saved through him (3:17). According to Jesus, an unmistakable signal of his approaching hour is given when the Gentiles begin to seek him out (12:20-26). Further, an editorial comment introduced by the Evangelist at 11:52 nearly reproduces the implied meaning of 10:16, when the earlier utterance of Jesus is understood in universal terms. In the view of the Fourth Evangelist, Jesus will not die only to benefit the nation of Israel, as the high priest seemed to think; rather, "Jesus was about to die . . . not for the nation only, but to gather into one the dispersed children of God" (11:51-52). The vocabulary of gathering used here (συναγωγή) is significant.

We may also take note of the way in which the image of Jesus as the

---

32. Rudolf Bultmann went even further than this, perceiving in verse 26 evidence of a Gnostic understanding of the flock as a pre-temporal and, therefore, predestined community of the saved. See Bultmann, *The Gospel of John: A Commentary,* ed. R. W. N. Hoare and J. K. Riches, trans. G. R. Beasley-Murray (Philadelphia: Westminster, 1971), pp. 373-75.

door or gate is handled within the shepherd discourse. When Jesus speaks of himself by means of this figure, the fences set around his pastureland may well be fixed in place but the question of access has been left wide open: "I am the gate. *Whoever* enters by me will be saved, and will come in and go out and find pasture" (10:9). In this way, the broad promise of 3:16 is confirmed: "For God so loved the world that he gave his only Son, so that *everyone who believes in him* may not perish but may have eternal life."

Rudolf Schnackenburg is quite right to observe concerning the image of the shepherd in John 10 that this figure "bears no ruler-like features."[33] As such, Jesus' approach to shepherding is exceptional, especially when compared to the usual way this metaphor is understood in the rest of Scripture.[34] The Good Shepherd of John 10 models a leadership style based on mutual trust, rather than on the exercise of authority or the maintenance of order within the people of God. Remarkably, all four of the shepherding functions discussed earlier are to be found in the shepherd discourse of John 10, and they appear to be in balance with each other, a fact that contributes to the impression that this is the most complete rendering of the image contained in the New Testament. The shepherd guides (10:3-5). With the provision of good pasture and abundant life (10:9-10), the fundamental needs of the sheep are met. Protection is indicated by Jesus' promise that no one will be able to snatch the sheep given by the Father out of his hand (10:28-29). Finally, in the concern expressed for "other" sheep in 10:16, an indication is given of the shepherd's future work of gathering the lost. From the perspective of John's Gospel, the process of gathering enters into its decisive stage at the point of Jesus' resurrection: "And I, when I am lifted up from the earth, will draw all people to myself" (12:32). Does the evangelist intend for the reader to recall here the post-exilic prophecy of Isaiah 56? One cannot be sure, but certainly this action of the Good Shepherd fulfills the promise of God recorded there: "I will gather others to them besides those already gathered" (Isa. 56:8).

33. Rudolf Schnackenburg, *The Gospel according to St. John*, trans. Kevin Smyth (New York: Crossroad, 1990), vol. 2, p. 295.

34. Cf. the still useful summary provided by J. G. S. S. Thomson, "The Shepherd-Ruler Concept in the OT and Its Application in the NT," *SJT* 8 (1955): 406-18.

Peter the Shepherd

The exegetical section of this chapter will now conclude with a second, more extended, look at the passage with which we began, Jesus' call to Peter to feed and tend his sheep (John 21:15-17). Earlier, my intention was to show only that the early church traced back to Jesus its initial warrant to appropriate the image of the shepherd as a suitable figure of ministerial vocation. It remains now for us to explore further the content of the commission given to Peter and to consider its possible missionary import.

To attempt to define more precisely the pastoral office to which Jesus called Peter means immediately to confront a host of difficult interpretive questions. What ministry tasks are implied in the command to "feed" the sheep that belong to Jesus? Are these tasks different from what is indicated by the instruction to "tend" sheep? Does it matter that not one but three words were used to designate the objects of Peter's pastoral concern ("lambs," "sheep," and "little sheep")? What is the connection between these verses and the first scene in John 21, where the setting for the dialogue between Jesus and Peter is described and some preliminary action involving Peter, Jesus, and some other disciples takes place? What is the significance of the material that follows verses 15-17? Finally, how does this set of commands to Peter relate to the commission given to all the disciples in John 20?

As a way to begin to address such questions, we will look first at the direct speech exchanged between Peter and Jesus in John 21:15-17. Commentators have long deliberated over the rich but subtle vocabulary of these verses. Perhaps nowhere else in the New Testament are so many closely related words bunched together. Are the alternative terms offered for love (ἀγαπάω, φιλέω), sheep (ἀρνίον, πρόβατον, προβάτιον), knowing (οἶδα, γινώσκω), and pastoral care (βόσκω, ποιμαίνω) meant to signify discernible nuances in meaning or just variations in style?[35]

By and large, modern scholarship recognizes no critical semantic differences among these terms as they are employed in this passage.[36] Even

35. The last of the three terms mentioned for sheep (προβάτιον) is not attested in all the manuscripts.

36. This was the conclusion of Bultmann, *Gospel of John,* pp. 711-12, which has not been seriously challenged in the meantime. Raymond Brown, *The Gospel according to John (13–21): Introduction, Translation, and Notes* (Garden City, N.Y.: Doubleday, 1970), pp. 1102-6, and Schnackenburg, *Gospel according to St. John,* vol. 3, pp. 362-63, both indicate their agreement with Bultmann on this point.

the two words used here for shepherding are held to be practically synony-
mous, since they probably represent slightly different dimensions of a single Aramaic verbal idea *(ra'ah)* that encompasses within its broad conceptual field of meaning a wide range of pastoral activities (feeding, guarding,
guiding, gathering, searching, judging, and so on). Taken together, the two
Greek verbs for shepherding ("feeding" and "tending") may simply be a
means by which to approximate the whole of the pastor's task.[37] On the
other hand, the threefold command to Peter to act the part of the shepherd
(corresponding in form to the three sets of questions and answers exchanged between Jesus and Peter) is usually taken as more than a stylistic
flourish. At a minimum, we may understand a kind of rehabilitation to be
taking place in 21:15-17, a scene of reinstatement in which Peter is restored
to a position of respectability within the community after his three shame-
ful denials of Jesus during the Passion.[38]

Is Peter's commission in any sense a call to mission? A long tradition
of exegesis (especially within the Roman Catholic Church, but not only
there) has generally preferred to see here a solemn transfer of dominical
authority to Peter, effected in order that the "Vicar of Christ" and his successors might be empowered to exercise jurisdiction over Jesus' flock, understood as the church. According to this reading of John 21:15-17, Jesus intended to install Peter into a pastoral "office" that essentially anticipated in
its prerogatives the claims to primacy developed much later for the papacy.
It is not necessary to imagine abstractly the results of such an exegesis. In
1515/1516, Raphael of Urbino created a classic illustration of the scene along
these lines in the form of a "cartoon" or pattern in reverse that was used to
weave one of a set of ten tapestries prepared as decorations for the Sistine
Chapel (fig. 23).[39] In this picture, a number of visual clues recall the seaside

37. This is the view of Grant R. Osborne, "John 21: A Test Case for History and Redaction in the Resurrection Narratives," in *Gospel Perspectives: Studies of History and Tradition
in the Four Gospels*, ed. R. T. France and David Wenham, vol. 2 (Sheffield: JSOT, 1981), pp.
308-9, which confirms the finding of Brown, *Gospel according to John*, p. 1105.

38. Brown, *Gospel according to John*, pp. 1110-12, reviews the major positions taken on
the issue of Peter's "rehabilitation." We may note, with many other interpreters, that just before the dialogue begins, a strong linguistic link back to the scene of Peter's betrayal is supplied by a reference to the "charcoal fire" that burned on the beach (21:9). The same word occurs in the New Testament only one other time — in John's description of the courtyard of
the High Priest (18:18), where Peter denies Jesus three times.

39. Sharon Fermor has recently published a brief study of Raphael's tapestry car-

Fig. 23. *Christ's Charge to Peter,* by Raphael. Cartoon for Sistine Chapel tapestry, Rome (1515/1516)

context of the commissioning, including a bit of fishing tackle in the prow of a boat and the suggestion of a lakeshore in the background. Consistent with John's story, Peter is singled out from a larger group of disciples. He alone kneels and it is to him that Jesus points, while also gesturing to a small herd of sheep grazing behind him. Thus is Peter made the tender of Jesus' sheep.

The earliest known description of the tapestry woven from Raphael's design of this scene refers to it as the "Donation of the Keys."[40] This designation is accurate, if not official, due to the fact that the artist has chosen to represent the kneeling Peter with two keys in his hands. The keys, of course, are a vivid reminder of another commissioning scene, the one portrayed in

toons. Her book, *The Raphael Tapestry Cartoons: Narrative, Decoration, Design* (London: Scala, 1996), includes a superb set of illustrations that encompasses both the seven surviving cartoons and the tapestries woven from them. The definitive scholarly study of this subject continues to be John K. G. Shearman, *Raphael's Cartoons in the Collection of Her Majesty the Queen, and the Tapestries for the Sistine Chapel* (London: Phaidon, 1972).

40. Shearman, *Raphael's Cartoons,* p. 55. A more formal designation of the scene is "Christ's Charge to Peter."

Matthew 16:17-19, where Jesus promises to give Peter the "keys of the kingdom of heaven" as a symbol of his power to "bind and loose." No reference to keys is made in John 21; this element has to be imported from elsewhere.[41] What Raphael has done is to conflate two separate passages drawn from different Gospels, each of which features Peter as a foundational figure within the early Christian community.[42] In this way, a suggestion is made that the resurrection appearance by the shore reported in John 21 was the occasion on which the earlier promise of the keys was fulfilled. The net result of Raphael's approach was to subordinate the Johannine text to that of Matthew 16, so that the former is read through the latter. The ambiguity of the exchange between Jesus and Peter in John 21:15-17 is thus resolved. Whereas the dialogue did not indicate which of the shepherding functions Peter would assume or highlight as the caretaker of Jesus' sheep, the tapestry focuses the viewer's attention on one overriding consideration: the apostle's authority to govern. Peter will be a shepherd by exercising the power of the keys, which the Catholic church of the Renaissance most certainly understood as the right to rule the church as it then existed, even if that right was not yet universally recognized within Christendom.

When Raphael included near the center of his landscape background a miniature scene (fig. 24, detail) in which a tiny shepherd is shown leading a group of even smaller sheep along a country lane, he reminds us that there are alternative ways to approach the subject of Christ's charge to Peter. This very minor element in the tableau of the tapestry cartoon appears to be a recollection of John 10:3-4.[43] Its presence prompts one to ask how John 21:15-17 could be interpreted without the intrusion of non-Johannine

41. According to John 20:23, the risen Christ gave the power to "forgive" or "retain" sins to the disciples as a group, rather than to just one of them. Cf. also Matthew 18:18, where the power to "bind" and "loose" is conferred on the community as a whole.

42. Raphael was no innovator in this regard. When he adopted this line of interpretation, the artist was following a well-worn exegetical track, no doubt also favored by his patron, Pope Leo X. For example, Shearman, *Raphael's Cartoons*, p. 119, is convinced that Raphael was intimately familiar with Donatello's *Ascension*, a relief in which the giving of the keys takes place in the context of a resurrection appearance. Shearman further asserts that another famous Roman relief, located in the Ciborium of Sixtus IV and known as the *Donation of the Keys*, was the "principal model" for several of the figurative elements in Raphael's treatment of Peter's charge.

43. "The gatekeeper opens the gate for him, and the sheep hear his voice. He calls his own sheep by name and leads them out. When he has brought out all his own, he goes ahead of them, and the sheep follow him because they know his voice."

Fig. 24. Detail of
Christ's Charge to Peter

material, like Matthew 16:17-19. Certainly, if one were to rely primarily on data drawn from the Fourth Gospel, the Good Shepherd discourse would figure prominently. Jesus had already explained with reference to himself what the task of shepherding entails. Presumably, it is to the whole of this vocation that Jesus calls Peter. And, perhaps, this role is part of what Jesus has in mind when he commands Peter after the dialogue to follow him (21:19, 22).[44] As we have seen, the ideal shepherd of John 10 does not rule or govern. Shepherds who imitate this model seek rather to guide, provide for, protect, and gather sheep. This last activity is the part of shepherding that unequivocally connects it directly to mission.

44. I perceive several levels of meaning behind the command to follow. First, Peter is exhorted to follow Jesus as a disciple (cf. John 1:43). Second, he will imitate Jesus as a courageous witness to the truth and so experience a martyr's death (John 21:18-19). Third, Peter is to be a faithful shepherd, whose steadfastness in the end would prove that he was no false hireling, apt to run away when the flock was threatened (cf. John 10:12-13).

Finally, some additional support for a missiological reading of John 21:15-17 may be drawn from its immediate literary context. Especially pertinent are the initial verses in John 21 that set the scene of the dialogue (21:1-14). The chapter begins with the disciples engaged in fishing. After a fruitless night of effort (21:3), Jesus appears and tells them where to cast their nets (21:6a). The result is a miraculous haul of fish (21:6b, 11), which commentators at least since Jerome have taken to be a prefiguring of the church's missionary success. How are fishing and shepherding related to each other? At first glance, it would seem that they are completely different actions. Fishing is an apostolic function; tending sheep is an ecclesiastical concern. Raymond Brown sums up the logical problem in this way: "one can catch fish, but fishermen do not take care of fish the way shepherds take care of sheep."[45]

Strictly speaking, Brown is no doubt correct, yet one cannot deny that subtle filaments stretch out from each metaphor in the direction of the other and serve to tie them together. For example, the great catch of 153 large fish indicated in 21:11 (a sure sign of missionary success) is accomplished without breaking the net (a patent symbol of church unity). Peter, of course, plays a dual role. He is the one Jesus designates to be pastor in 21:15-17, after the apostle took the lead in the second phase of the fishing expedition by hauling in the teeming mass of fish. Most decisively, the idea of gathering is common to both of these actions. Shepherding and fishing may not be two sides of the same coin, but they ought not to be entirely separated from each other either, as though antithetical or completely isolated stages in the life of the church. We know that the experience of the community behind the Fourth Gospel had already opened it up to the possibility of a Gentile mission (12:20-26) and the prospect of outreach to the Samaritans (4:1-42). Certainly, the book's christological frame of reference pushes in the direction of the universal. Viewed through the lens of Johannine christology, the image of the shepherd has the potential to become a distinctive means by which to express a Christian intention to approach the world outside of the church with the Good News of Jesus' life, death, and resurrection.

45. Brown, *Gospel according to John*, p. 1084.

Missionary Poimenics

In his comprehensive two-volume handbook that describes the modern field of missiology, Jan A. B. Jongeneel includes a section on pastoral care. This he dubs "missionary poimenics," following the usage of François E. Daubanton.[46] As Jongeneel defines the topic, missionary poimenics is that branch of the theology of mission that describes "the systematic study of the missionary office and functions of the *poimen,* the *pastor,* the shepherd."[47] Missionary poimenics may be distinguished from more conventional forms of pastoral care by its wide field of vision. A missionary pastor is concerned not only for the personal needs of church members, but for the whole community from which they come. The routine transactions of parish life, while not unimportant, are not allowed to monopolize the pastoral horizon of the congregation nor to obscure its fundamental identity as a corporate witness to the gospel. Seen from this perspective, the pastorate can become a missionary vocation, whose total working brief necessarily includes concern for non-Christians and social realities outside the church.

The apostolic potential of the church's pastoral ministry is not easily realized in practice, however. Powerful opposing tendencies have to be overcome. If Christians believe, for example, that they are perpetually alienated strangers while on earth, only waiting to be repatriated to their heavenly home, or transients aching to reach a Promised Land located somewhere else, they and their pastors will have little incentive to become fully engaged with the immediate context in which they find themselves.

By the same token, Israel in the Old Testament consistently applied the image of the sojourner to itself. The story of Abraham, memory of the long residence in Egypt, and the experience of the Exile all served to rein-

46. Jan A. B Jongeneel, *Philosophy, Science, and Theology of Mission in the 19th and 20th Centuries: A Missiological Encyclopedia,* vol. 2 (Frankfurt am Main: Peter Lang, 1997), pp. 291-306. Jongeneel also provides documentation for several alternative names that have been used to designate this subdiscipline of missiology, including "mission pastoral theology" (J. Schmidlin), "missionary pastoralia" *(IRM),* "pastoral evangelism" (S. Southard), and "intercultural pastoral care" (W. J. Hollenweger).

47. Jongeneel, *Philosophy, Science, and Theology of Mission,* vol. 2, p. 291 (italics in the original). Jongeneel goes on to describe this kind of pastoral theology, which he sees rooted in Jesus Christ's compassion for humanity, as "the form and essence of the *pastorate to non-Christians*" (p. 292; italics again in the original).

force the sense that Israel was a unique people on pilgrimage, whose identity derived particularly from its vertical relationship with God. Perhaps as a result of this self-perception, Israel forged few constructive relationships cross-culturally with its regional neighbors. The other nations and peoples with whom the Israelites came into contact almost uniformly are portrayed as hostile threats and/or sources of temptation for the people of God.[48] It is no wonder that Israel's ministers — the priesthood — ended up completely focused on the special cultic needs of a people set apart, showing little active interest in the welfare of the neighbor or the good of the greater neighborhood.

Christianity, too, has known times in which a pastoral theology of social disengagement seemed to be warranted. On occasion, an overwhelming expectation that the Messiah's return was imminent or the experience of severe persecution has led different parts of the church to withdraw from participation in history, often in order to preserve the community's integrity or survival. Of course, Christian sectarianism is by no means completely unscriptural.[49] Nevertheless, we find in the New Testament that this perspective is rarely, if ever, presented alone. The church's theologians knew instinctively from the beginning that the body of Christ could not fulfill its purpose without reference to the world. Truly Christian faith cannot be practiced outside of time. Even during periods of unremitting persecution, the mainstream of the early church vigorously resisted the idea of devolving into a conventicle or some form of secret society that coveted anonymity for the sake of its own security in a strange and hostile land.

Thus, we read in the book of Hebrews about an itinerant community of persecuted "strangers and foreigners on the earth," ardently longing for their heavenly home, a "better country" prepared for them by God (11:13-16), who are nevertheless told to face the world and embrace whatever it has in store for them. As the writer of Hebrews puts it, because Jesus suffered "outside the city gate," the church must be ready to venture abroad, to "go to him *outside the camp* and bear the abuse he endured" (Heb. 13:12-

---

48. The intriguing figure of Melchizedek (Gen. 14) is the exception that proves the rule.

49. See, for example, the provocative discussion of Johannine sectarianism recently put forward by Robert H. Gundry in *Jesus the Word according to John the Sectarian: A Paleofundamentalist Manifesto for Contemporary Evangelicalism, Especially Its Elites, in North America* (Grand Rapids: Eerdmans, 2002), pp. 51-70.

13).[50] Another place where the language of estrangement seems at first to define the church's situation is 1 Peter, a letter addressed to "exiles of the Dispersion" (1:1). These are "a chosen race, a royal priesthood, a holy nation, God's own people" (2:9), all terms of exclusivity, to be sure. Even so, as "aliens and exiles" (2:11), they remained accountable for their conduct in the world.

The author of 1 Peter repeatedly extols exemplary public behavior as a duty of faith, not only because it neutralizes unjust accusations that might be made against groups of Christian believers, but also because the church's wider reputation is bound to reflect on the character of the Lord they worship. In this epistle, "honorable" conduct among the Gentiles (2:12) is a missionary concern, an issue of apologetics. The writer knows that many on the outside are first introduced to Jesus and the one who sent him by means of the church's public profile and the quality of its ministry in the world. In addition, God's own people must be prepared, at all times, "to make your defense to anyone who demands from you an accounting for the hope that is in you" (3:15).

Among those living nearer to our own time who have attempted to probe at the deepest level what it might mean to be a missionary pastor, the example of C. F. Andrews stands out. In the first half of the twentieth century, Andrews (1871-1940) was a world-famous Christian missionary, on the order of a David Livingstone or an Albert Schweitzer.[51] His was an extraordinary readiness, widely recognized during his lifetime and remembered long afterward, to open himself up to the cultures, religions, and political aspirations of India and her people. His closest friends were not fellow missionaries from Britain and the West but Indians from a variety of religious backgrounds, including people like Gandhi, the poet Rabindranath Tagore, and the Muslim intellectual Mauvli Zaka Ullah.

Andrews was a fervent trade unionist, unwavering in his commitment to the urban poor, whether those of London or Calcutta. He became a proponent of Indian nationalism, much to the chagrin of his fellow Anglo-Indians. Dissatisfied with conventional patterns of missionary service in India, he left the Cambridge Mission to Delhi in 1914 and joined

50. The implications of Christ having died at the periphery of the city are probed with remarkable insight from the perspective of mission theology in Orlando E. Costas, *Christ outside the Gate: Mission beyond Christendom* (Maryknoll, N.Y.: Orbis, 1982).

51. This is the judgment of Timothy Yates, *Christian Mission in the Twentieth Century* (Cambridge: Cambridge University Press, 1994), p. 74.

Tagore's ashram as a Christian layperson. There is every reason to believe that Andrews did not at that time imagine himself to have stopped being a Christian missionary. To the contrary, it was in order to fulfill his missionary vocation more completely that Andrews felt it necessary to abandon the privileges of the Anglican priesthood and to step outside the social circles of the religious establishment that ministered to imperial India.[52]

The impressive career of C. F. Andrews was shaped by a distinctive vision of pastoral action, anchored in a life of intentional prayer. Thanks to an invitation extended to him near the end of his life by Cambridge University to deliver a set of University Lectures in pastoral theology, we have the means to grasp what Andrews, in hindsight, thought he had been doing. The lectures were duly presented in 1937. Afterward, back in India, he revised and expanded his text, which was eventually published in monograph form as *The Good Shepherd*. The title of the book not only provides a guiding image for Andrews's exposition of his topic but also points to his high regard for the Johannine perspective within the New Testament.[53]

Two qualities in particular mark the pastoral theology of C. F. Andrews and call for comment here. The first is the utter seriousness with which he took Ezekiel 34:2-6 as a normative template for Christian mission.[54] In fact, this text roughly supplies the outline for the second half of the book, which is designated "the practical work."[55] Following the

---

52. Andrews did not completely dissociate himself from the church during this long period of lay ministry. In addition, he returned to the priesthood in 1936.

53. Under the influence of B. F. Westcott at Cambridge, Andrews imbibed early from his undergraduate milieu a deep-set appreciation for the Fourth Gospel. The Johannine tilt of Andrews's theology is often pointed out. See, for example, Eric J. Sharpe, "The Legacy of C. F. Andrews," *IBMR* 9 (1985): 117-18.

54. The text of the passage is as follows: "Ah, you shepherds of Israel who have been feeding yourselves! Should not shepherds feed the sheep? You eat the fat, you clothe yourselves with the wool, you slaughter the fatlings; but you do not feed the sheep. You have not strengthened the weak, you have not healed the sick, you have not bound up the injured, you have not brought back the strayed, you have not sought the lost, but with force and harshness you have ruled them. So they were scattered, because there was no shepherd; and scattered, they became food for all the wild animals. My sheep were scattered, they wandered over all the mountains and on every high hill; my sheep were scattered over all the face of the earth, with no one to search or seek for them."

55. The first part of the book takes up the matter of prayer, under the heading of "personal preparation."

prophet's schema, the ideal pastor feeds sheep, which implied to Andrews a loving ministry at home and abroad among the young. True shepherds must also respond to human need and so work to realize just social relations. This is how they act to strengthen the weak, heal the sick, and bind up the broken. Andrews understood this part of his own call to be a specific summons to enter into India's struggle against what he believed were the intertwined evils of imperialism, militarism, and predatory capitalism. Finally, to seek the lost, strayed, and scattered meant to attend to those forgotten by society, in particular the poor multitudes for whom Jesus himself had expressed his compassion as their pastor (Matt. 9:36).

The spatial orientation of Andrews's pastoral theology is the second remarkable feature of his approach. He was constantly prompted by the circumstances of his life and theological outlook to seek after "other sheep," outside and far beyond the traditional folds of European Christianity. In *The Good Shepherd,* Andrews captures an indispensable quality of missionary shepherding, its outward-facing aspect, when he observes:

> We must never be content . . . with the small local area in which we live, or the school in which we teach, as if that were our one narrow field of work. We must, as the true ministers of our Saviour Jesus Christ, have the *mind* of the Saviour, and think further still with hearts full of compassion concerning those multitudes who are the outcast among mankind and remain outside the loving care of any pastor or shepherd. Jesus Christ, we are told, came into the world "to seek and to save that which is lost"; and there are countless millions of poor and distressed people to-day, all over the world, who need the Shepherd's care and have not yet found it.[56]

56. C. F. Andrews, *The Good Shepherd* (London: Harper, 1940), pp. 164-65 (emphasis in original). This was not a late-in-life insight for Andrews, but a long-held conviction. In a sermon preached some thirty years before he gave these lectures, Andrews spoke of how his understanding of the Christian faith had already begun to expand during his first decade in India: "As my outlook has widened, I have found Christ in strange, unlooked-for places, far beyond the boundary of sect or dogma, of church or chapel, far beyond the formal definition of man's devising, or of man's exclusive pride. . . . In South Africa, I found Christ's presence . . . far more intimately . . . in the Indian and Kaffir locations placed outside the cities of the Rand, than in those cities themselves built up of gold with all its fatal curse upon it." Quoted in Daniel O'Connor, *Gospel, Raj and Swaraj: The Missionary Years of C. F. Andrews, 1904-14* (Frankfurt am Main: Peter Lang, 1990), p. 288.

It must be emphasized that Andrews did not assume a simple subject-object relationship to the "other sheep" for whom he searched in the name of Jesus. In keeping with his appreciation for the Logos-theology of the Fourth Gospel, he was quite prepared to discover in the course of his pastoral work that Jesus had preceded him as the true light and life of humankind:

> Not seldom have I seen, almost objectively, Christ looking at me through the eyes of someone who had come to me eager to find God. As we talked together our hearts would burn within us and Christ would be there invisibly in our midst.[57]

Further, one should not suppose that Andrews was proposing a view of Christianity as one among many equally true religious paths, in the manner of a late-twentieth-century pluralist, or that he intended to assign to Hinduism a preliminary, but ultimately discardable, role of preparation for the gospel, as the fulfillment theorists of his own day advocated. Instead, Andrews was looking for subtle signs of Christ's presence in unexpected places while seeking after creative ways to make the gospel known, even as he interacted on a daily basis with every class of person to be found in India. He was zealous most of all to see the rise of novel and distinctively Indian forms of Christianity. After just a few years on the subcontinent, he had come to the conclusion that the usual appurtenances of Christianity to which Europeans had grown accustomed were entirely unsuited to India. Johannine theology had provided Andrews a license and the image of the shepherd an effective means for him to explore new ways of extending pastoral care to "that world outside" of settled Christendom.[58]

It remains, finally, to suggest an appropriate way to represent missionary shepherding in graphic form. To be consistent with the interpretation developed above, this image of mission requires the artist to respect the dynamic aspect of tending sheep, which is felt most acutely in the expectation that good shepherding involves gathering sheep. At the same time, we have to be mindful of our historical situation. Depictions of Jesus the Good Shepherd, carrying a lost sheep on his shoulders (cf. fig. 21, above), may not convey the same impression today as they did in the con-

57. Andrews, *Good Shepherd*, p. 197.
58. Andrews, *Good Shepherd*, p. 196.

Fig. 25. *The Lost Sheep*, by Fan Pu.
Traditional Chinese papercut (late twentieth century)

text of early Christianity, before the post-Constantinian church began to acquire substantial influence and power in the civil realm. Some might even find the idea of a knowing shepherd transporting a dumb animal to a location of the rescuer's choice a repulsive notion, the very antithesis of truly Christian mission or, possibly, a back door through which the inveterate character of the Shepherd-Ruler could make another appearance.

Fan Pu's papercut, *The Lost Sheep* (fig. 25), seems to offer a healthy balancing of these concerns.[59] In the shepherd's outstretched arm, one can

59. Fan Pu is former director of the Amity Christian Art Center in Nanjing, People's Republic of China. Since 1980, she has been at the forefront of a growing number of Christian artists in China who are using this traditional form of folk art as a means to illustrate a broad variety of biblical stories and Christian religious themes. In a recent article on her art and the philosophy behind it, Fan Pu has explained that she sees herself engaging in basic issues of contextualization as she seeks to spread the Christian message by means of this pre-Christian

perceive a determination to extend the reach of Christian pastoral compassion. The staff is present, but it is not imposed as a symbol of authority or discipline. The shepherd's simple clothing bespeaks a humble task, far removed from the exercise of power. The background of the scene communicates a strong impression of distant isolation. This sheep is lost, without sufficient resources of its own to cope in an unforgiving environment, where brambles threaten to ensnare and immobilize disoriented wayfarers. The searcher beckons, but the picture leaves room for the sheep to react to the shepherd's gesture in the symbolic gap that separates the two figures. A positive response from the sheep depends in part on whether or not Jesus' voice has been heard in the human shepherd's call.

Missionary shepherding is just like this — an intention to demonstrate care for those living beyond the range of traditional ministries. No stray sheep need stay lost, if enough missionary shepherds are willing to expand and develop their concept of pastoral service. In so doing, contemporary disciples offer their reply to the still-active missionary command of Jesus to feed and tend his scattered flock.

art form. See "New Wine in Old Bottles: Filling Traditional Papercuts with Christian Spirit," which may be found on the website of the Amity News Service (China Christian Council) at http://www.amitynewsservice.org/page.php?page=712&p.

chapter 6

Building and Planting

Paul the Apostle

The figure of Paul looms large within the history of Christian mission. Luke's account in the Acts of the Apostles establishes beyond a doubt that Paul was a significant shaper of the early church's destiny, apparently surpassing in influence all of Jesus' original disciples except possibly Peter. Paul admits that he sought at the beginning of his missionary career to win the approval of Peter and the other "pillar apostles" for his formulation of their shared message (Gal. 2:9). Yet, in the end, it was he and not they who provided the largest direct contribution to the canonical corpus of the New Testament. Even more decisively, it was Paul's version of the gospel that eventually came to dominate the church's subsequent understanding of its identity and mission, rather than any Jewish Christian theological framework. With the passage of time, Paul's capacity to stimulate thinking, debate, and missionary action has been proven more than once. It is not unreasonable now to seek further inspiration from Paul with respect to our growing collection of mission images.

A great part of Paul's genius lay in his ability to use language. Whatever defects he may have had as a speaker, his ability to communicate powerfully in writing has rarely been questioned, even by his critics. The epistles of Paul are infused throughout with vivid expressions, sharp turns of phrase, aptly chosen quotations, and a liberal dose of metaphor. The purpose of this chapter is to sift through the rich store of Paul's linguistic treasure house in order to identify yet one more distinctive way the earliest followers of Jesus conceptualized their mission. Of particular interest to our investigation are those places in Paul's correspondence where he self-consciously reflects on his own activities. These passages are like little windows that allow us to observe unseen a leading first-century missioner as he struggles to explain to a shifting set of distant interlocutors the meaning of what he was attempting to accomplish.

In this respect, at least, Paul has no equivalent in the entire New Testament. His surviving correspondence is intimate to a degree not shared by any other writer. The modern reader of Paul's epistles also benefits not a little from the fact that the apostle faced substantial opposition to his leadership within the Christian community at nearly every turn. These circumstances forced him to clarify his intentions and to justify his approach to ministry and mission in the name of Christ. As a result, Paul was obliged not only to work out a theologically coherent point of view that addressed crucial issues of faith and practice, but also to consider carefully the form of his apostolate and how he wanted it to be perceived.

Before a proper examination of Paul's efforts to interpret his missionary enterprise can be attempted, it is necessary to begin by describing briefly the work he was actually doing. Over the course of his long service on behalf of the gospel, how did he go about fulfilling his missionary vocation? What were the chief undertakings and primary roles that made up Paul's apostolate? It will also be helpful to discuss as a preliminary matter the most important claims and charges made by Paul's opponents concerning the quality and character of his leadership in mission. Only with these data in clear view will it be possible to assess and evaluate the various figures of speech Paul used to portray his life's overriding occupation. Eventually, I hope to show that the paired metaphors of building and planting epitomize the heart of Paul's missionary self-understanding, the more so when the whole of his work on behalf of the gospel is taken into consideration.

Over the course of an intense and active career, Paul responded to his missionary calling on several levels simultaneously. Although successfully integrated in his person, these different dimensions of Paul's apostleship can nevertheless be distinguished from each other.

Paul the Evangelist

First of all, Paul was an evangelist. At a minimum, this means that he proclaimed the gospel in public and private settings, while helping groups of believers in a variety of circumstances to organize themselves together into worshiping communities. Oddly enough, we can assign this role to Paul in spite of the fact that not one of the apostle's missionary sermons has been preserved in the New Testament. As noted earlier, the speeches attributed to Paul in Acts are for the most part composed by Luke, although fleeting reminiscences of actual Pauline kerygma may perhaps be detected here and there.[1] The extant letters of Paul contained in the New Testament are not missionary documents either, strictly speaking. These were addressed to already-formed local churches or fellow believers and so cannot be taken as illustrations of the way Paul presented the gospel to first-time hearers.

Despite the non-missionary character of his letters, they still provide solid evidence of Paul's having performed the most basic tasks of evangelism. For example, Paul makes frequent reference in them to his function as a preacher or proclaimer of the gospel. Indeed, in Paul's mind, this was the primary purpose for which he was made an apostle: "God, who had set me apart before I was born and called me through his grace, was pleased to reveal his Son to me, so that I might proclaim him among the Gentiles" (Gal. 1:15-16). The priority of preaching within Paul's apostolic brief is clearly asserted in his first letter to the Corinthians: "For Christ did not send me to baptize but to proclaim the gospel . . ." (1:17). As Paul explains elsewhere in the same letter, he considered himself under obligation to preach the Good News, since this was the foundation of the commission entrusted to him by Christ:

> If I proclaim the gospel, this gives me no ground for boasting, for an obligation is laid on me, and woe to me if I do not proclaim the gospel! (1 Cor. 9:16)[2]

1. See p. 55, esp. note 23, in this volume.

2. Paul's sense of apostolic responsibility is reinforced by his conviction that the preached word is an indispensable part of God's economy of salvation. His impassioned argument in Romans 10 makes this case in no uncertain terms: "But how are they to call on one in whom they have not believed? And how are they to believe in one of whom they have never heard? And how are they to hear without someone to proclaim him? . . . So faith comes from what is heard, and what is heard comes through the word of Christ" (10:14-15, 17).

Evidently, Paul did not *always* have in mind situations of initial evangelization when he employed the vocabulary of proclamation to describe his ministry. His eagerness to preach the gospel in Rome (Rom. 1:15), for instance, is declared just after an acknowledgment that their faith was already known throughout the world (Rom. 1:8). Even so, Paul insists that he prefers to work in those places where Christ has not yet been named (Rom. 15:20), which meant for him lands beyond the immediate reach of existing congregations (2 Cor. 10:16).

Besides preaching, Paul engaged in other activities that prepared the way for the formation of local churches. Notwithstanding his protest in 1 Corinthians 1:17, Paul does admit to having baptized several individuals and the "household of Stephanas" while in Corinth (1 Cor. 1:14-16). The letters also show Paul paying close attention to the ongoing leadership needs of the congregations he had founded. It would be a mistake to interpret Paul's continuing contact with the churches through letters or follow-up visits simply as an attempt to control their behavior.[3] Paul had a legitimate concern for the long-term viability of these nascent communities of faith, which could only be realized if a succeeding generation of leaders was allowed to emerge. Paul contributed directly to this development by enlisting co-workers at every stage of his missionary venture. Thus, in the letters one observes Paul consistently extending words of recognition and appreciation for the ministry of others (cf. Rom. 16).

W. Paul Bowers understands Paul's working definition of his own mission to include an aspect of nurture: "A distinguishing dimension of the Pauline mission is that it found its fullest sense of completion neither in an evangelistic preaching tour nor in individual conversions but only in the presence of firmly established churches."[4] Given the nature of the letters as pastoral documents, Bowers is certainly correct to urge this approach to Paul's practice of ministry. Still, we must continue to remind ourselves that Paul's ecclesiology did not develop separately from or outgrow his missiology. Paul not only hoped to leave a legacy of healthy

3. See Elizabeth A. Castelli, *Imitating Paul: A Discourse of Power* (Louisville: Westminster/John Knox, 1991), for a "Foucauldian reading" of Paul's actions and teaching that assumes on his part an overweening desire to dominate the churches, in order to stamp out difference and produce sameness in the interest of an enforced orthodoxy among Christians.

4. W. Paul Bowers, "Mission," *DPL*:610. A fuller statement of this argument is presented in Bowers, "Fulfilling the Gospel: The Scope of Pauline Mission," *JETS* 30 (1987): 185-98.

congregations behind him but also yearned to see established communities of faith actively participate with him in a mission of further outreach. This was the substance of his proposal to the church at Rome, when he suggested a flying visit to them on his way to Spain (Rom. 15:28-29). A similar aspiration seems to lie behind a difficult passage in 2 Corinthians, where Paul explicitly connects the growth of faith in Corinth to his future plans for mission: "our hope is that, as your faith increases, our sphere of action among you may be greatly enlarged, so that we may proclaim the good news in lands beyond you, without boasting of work already done in someone else's sphere of action" (2 Cor. 10:15-16). Whatever else may have been at issue here (including the interference of others in Paul's Corinthian parish and the proper grounds of boasting), one thing seems to be clear: as with the congregation at Rome, Paul looked forward to the day when the Corinthians would become mature enough in faith to collaborate with him in the pioneer work he continued to regard as his first priority.

Paul the Mission Strategist

At some point, Paul's interest in practical cooperation shades into a deliberate intention to plan carefully for mission. Thus, Paul the evangelist takes on the additional role of mission strategist. Hints that Paul may have learned early on to think in strategic terms about mission surface in the aftermath of the Jerusalem conference, reported at length by Luke in Acts 15. Paul's briefer account in Galatians, probably written quite soon after the gathering, portrays the decision to split responsibility for separate missions to Jews and Gentiles as a finely balanced and theologically appropriate resolution of conflicting priorities. As he put it, "I had been entrusted with the gospel for the uncircumcised, just as Peter had been entrusted with the gospel for the circumcised" (Gal. 2:7). The net effect of the Jerusalem meeting was that two equal parts of a single mission in service to the same gospel were enabled to operate interdependently. The right hand of fellowship extended by Peter, James, and John to Barnabas and Paul symbolized the unity of their parallel efforts, as well as the tacit agreement of the Jerusalem church to Paul's gospel of freedom for the Gentiles. For his part, Paul made the collection of support for "the poor" in Jerusalem (Gal. 2:10) an essential element of his larger agenda for mission. Considered from the perspective of strategic planning, the Jerusalem agreement represented a well-conceived framework for future outreach, based as it was on an efficient division of labor that conceivably could accommodate serious differences in theological outlook while preserving unity.[5]

Paul's missionary tactics likewise imply an awareness of the telltale link that connects methodology to purpose. The most obvious of his choices, often noted, was the crucial decision to advance the evangelization of whole regions within the Roman Empire by planting dynamic churches in key cities.[6] The itineraries in Acts clearly show that although Paul covered huge distances on his journeys, he spent the bulk of his time in just a few places. This approach capitalized on the social, political, and economic importance of provincial centers like Ephesus and Corinth, busy hubs of trade and travel to which numerous inhabitants from the countryside surrounding them were inevitably drawn for one reason or another.[7]

Did the first generation of urban Christians actually participate in the evangelization of towns and villages located near them in the Greco-Roman hinterlands? Paul gives us reason to think so. In his first letter to the Thessalonians, he gives thanks especially for their vibrant faith, which he sees radiating outward from the metropolis with wonderful effect:

> For the word of the Lord has sounded forth from you not only in Macedonia and Achaia, but in every place your faith in God has become known, so that we have no need to speak about it. For the people of

---

5. Subsequent events in Antioch (cf. Gal. 2:11-21) soon brought to light a serious shortcoming in this strategy. Which set of rules would be followed in the case of mixed congregations?

6. David J. Bosch summarizes a large mass of the relevant New Testament literature in *Transforming Mission: Paradigm Shifts in Theology of Mission* (Maryknoll, N.Y.: Orbis, 1991), pp. 129-31. Much earlier, in a provocative book entitled *Missionary Methods: St. Paul's or Ours?* (Grand Rapids: Eerdmans, 1962 [1927]), Roland Allen had praised this aspect of Paul's missionary strategy, likening the congregations he had established in places like Thessalonica, Corinth, Philippi, and Ephesus to "mints from which the new coin of the Gospel was spread in every direction" (p. 17). Most recently, Eckhard Schnabel has offered a remarkably thorough review of the strategic and tactical aspects of Paul's approach to mission. See his *Early Christian Mission* (Downers Grove, Ill.: InterVarsity, 2004), pp. 1292-1475 ("Missionary Tactics and Communication").

7. On the importance of these cities for purposes of commerce and communication across the Roman Empire, see M. P. Charlesworth, *Trade-Routes and Commerce of the Roman Empire*, second ed. (Cambridge: University Press, 1926), pp. 76-96, 114-29.

those regions report about us what kind of welcome we had among you, and how you turned to God from idols, to serve a living and true God. (1:8-9)[8]

This is a remarkable piece of testimony. Paul is commending the Thessalonians for the fact that he had heard reports of their faith from un-named third parties living in Macedonia and Greece. He clearly takes de-light in the news that the message he preached to them was continuing to echo far and wide by means of *their* witness. Paul could consider the Thessalonians to be a community divinely chosen (1:4) in two respects: first to receive the gospel and then to share it.

The letter of Colossians offers a more detailed look at the underlying process by which new congregations came into being outside the major cities where Paul had initially concentrated his attention. The principal figure in this story is Epaphras, a "beloved fellow servant" of Paul's who is warmly praised in Colossians as a "faithful minister of Christ" (1:7). From Colossians 4:12, we learn that Epaphras was a native of Colossae ("Epaphras, who is one of you . . ."). Epaphras is further identified as the one from whom the Colossians first heard the gospel (1:5-7), and, in a sub-sequent passage, he is credited for his "hard work" on behalf of the gospel in Laodicea, Hierapolis, and Colossae itself (4:12-13). Most interpreters of the letter understand this language to mean that Epaphras was the one who founded the first congregations in this cluster of small towns located up the Lycus valley not far from Ephesus. In so doing, he may have been a missionary agent acting under the direct supervision of Paul, or, perhaps,

---

8. The suggestion — surely hyperbole — that the preaching of the Thessalonians had rendered further proclamation by Paul unnecessary in two entire provinces is perhaps the highest compliment the apostle could possibly have paid them. On the implications of the Thessalonian witness, see James P. Ware, "The Thessalonians As a Missionary Congregation: 1 Thessalonians 1,5-8," *ZNW* 83 (1992): 126-31. I. Howard Marshall discusses the role of con-gregations in Paul's mission more broadly in "Who Were the Evangelists?" in *The Mission of the Early Church to Jews and Gentiles,* ed. Jostein Ådna and Hans Kvalbein, WUNT 127 (Tübingen: Mohr Siebeck, 2000), pp. 251-63, as does Eckhard Schnabel, *Early Christian Mis-sion,* pp. 1451-1559. Ware argues further in "'Holding Forth the Word of Life': Paul and the Mission of the Church in the Letter to the Philippians in the Context of Second Temple Ju-daism" (Ph.D. diss., Yale University, 1996) that Paul expected the congregations he had founded (at Philippi and elsewhere) to be active agents of mission to the Gentiles, in keeping with their fundamental identity as new "mediatorial communities" established for the salva-tion of the nations.

he was working more independently.[9] In either case, it seems virtually certain that Epaphras came under Paul's influence at Ephesus, and it was probably in Ephesus that the two of them were imprisoned together for a time (cf. Philem. 23).[10] The reason why Epaphras came to Ephesus in the first place is unknown. Business interests may have pulled him to the city, but this cannot be established on the basis of the few prosopographical details offered in the epistles. What Colossians does show is that Ephesus had begun already in the time of Paul to function as a "Zentrumsmission" for the province of Asia.[11]

Paul's choice of a trade and his decision to keep practicing it toward the end of his career alert us to a final set of strategic considerations that should be mentioned here. We know from the letters that he engaged in manual labor of some kind, which Luke identifies as tent-making (Acts 18:3; cf. 1 Cor. 4:12; 1 Thess. 2:9; 2 Thess. 3:7-8). At first, Paul may have worked out of necessity during the long, lean years spent in Arabia, Damascus, and the "regions of Syria and Cilicia" (Gal. 1:17, 21). As time wore on, he would discover that his highly portable skill was ideally suited to the mobile lifestyle of an itinerant evangelist, whose long-range travels propelled him back and forth across Asia Minor. An experienced tent-maker could expect to find employment throughout the Greco-Roman world (as Paul did with Prisca and Aquila in Corinth). Moreover, the few tools needed for this simple occupation were easily carried from place to place. It has been suggested that the tent-maker's workshop would have provided Paul with an expedient venue for informal missionary preaching, since it afforded him an opportunity to present the claims of the gospel to unbe-

9. Taken together, the positive descriptors applied to Epaphras in Colossians ("our beloved fellow servant," "faithful minister of Christ," and "servant of Christ Jesus") might lead one to conclude that his relationship to Paul was more collegial than subordinate. On the other hand, Epaphras seems in some way to be reporting to Paul (cf. Col. 1:8). A complicating factor is introduced at Colossians 1:7, where some manuscripts indicate plainly that Epaphras was Paul's agent ("a faithful minister of Christ *on our behalf*"), but others do not (". . . on *your* behalf").

10. See Jerome Murphy-O'Connor, *Paul: A Critical Life* (Oxford: Clarendon, 1996), pp. 175-79, for a review of the evidence regarding the provenance of the prison epistles (Ephesians, Philippians, Colossians, and Philemon). If Murphy-O'Connor's construal of the data is correct, then Epaphras and Paul were imprisoned together in Ephesus.

11. Cf. Wolf-Henning Ollrog, *Paulus und seine Mitarbeiter: Untersuchungen zu Theorie und Praxis der paulinischen Mission* (Neukirchen-Vluyn: Neukirchener Verlag, 1979), pp. 125-29.

lieving co-workers and a steady stream of customers in a relaxed context of everyday conversation.[12] If so, Paul's workplace might well have functioned as a third major social setting for his evangelistic activities, as important to the fulfillment of his vocation as the synagogue encounters and house meetings more specifically described in Acts and the epistles.

Curiously, Paul never discusses his trade with respect to its practical advantages. His interest focuses rather on the theological significance of his manual labor.[13] From the letters, we know that Paul's decision to keep working perplexed some of his correspondents and perhaps angered or embarrassed others. Part of the problem lay in the fact that tent-makers and other artisans — as a class of workers — were not highly esteemed in first-century Greco-Roman society. Paul seems to acknowledge this prejudice, perhaps exploited by opponents in Corinth, when he asks rhetorically about his policy of self-support, "Did I commit a sin by humbling myself so that you might be exalted, because I proclaimed God's good news to you free of charge?" (2 Cor. 11:7).[14] Complicating the issue, Paul and his congregations seem to agree that he was entitled *not* to work. Like a house philosopher or resident intellectual, Paul had a "right" to claim support from the congregations he had founded.[15] On top of this, in Corinth, if not also elsewhere, it appears that benefactors stood by ready to subsidize a full-time ministry, but Paul refused their help, risking insult, even as he accepted gifts from other sources (Phil. 4:14-19; 2 Cor. 11:8).[16]

12. Ronald F. Hock, "The Workshop As a Social Setting for Paul's Missionary Preaching," *CBQ* 41 (1979): 438-50. See also Hock, *The Social Context of Paul's Ministry: Tentmaking and Apostleship* (Philadelphia: Fortress, 1980); Abraham J. Malherbe, *Paul and the Thessalonians: The Philosophic Tradition of Pastoral Care* (Philadelphia: Fortress, 1987), esp. pp. 5-33; and Murphy-O'Connor, *Paul*, pp. 85-89.

13. I am leaving to the side Paul's minor argument about the moral virtue of working with one's hands (cf. 1 Thess. 4:11-12; 5:14), since the problem of "idlers" he addresses in this way does not seem to be widespread.

14. The low status of Paul's trade is discussed in Ronald Hock, "Paul's Tentmaking and the Problem of His Social Class," *JBL* 97 (1978): 555-64. Among those who have also worked insightfully on this problem, two scholars in particular have helped me to understand better the intricacies of the Corinthian social setting: Gerd Theissen, *The Social Setting of Pauline Christianity: Essays on Corinth*, ed. and trans. John H. Schütz (Philadelphia: Fortress, 1982), and Dale B. Martin, *The Corinthian Body* (New Haven: Yale University Press, 1995).

15. Paul mentions his "right" to be supported in 2 Thessalonians 3:9. A more developed argument of the same point is presented in 1 Corinthians 9:3-18.

16. For a discussion of the apparent inconsistency of Paul's approach to apostolic

From an analysis of Paul's social setting, we thus learn that powerful disincentives pushed hard against Paul's intention to continue plying his trade. One suspects that neither whim nor conceit could have withstood these pressures. Paul justifies his resolve by rooting the basis of his practice in the nature of the gospel itself. At the center of Paul's argument is an assertion that by earning his own livelihood (or, at least, a good portion of it), he has acted to relieve the churches from any burden his support might have caused them.[17] In the case of the Corinthian congregation in particular, Paul's assertion has to mean more than a concern for their financial well-being, since it appears that potential patrons were not wanting in this situation.

The analysis of Dale Martin cuts to what I think is the heart of Paul's rhetorical strategy: "Paul takes on manual labor *because* of (not in spite of) his view that it is demeaning."[18] The work Paul does with his hands is an expression of "self-lowering," as Martin puts it, which makes sense precisely because it offers a way for the apostle to illustrate something important about the gospel. To upper-class Corinthians, Paul was teaching them that the Christian life may require personal sacrifice, a decidedly counter-intuitive proposal for those used to exercising their social power.[19] Concurrently, Paul's embrace of "slavish" labor kept him in daily contact with the lower classes, which served to demonstrate that the gospel had a claim on them, too.[20] For the benefit of all, Paul's missionary praxis recalled the example of Jesus, who "emptied himself, taking the

maintenance, see Margaret E. Thrall, *A Critical and Exegetical Commentary on the Second Epistle to the Corinthians,* vol. 2 (Edinburgh: T&T Clark, 2000), pp. 699-708.

17. The key passages are 1 Thessalonians 2:9 ("You remember our labor and toil, brothers and sisters; we worked night and day, so that we might not burden any of you while we proclaimed to you the gospel of God") and 2 Thessalonians 3:8 ("We did not eat anyone's bread without paying for it; but with toil and labor we worked night and day, so that we might not burden any of you"). Cf. 2 Corinthians 11:9 and 12:14-16.

18. Dale B. Martin, *Slavery As Salvation: The Metaphor of Slavery in Pauline Christianity* (New Haven: Yale University Press, 1990), p. 124 (emphasis in the original).

19. This is why Paul includes the circumstances of his "toil" and "labor" among the hardships he has had to endure on behalf of the Corinthians for the sake of the gospel (cf. 1 Cor. 4:12; 2 Cor. 6:5; 11:23, 27).

20. Thus, Paul's claim that he made himself weak to win "the weak" (1 Cor. 9:22) meant that he was deliberately lowering himself in the eyes of society, in order to present the gospel to those nearer to the bottom of the social ladder. Again, see Martin, *Slavery As Salvation,* pp. 118-24.

form of a slave" (Phil. 2:7). In this respect, Paul's strategy for mission was bold, not least because it dared to show how a powerful message of salvation could overturn even the most entrenched expectations of social convention.

Paul the Missionary Theologian

Theological vision is the third dimension of Paul's apostolic vocation, the component that guided his choice of strategies and provided daily missionary practice with an ultimate frame of reference. Paul answered this aspect of his call by developing into a missionary theologian. As such, he modeled a habit of critical reflection on evangelistic technique that continues to be worthy of imitation. Paul's status as a theologian hardly needs to be established here. He was, as an authoritative interpreter of his thought has written recently, "the first and greatest Christian theologian."[21] Still, a few words about this element of Paul's agenda might be appropriate, especially if they help us to grasp the larger intellectual context in which Paul was operating.

The cataclysm of Paul's conversion immediately presented him with two new facts that demanded theological explanation. The first of these was the resurrection of Jesus, an event that became real for Paul when he encountered the living Christ in a vision (1 Cor. 9:1; 15:8). The second was Paul's inner conviction that God had called him to be an apostle to the Gentiles (Gal. 1:15-16). A lifetime of faithful questioning followed this defining moment, as Paul sought to reconcile an inherited tradition of religious insight with his own extraordinary experience. Eventually, he also had to come to terms with the claims made by the community of faith he had so zealously persecuted as Saul the Pharisee, since these, too, professed loyalty to the Risen One whom Paul had seen.

Paul tells us very little about the gestational process by which his mature theology came into being. While insisting that the first apostles, still resident in Jerusalem, did *not* instruct him directly, Paul leaves open the possibility of catechesis among the Christians in Damascus.[22] It could be

---

21. James D. G. Dunn, *The Theology of Paul the Apostle* (Grand Rapids: Eerdmans, 1998), p. 2.

22. "I did not confer with any human being, nor did I go up to Jerusalem to those

that Barnabas, Paul's senior partner in the first organized efforts to share the gospel with Gentiles, was another significant factor in his development as a missionary theologian.[23] Whatever outside forces may have contributed to the ripening of his theological point of view, the voice one hears already in the earliest extant letter attributable to Paul (1 Thessalonians, usually dated c. 50 CE) is both distinctive and well-seasoned. Paul has a firm grasp on the message he wants to share with those ready to receive it, but especially the Gentiles. The dazzling figure, whose sudden appearance more than a dozen years earlier had blinded the willful Pharisee on the road to Damascus, had by this time acquired a more complete identity. Paul now knew and proclaimed him as "the Lord Jesus Christ" (1 Thess. 1:1), God's Son (1:10), whose death "for us" (5:10) and subsequent resurrection was the sure basis of Christian hope.

The rest of Paul's epistolary corpus bears witness to a theology that is consistent with itself but not so monochromatic that it has to be applied like whitewash over every vertical surface Paul happens to encounter in the course of his subsequent work and travel. Paul's theology has texture — and an apostolic edge — precisely because its author continued to conceive of himself as a preacher of the gospel still under obligation to extend

---

who were already apostles before me, but I went away at once into Arabia, and afterwards I returned to Damascus" (Gal. 1:16-17). In his own way, Luke seems to confirm this reading of Paul's sketchy account. As the story of his conversion is told the first two times in Acts, Paul is confounded rather than enlightened by what happens to him on the road to Damascus. Blind and helpless, he has to be led "by the hand" into the city (Acts 9:8). Ananias, a member of the congregation at Damascus, is the means by which Paul learns that it was "the Lord Jesus" who appeared to him (9:17). Subsequently, Ananias is identified as the one who first connected what had happened to Paul with "the God of our ancestors" (22:14). It is possible that Luke meant to represent the whole of the Damascus community through the figure of Ananias. Galatians 1:18 suggests that Paul stayed in Damascus for a period of three years.

23. The seniority of Barnabas must be inferred from details contained in the Acts narrative, like the fact that the name of Barnabas comes first when linked to that of Paul still called Saul (Acts 13:1-12). Luke's treatment of the early Gentile mission suggests further that Barnabas may have served as Paul's mentor at the beginning of their collaboration together, first by acting to introduce Paul to the apostles in Jerusalem (Acts 9:26-27) and then by taking the initiative to include him in the work already underway at Antioch (Acts 11:22-26). What Paul says about Barnabas in the epistles does not rule out this interpretation of their early relationship. On the other hand, later disagreements with Barnabas (cf. Gal. 2:11-13; Acts 15:36-41) may have contributed to a reluctance on Paul's part to draw attention to any possible debt owed to his first colleague in mission.

the reach of God's word. Even Romans, supposedly the most didactic and timelessly systematic of Paul's letters, is written with a view to the *next* phase of Paul's missionary activity.[24] Simply put, Paul never stops being a missionary!

Another way to appreciate the missionary character of Paul's theology is by observing the manner in which he responded to the various pastoral crises brought to his attention. Local disputes over food in Corinth, for example, become occasions to discuss freedom in Christ. When outsiders challenge Paul's authority in Galatia, he turns a potential power struggle into a debate over the Law. Paul never lets go of the big issues that ought to lead the way when the church perceives itself to be in a missionary situation. His concentration is steadily maintained on matters of gospel and culture, Christ and the religious aspirations of humankind, the power of sin and God's provision for salvation. Thus, Paul is not interested in congregational micro-management for its own sake. To the end, he is working to create and strengthen communities of believers, who will themselves become participants with him in God's mission. The analysis of Nils Dahl is right on target: "[Paul] argues theologically in order to make the missionary congregations understand their own place within the divine economy, what God has granted and promised to them and therefore also what he can expect of them."[25]

24. J. Christiaan Beker highlights the "contingency" of Romans in *Paul the Apostle: The Triumph of God in Life and Thought* (Philadelphia: Fortress, 1980), pp. 59-108.

25. Nils A. Dahl, "The Missionary Theology in the Epistle to the Romans," in *Studies in Paul: Theology for the Early Christian Mission,* assisted by Paul Donahue (Minneapolis: Augsburg, 1977), p. 71. More recently, Michael D. Barram has drawn attention to Paul's "broadly-conceived" missionary purpose as the basis of his moral instruction to the churches. In this reading of Paul, the apostle's interest in proper conduct is an integral aspect of his total mission, which throughout remained focused on the salvation of Jews and Gentiles. Thus, Paul concludes his discourse regarding food sacrificed to idols with a statement that expresses his concern for the salvation of those outside the church: "So, whether you eat or drink, or whatever you do, do everything for the glory of God. Give no offense to Jews or to Greeks or to the church of God, just as I try to please everyone in everything I do, not seeking my own advantage, but that of many, so that they may be saved. Be imitators of me, as I am of Christ" (1 Cor. 10:31–11:1). Cf. Barram, "'In Order That They May Be Saved': Mission and Moral Reflection in Paul" (Ph.D. diss., Union Theological Seminary and Presbyterian School of Christian Education, 2001).

Interpreting Paul's Mission

We move now from the task of describing Paul's work to the question of its portrayal. This is not a concern foreign to the texts under examination in this chapter. Paul's letters show the apostle to be fully engaged with the problem of how to represent his missionary activity. At issue was Paul's reputation, plus the future direction of the congregations he had helped to bring into being. Paul might have been content to let his work speak for itself, trusting in the Spirit's power to guide Christian reflection, had he not been made aware of other actors, already quite busy, who sought to shape the perceptions of his correspondents in ways he thought harmful. From Paul's perspective, false characterizations of his ministry were circulating in the churches. Since he believed that these misrepresentations threatened to undermine faith in the gospel itself, Paul felt compelled to respond with alternative readings of his approach to mission.

The matter of Paul's opponents is complex and has been discussed many times at great length elsewhere.[26] Here, our focus necessarily remains on just one narrow aspect of this topic: the impressions of Paul the missionary created by those who vied with him for leadership over the congregations he had founded. When Paul attempts to portray his ministry, these impressions form a crucial part of the total context in which he must communicate. To be successful in these circumstances, Paul is obliged not only to express his intentions in a positive way but also to blunt the charges of his critics.

One can assume that Paul had some knowledge of what others were saying about him, because supporters in the various churches were eager to keep him informed (cf. "Chloe's people" in 1 Cor. 1:11).[27] In addition,

26. A number of full-scale treatments of the problem have been rendered over the past 170 years, beginning with the seminal study of Ferdinand Christian Baur, "Die Christuspartei in der korinthischen Gemeinde . . . ," first published in 1831. Baur's original essay has been republished in *Ausgewählte Werke in Einzelausgaben*, ed. Klaus Scholder (Stuttgart: Frommenn, 1963), vol. 1, pp. 1-146. See also Baur, *Paul, the Apostle of Jesus Christ, His Life and Work, His Epistles and His Doctrine: A Contribution to the Critical History of Primitive Christianity*, ed. and trans. Eduard Zeller and Allan Menzies, second ed., 2 vols. (London: Williams and Norgate, 1875-1876).

27. One cannot assume that Paul's knowledge was always accurate. Either Paul or his informants may have misunderstood what they had heard. The possibility of deliberate distortion or exaggeration is also present. After all, when Paul reports the comments and criti-

when Paul dispatched subordinates like Timothy and Titus with messages and instructions to relay to others, he could count on them to return with eyewitness reports concerning the latest situation in the churches they had visited. Modern readers are at a disadvantage in this respect, since the views of Paul's opponents must be reconstructed on the basis of what can be gleaned second-hand from Paul's correspondence. A cautious approach will be followed here, with a minimum of speculation offered on the exact identity or specific beliefs of Paul's competitors.[28]

Throughout his career, Paul had to confront misgivings about his right to be considered an apostle in the fullest possible sense. The issue arose in two different ways, broadly speaking. First, in order to claim the apostolic status commonly accorded to Peter and others who led the community in Jerusalem, Paul needed to show that he was their equal. This was a difficult test to meet, because there were obvious and undeniable differences between them. Unlike the original group of apostles, Paul had not been a follower of the earthly Jesus, nor was he among those known to have been commissioned to announce the Good News in the immediate aftermath of the crucifixion and resurrection. He had not participated in the miracle of Pentecost, when the Holy Spirit had made its dramatic first appearance. By his own admission, it was Paul who sought the recognition of the Jerusalem apostles for his ministry and not vice versa, thus implying that they were the higher authority (Gal. 1:18-19; 2:9). Then, when he began to preach, Paul's gospel to the uncircumcised appeared to be at variance with what Peter, James, and John were proclaiming in Jerusalem. Had the former persecutor of the church misunderstood the substance of the message originally entrusted to the Twelve? How could he now claim equivalence with those through whom the community had surely seen the Spirit in action?

Paul's answer to this challenge was grounded in the experience of his call. He could presume to claim parity with the other apostles only because Jesus had also appeared to him (1 Cor. 15:5-9). If Paul had what seemed to

cisms of his opponents, he does so while trying to persuade his correspondents to dissociate themselves from such views.

28. Pauline scholars continue to debate these questions vigorously, without appearing to reach a consensus. For a forceful restatement of Baur's original thesis, see Michael D. Goulder, *Paul and the Competing Mission in Corinth* (Peabody: Hendrickson, 2001). On the variety of methods that have been followed by scholars seeking to identify Paul's antagonists, see Jerry L. Sumney, *Identifying Paul's Opponents: The Question of Method in 2 Corinthians* (Sheffield: JSOT, 1990).

some to be another gospel to preach, the problem was not of Paul's own making, nor was it his alone to resolve. The risen Christ had called him to preach the gospel to the Gentiles, without demanding that the Gentiles first become Jews. In this way, according to Paul, Christ himself had created a new milestone in the history of salvation and a novel twist on the theme of missionary vocation. Paul understood the gospel he preached to be an invitation to all believers — whether Jewish or Gentile in background — to integrate this new fact into their understanding of God's purposes.

A second set of concerns revolved around Paul's conduct as an apostle. Especially in the Corinthian context, ambitious rivals were eager to sow seeds of doubt, from which suspicions could grow that Paul was some kind of fraud since he did not exhibit all of the personal qualities one should expect to see in a true apostle.[29] A recurrent complaint was that Paul failed to impress as a speaker. This was something on which Paul and his critics seemed to agree. Paul relates the basic charge against him by means of a direct quote, possibly obtained by one of his informants: "For they say, 'His letters are weighty and strong, but his bodily presence is weak, and his speech contemptible'" (2 Cor. 10:10). A few verses later Paul reluctantly concedes the truth of the accusation, while dismissing its significance: "I may be untrained in speech, but not in knowledge; certainly in every way and in all things we have made this evident to you" (2 Cor. 11:6).

As for the problem of his "weak" physical appearance, the apostle had no doubt heard this reproach more than once. In his letter to the Galatians, he had had to acknowledge the shame of an undisclosed "physical infirmity" that had been an embarrassment to all of them (Gal. 4:13-14). This may or may not have been the same condition Paul later referred to as his "thorn in the flesh" (2 Cor. 12:7). Paul's various audiences were predisposed to assume that physical strength and vigor enhanced the power of one's rhetoric.[30] A public speaker could earn respect with convincing ges-

---

29. We cannot assume, however, that a prevailing set of expectations had already coalesced in the early church around the idea of the Christian apostolate. Paul and his opponents were not only comparing their individual performances but were also arguing over the standards by which they ought to be judged. On this point, see Dieter Georgi, *The Opponents of Paul in Second Corinthians* (Philadelphia: Fortress, 1986), pp. 32-39.

30. The link between a strong physical appearance and success in Greco-Roman oratory has been noted by a number of scholars recently. See, for example, Stephen M. Pogoloff, *Logos and Sophia: The Rhetorical Situation of 1 Corinthians*, SBLDS 134 (Atlanta: Scholars, 1992), pp. 147-49.

tures, a well-modulated voice, and an authoritative bearing, all of which required firm control over one's body. Obvious signs of anxiety, uncertainty, or physical disability, on the other hand, could trigger ridicule or disdain from one's audience. Paul's admittedly feeble oratory, especially when delivered "in weakness and in fear and in much trembling" (1 Cor. 2:3), was not likely to inspire confidence.

Other behaviors further reduced Paul's stature in the eyes of his critics. He would not accept payment for his gospel work among the Corinthians, preferring instead to degrade himself by performing manual labor, as noted above. Paul showed sensitivity to the impression created by this decision. Was it a sin, he asks the Corinthians (2 Cor. 11:7), to abase himself in this way? Yet, despite the risk of insult, he could not bring himself to accept financial support from the church in Corinth, since the practice of patronage in their context implied the right to bestow honor and recognition by those able to provide maintenance. For much the same reason, Paul declined to legitimate his ministry by producing letters of recommendation (2 Cor. 3:1-3). If the authority of his apostleship truly rested on the call of Christ, as he claimed, such letters would be superfluous.

So Paul refused to get into a bidding war with his antagonists in Corinth. But by rejecting their proposed terms of comparison, he also denied himself access to a fundamental New Testament image of mission, that of the proclaimer as orator. This is ironic, given the fact that the public rhetor was one of the leading roles assigned to Paul by Luke. As we saw in Chapter Two, Paul comes across in Acts as an accomplished speaker, quite able to hold his own in a variety of contexts. He could speak the truth to power (for example, to the Jerusalem council, the governor Felix, or King Agrippa), engage sophisticated audiences like the Athenian philosophers (Acts 17), or calmly face down a hostile mob (Acts 22). The Paul we meet in Acts is a bold and confident figure, eager (and apparently able) to make a powerful apology on behalf of the Christian faith, regardless of the circumstances. Luke shows no awareness of Paul's anguished struggle to express himself in person. That part of Paul's story can be glossed over, because his more talkative and verbally persuasive opponents simply do not appear in the narrative of Acts.[31]

---

31. Luke does make room in his story for one potential rival to Paul: the naturally gifted controversialist from Alexandria, Apollos (Acts 18:24-28). Apollos's forensic skills are clearly acknowledged in Luke's careful treatment, but his ignorance of the Holy Spirit seems to constitute an offsetting (albeit correctable) deficiency that diminishes his stature and im-

If not as a compelling debater, then how did Paul choose to represent his missionary activities and sense of vocation? In the letters, one finds Paul applying over a dozen different roles to himself, in order to explain the nature of his apostolate. These seem to fall into three different groups, the first of which coalesces around the concept of *subordination*. The key terms here are slave (δοῦλος), servant/minister (διάκονος), servant/helper (ὑπηρέτης), steward (οἰκονόμος), and ambassador (πρεσβεία). Each of these designations implies a position of inferiority and accountability to some other more powerful actor. When Paul uses the language of slavery or servanthood for himself, he usually does so as a way to indicate his complete subjection to Christ or unqualified dedication to God's cause.[32] The idea of stewardship likewise communicates the notion of putting oneself in the service of another, and it is appropriate to recall that it was not unusual for slaves to be appointed stewards in Greco-Roman society. A slave-steward could be given considerable authority within the household of the master, in which case the social status of the position increased. Yet, when Paul appropriates the image of stewardship for his ministry, he tends to emphasize the sense of responsibility that came with his commission, rather than his power to act as Christ's proxy:

> Think of us in this way, as servants [ὑπηρέτας] of Christ and stewards [οἰκονόμους] of God's mysteries. Moreover, it is required of stewards that they be found trustworthy. (1 Cor. 4:1-2; cf. 9:17)

---

portance. Ultimately, Luke blends the contributions of Apollos into a larger scheme of mission that remains firmly under the direction of Paul.

32. Thus, "Paul, a servant [or slave] of Jesus Christ, called to be an apostle . . ." (Rom. 1:1; cf. Phil. 1:1; Gal. 1:10). Or, "as servants of God we have commended ourselves in every way: through great endurance, in afflictions, hardships, calamities . . ." (2 Cor. 6:4; cf. 1 Cor. 3:5; 2 Cor. 11:23). Martin, *Slavery As Salvation,* understands Paul's claim to slave status to be an assertion of authority, because the slaves of high-status patrons could and did exercise considerable power in Greco-Roman society (on this, see esp. pp. 1-49). Martin's elegant and largely persuasive argument certainly helps to explain Paul's meaning in 1 Corinthians 9:19, where the apostle declares that he has made himself "a slave to all," in order to "win more" to the gospel. While agreeing with Martin that slavery to Christ connotes more than humiliation for Paul and that his determination to do manual work, a deliberate act of "self-lowering," was probably used in 1 Corinthians as an example to teach high-status Christians in the community to set aside their own interests for the sake of the weak, I am not convinced that Paul uses this metaphor generally to signal his right to lead and to exercise authority. The primary idea behind Paul's slavery to Christ, I believe, is rather his complete submission to and total identification with the one who called him into mission.

Empowered stewards resemble ambassadors, especially when the latter are understood to be authorized agents of a sovereign power. In neither case, however, is the idea of subordination lost when Paul applies these roles to himself. Thus, the instrumentality of the ambassador's position — not the extent of the ambassador's influence — is the aspect highlighted in the one passage where the concept appears in Paul's undisputed letters: "So we [Paul and Timothy] are ambassadors for Christ, since God is making his appeal through us; we entreat you on behalf of Christ, be reconciled to God" (2 Cor. 5:20).[33]

Paul also assigned to himself a set of *parental* roles. At times, for example, he presumed to speak to the congregations he had founded as their wise father: "As you know, we dealt with each one of you like a father with his children, urging and encouraging you and pleading that you lead a life worthy of God, who calls you into his own kingdom and glory" (1 Thess. 2:11-12; cf. 2 Cor. 6:13).[34] Paul does not overlook the harsher side of first-century fatherhood, including the threat of punishment for wayward children who refuse to heed sound advice. The father as disciplinarian is on view in 1 Corinthians 4:

> I am not writing this to make you ashamed, but to admonish you as my beloved children. . . . But some of you, thinking that I am not coming to you, have become arrogant. . . . What would you prefer? Am I to come to you with a stick, or with love in a spirit of gentleness? (1 Cor. 4:14, 18, 21)

Paul was not afraid to apply to himself maternal roles of nurture vis-à-vis these same congregations. Thus, he could invoke the image of the gentle nurse, who cared lovingly for the children placed in her care (1 Thess. 2:7). Or, he could liken his ministry to that of a nursing mother, who fed "infants in Christ" with milk, until they were ready for solid food (1 Cor. 3:1-2). Perhaps the most daring image Paul employs in conjunction

33. Cf. Ephesians 6:20, where Paul refers to himself as "an ambassador in chains."

34. Here, the fact that Paul had literally introduced these congregations to the gospel by his missionary activity is the basis of his conceptual language. In a very real sense, he had become their "father in Christ Jesus through the gospel," as he put it in 1 Corinthians 4:15 (RSV). A similar understanding seems to lie behind Paul's assertion to Philemon that he had become the father of Onesimus during the time they shared together in prison (Philem. 10).

with his apostolic office is that of a mother near the end of her term of pregnancy, straining to give birth: "My little children, for whom I am again in the pain of childbirth until Christ is formed in you" (Gal. 4:19).[35]

Parental images seem to stand in opposition to the idea of subordination. In Paul's day, mothers and (especially) fathers were authority figures, who normally spoke "down" to their dependent children, while slaves and other trusted retainers looked "up" to the powerful patrons from whom they received their orders. In the context of Paul's ministry, each approach had something important to say about his missionary identity, but neither is comprehensive in the sense that the totality of Paul's work could be summed up and expressed through it. What these two sets of images have in common is their focus on human relationships, with the extended family under God's care as their assumed setting.[36] What is missing is an explicit reference to the process by which these relationships were first established. The faith communities Paul attempted to advise and strengthen as Christ's slave and as a parent to believers were not spontaneously generated. They had to be created. This implies a need to consider the full range of apostolic activities conducted by Paul through which initial evangelization took place, as well as the developmental phase that followed. As Paul employs them, the images of *building and planting* hold promise as ways to represent this part of his work, without sacrificing the interpretive insights offered by these metaphors of submission and nurture. The roles associated with this pair of images constitute a third way Paul chose to portray his mission.

---

35. On this last image, see the analysis of Beverly R. Gaventa, "The Maternity of Paul: An Exegetical Study of Galatians 4:19," in *The Conversation Continues: Studies in Paul and John in Honor of J. Louis Martyn*, ed. Robert T. Fortna and Beverly R. Gaventa (Nashville: Abingdon, 1990), pp. 189-201. More recently, Gaventa has examined the image of nursing that mother Paul applies to himself in 1 Corinthians 3, asking what this might say about the character of his apostolic ministry. See "Mother's Milk and Ministry in 1 Corinthians 3," in *Theology and Ethics in Paul and His Interpreters: Essays in Honor of Victor Paul Furnish*, ed. Eugene H. Lovering Jr. and Jerry L. Sumney (Nashville: Abingdon, 1996), pp. 101-13. Gaventa discusses Paul's maternal imagery more generally in "Our Mother St. Paul: Toward the Recovery of a Neglected Theme," *Princeton Seminary Bulletin* 17 (1996): 29-44.

36. At first glance, the ambassador's role, normally performed against a backdrop of power politics, does not seem to fit here. Paul employs it, however, in a much wider social sense than this, with reconciliation between estranged parties the hoped-for outcome of his embassy with Timothy.

Building and Planting

Paul makes heavy use of construction terminology in the Corinthian correspondence. In fact, as Margaret M. Mitchell has observed, the metaphor of building is the "predominant image" of 1 Corinthians.[37] The reason behind Paul's choice of language is obvious. The two canonical letters show that factional conflict in one form or another was a constant feature of church life in Corinth. Between the start of Paul's work in the city and the writing of 1 Corinthians, a dangerous and disputatious spirit had taken hold within the small body of the fellowship there. The slogans Paul quotes in 1 Corinthians 1:12 ("I belong to Paul . . . Apollos . . . Cephas . . . Christ") appear to prefigure an impending collapse of their common identity, as rival parties and interests jostled for advantage within the church body politic. Eventually, ambitious outsiders (for example, the "super-apostles" of 2 Corinthians 10–13) would come on the scene and attempt to exploit for their own purposes a deeply rooted pattern of party strife and competition. The building imagery Paul employs throughout the Corinthian correspondence proved to be a theologically suitable way for him to respond to the sad fact of their persistent discord.

After thoroughly rebuking the church at Corinth for its worldly factionalism (1 Cor. 1:10–3:4), Paul begins to make his case for unity in the face of incipient division by means of an agricultural metaphor, introduced in 1 Corinthians 3:5-9. With respect to their beginning as a community of faith, how should the Corinthians regard the two most prominent missionaries to have worked in their midst up to this point? Paul suggests a word-picture: his task has been to plant, while Apollos watered. The full implications of these designations are not spelled out, but the following observations may be briefly noted.[38]

---

37. Margaret M. Mitchell, *Paul and the Rhetoric of Reconciliation: An Exegetical Investigation of the Language and Composition of 1 Corinthians* (Tübingen: J. C. B. Mohr [Paul Siebeck], 1991), p. 104. Mitchell sees allusions in 1 Corinthians to the metaphor of building not only in words established on the root οικ- (e.g., οἰκοδομή, οἰκονόμος οἰκονομία) and references to foundation-laying (θεμέλιος), but also in terms like βεβαιόω ("to establish"), ἑδραῖος ("steadfast"), ἀμετακίνητος ("immovable"), ἵστημι ("to stand"), κραταιόομαι ("be strong"), and [συν]ἔργον ("work"). See her discussion, pp. 99-111. In any case, Paul's interest in "building up" the church in Corinth remains a primary concern throughout the Corinthian correspondence (cf. 2 Cor. 10:8; 12:19; 13:10).

38. What Paul plants, for example, is not specified (the word of God?). Also, no details are provided to clarify whether Paul has in mind the whole of what Apollos did in Corinth or just one particular part of his work.

First, Paul urges the Corinthians to consider his work and that of Apollos to be of equal value, despite their different emphases: "The one who plants and the one who waters have a common purpose" (3:8). Each received his assignment from the same source, and so they rightfully share in a common status, as servants (διάκονοι) of the Lord (3:5). Paul reinforces the idea of their subordination to God and their dependence on God's decisive presence in their work by calling attention to the fact that neither planters nor cultivators can guarantee a good result for their joint endeavor. According to Paul, growth in the natural world must be attributed finally to God's involvement, without which no amount of human industry can produce a worthwhile yield. By recognizing the indispensability of God, Paul removes all grounds for boasting of their accomplishments: "So neither the one who plants nor the one who waters is anything, but only God who gives the growth" (3:7). The missionary application lying immediately behind Paul's figure of speech is unmistakable. The two co-workers, operating under the aegis of God, are identified as the effective means by which the Corinthians had entered into faith (3:5). Through them, God laid claim to the Corinthian congregation as God's own field and building (3:9).

The questions of identity and purpose posed in 1 Corinthians 3:5 ("What then is Apollos? What is Paul?") are still hanging in the air when Paul shifts his symbolic focus from farming to construction. The new metaphor he uses to respond to these questions is similar but not identical to the figure he offered previously. There are still three human parties involved that can be differentiated from each other. In this case, Paul calls himself a "skilled master builder," whose job it is to lay a foundation consisting of Jesus Christ (3:10-11). Other missionary actors (including Apollos, but not necessarily limited to him) are identified as those who "build on" the foundation Paul has already laid in Corinth. The congregation, already likened to a building in verse 9, now becomes "God's temple," the dwelling place for God's Spirit (3:16-17).

Paul's move into the imaginative world of civil engineering requires a modification in the way God's role is conceived. Any notion of miraculous growth would be out of place in this context. Yet, even here, Paul manages to establish a relationship between these two different conceptual realms. The bridge that connects them is a shared eschatological horizon. Just as the planter and irrigator will receive "wages" in the future commensurate with the "labor" each one expends (3:8), those who add to Paul's foundation can expect a "reward" for their "work," if it survives the holocaust of the Last Day (3:12-14). Paul implies that God will supply the wages and rewards in each case, when the time comes. Substandard work that does not pass its final test will be lost, but the salvation of the worker is not thereby put into jeopardy (3:15). On the other hand, those who threaten the integrity of the building itself can expect to receive the full force of God's wrath: "If anyone destroys God's temple, God will destroy that person" (3:17).

The role Paul assigns to himself in his metaphor of building is carefully chosen. The "master builder" he claims to resemble is identified as the human initiator of God's building project. While the Greek term ἀρχιτέκτων might appear at first to suggest responsibility for overall building design and the supervision of workers, Paul shows interest in only one of the many functions commonly associated with the practice of architecture in his day: the laying of a proper foundation.[39] Two personal qualifications are included in Paul's self-description. One is that he is σοφός, which here should probably be translated "skilled" or "competent," provided that the ironic connection to Paul's earlier discussion of wisdom (1 Cor. 1:18–2:13) is not totally effaced. Paul is claiming to be wise, even as he excoriates those who trust in wisdom! This is a subtle bit of wordplay, by means of which Paul is able to recall for his readers the radical reversal of expectations implied in the folly of the cross. Paul's second qualification consists of a conviction that God had gifted him for this work: "According to the grace of God given to me . . ." (3:10). By linking his particular missionary charism to a divine source, Paul acknowledges once again that his apostolate depended entirely on God's prevenient activity (cf. 1 Cor. 3:5 and Gal. 1:15).

39. Contra Jay Shanor, who argues that, as ἀρχιτέκτων, Paul's primary responsibility was to oversee the coordination and general progress of the Corinthian building project by directing the less skilled craftsmen working under his supervision. Shanor, "Paul As Master Builder: Construction Terms in First Corinthians," *NTS* 34 (1988): 465-66. The technical studies Shanor cites establish that such an understanding of ἀρχιτέκτων may have held generally in Greco-Roman times, but not that this was Paul's intended meaning of the term. I do not find what Shanor calls the "authoritative posture" struck by Paul in First Corinthians to be relevant to the matter at hand. More pertinent, it seems to me, is the admonition in the passage itself that those building on Paul's foundation should take care how they go about their tasks (1 Cor. 3:10). Paul leaves no doubt that it is God, not he, who in the end will judge the quality of the work that they do.

What did Paul mean by "laying a foundation"? Hans Conzelmann focuses his attention too narrowly on Paul's personal standing in Corinth, I believe, when he says,

> The foundation is an understandable and widely used metaphor for the rudiments of doctrine. . . . By means of this assertion, Paul maintains his own authority, and at the same time upholds the criterion to which it is subject: κατὰ τὴν χάριν κτλ, "according to the grace, etc."[40]

To be sure, Paul stakes out a unique and crucial position for himself within the larger scheme of the Corinthian mission by means of the building metaphor. Early choices made in the process of evangelization inevitably affect the range of options available to those who follow in the work. If nothing else, the one laying the foundation of a building determines the likely parameters of its eventual shape, plus its initial orientation to the surrounding environment. Paul is not misrepresenting his role. In the case of Corinth, many in the city will have first heard of the gospel through his preaching. The apostle seems to have been the chief instrument by which the Good News initially became known on a wide scale within the community. Acts 18 confirms the impression created in the Corinthian letters that Paul was the indispensable member of an extraordinary team of missionaries that managed in just a few months to establish a viable set of house churches in this busy urban setting marked by competing religious traditions.

It would not be sufficient to portray Paul's contribution to the mission in terms of the body image he presents in 1 Corinthians 12. Paul's work did not merely complement the efforts of his fellow missioners in the same way that a foot participates equally with a hand or an eye in the total reality of the body. The language of construction employed by Paul implies a sequence of actions. Like the planter, whose work naturally precedes that of the irrigator, the foundation-layer does his or her work at the inception of the project and thus shapes the context within which others will labor, when they "build on" what has already been set into place.

Paul identifies the foundation he has laid in Corinth as Jesus Christ. Actually, he says more than this, declaring that "no one can lay any foun-

---

40. Hans Conzelmann, *1 Corinthians: A Commentary on the First Epistle to the Corinthians,* trans. James W. Leitch (Philadelphia: Fortress, 1975), p. 75.

dation other than the one that has been laid; that foundation is Jesus Christ" (3:11). What this means theologically for Paul is that he must stand against any attempt to insinuate for the common life of the Corinthian church an alternative premise to the one with which it began. That is to say, a building can have only one foundation, and it must be established at the outset of construction. Paul touches on this idea again in Romans 15:20, when he writes of his reluctance to preach the gospel where Christ has already been named, lest he build on a preexisting foundation laid by someone else.

Had another foundation been proposed for Corinth? In 1 Corinthians 1–4, it could be that Paul's sharp rejection of wisdom stems in part from his perception that some Corinthian Christians wished to make it a primary framework or a set of first principles for interpreting the gospel. If the word of the cross Paul preached in Corinth (1 Cor. 1:18) defines the Christian community at its most basic level, then human wisdom becomes relatively unimportant, a decidedly secondary consideration. This does not mean that wisdom as a product of human culture necessarily stands in absolute contradiction to the gospel, as though ontologically opposed to God's perspective. But it cannot function as the bedrock structure on which the church depends for its essential identity.

The fundamental elements of Paul's message — the content of the foundation in Jesus Christ laid in Corinth — are summarized in 1 Corinthians 15:3-5. The Corinthian fellowship was established on the basis of these bare affirmations, which Paul appears to regard as the Corinthian church's true apostolic foundation, held in common with the whole church:

- that Christ died for our sins in accordance with the Scriptures;
- that he was buried;
- that he was raised on the third day in accordance with the Scriptures; and
- that he appeared to Cephas, then to the Twelve.

On the basis of this foundation, additional building activity by missionaries and ministers could proceed in Corinth. As noted above, Paul expects that the quality of the later work will be judged on its own merits at the Last Day, and so God remains the ultimate evaluator of whatever else might be accomplished by the Corinthian Christians after Paul. The apostle does not propose by means of this figure of speech to assert a personal right to direct the efforts of future builders, but he has bequeathed to them a most valuable gift. Whatever the shape of the superstructure that eventually arises on this site, Paul counsels that confidence in the integrity of the whole project will still be justified, because its foundation is secure and strong. Thus, within the maelstrom of dissent that threatened to tear apart the church in Corinth, Paul appealed to his correspondents to hold fast to the gospel they had first received (1 Cor. 15:1-2). Properly anchored, the Christians in Corinth would find the strength needed to stand firm in their faith (15:58). A spiritually mature community (3:1-3), ready to participate fully in the work of evangelization that still lay ahead, would indeed embody, in the end, the definitive proof of Paul's apostolate (9:1-2).

Our analysis of Paul's missionary practice and its portrayal may now be brought to a conclusion. Before us stands a somewhat enigmatic figure, whose permanent legacy is beyond doubt, but whose short-term success may have been unevenly realized within the span of his lifetime. The breadth of the commission Paul attempted to fulfill is extraordinary by any reckoning. His vocation stretched to encompass an astonishing variety of tasks and aims, from outreach on a very personal scale to the devising of continent-wide strategies for evangelization and the articulation of a groundbreaking theology of mission. As he proceeded, Paul had to negotiate his way through an accumulated tangle of personal interests that did not always mesh well together.[41] So we see Paul the pioneer missionary resolved to extend the reach of the gospel to ever more distant populations in Europe, while continuing to tend to the ongoing pastoral needs of churches he had helped to establish; or, an independent Paul, who fiercely resists the interference of other apostles in his field, yet practices a thoroughly collaborative approach to mission. In times of crisis especially, Paul was quick to assert authority over "his" congregations, but he thought it important nevertheless to institute structures of leadership that would eventually render the role of founder superfluous. Then there is the eloquent testimony of Romans 9–11, which shows the apostle to the Gentiles near the end of his career still longing to witness the salvation of his fellow Jews.

The complexity indicated by these and other contending priorities within Paul's approach to mission almost defies visual representation. All

---

41. For what follows in this paragraph, I have benefited from the analysis of Georgi, *Opponents of Paul*, pp. 364-66.

the same, Paul managed to find an appropriate set of images by which to capture many of the nuances in style and substance that characterized his missionary practice. As a planter and builder, Paul did not imagine himself to be a solitary figure or self-sufficient missionary agent acting on an exclusive mandate from God. In the metaphor of planting, Paul proposes to work in partnership with fellow missionaries like Apollos on an equal footing. As a builder of the church in Corinth, Paul anticipates a continuing mission of collaboration between himself and the congregation. Paul clearly recognized that while foundations are crucial, because they secure the stability of buildings, it is the visible edifice that finally completes the construction process. Likewise, the planter's long-term success depends on the efforts of the irrigators and cultivators who follow.

The metaphors of building and planting employed in the Corinthian correspondence do leave room for Paul to claim and exercise a measure of authority. Given the zealousness with which Paul defends his apostolic commission in the letters, one can hardly be surprised by this. We must be precise, though, when describing the kind of authority signaled by these figures of speech. In Paul's usage, the planter and master builder are similar in that they *begin* new phases of mission work. Leadership here means to plan and initiate, to prepare the way for successors to carry on God's work, to improvise tactics for circumstances not previously encountered. These are not managerial functions. Nor is this another form of benevolent patriarchalism. Theologically and strategically, Paul was like a powerful force that pulled the church into uncharted territory. Where others might have been more cautious, Paul was willing to think creatively, risk failure, and test the artificial limits of geography, language, and ethnicity that threatened to hem in the gospel. Within the conceptual space defined by the metaphors of planting and building, this is a form of leadership that demands a high degree of trust from collaborators and colleagues, because initial decisions made on behalf of the whole team may well carry great weight into the future.

Paul's figures of speech also allow him to acknowledge God's sovereignty in mission, whether as the ultimate patron of the building project or the source of miraculous growth. By identifying himself and Apollos as servants of the divine will (1 Cor. 3:5; cf. 4:1), Paul pays heed to God's intimate involvement in the missionary process by which the Corinthian congregation came into being. By the same token, when he calls the church in Corinth "God's field, God's building" (3:9) or "God's temple" (3:16-17),

Paul recognizes God's perpetual right of ownership over the outcome of this process. The planting and building metaphors provide a way for Paul to hold in tension the values of collaboration and authority noted above with this notion of God's active presence in evangelization. The result is a fully rounded image of mission that most nearly represents the sum of Paul's missiological ideals and actual practice.

An Apostolic Model in a Post-Apostolic Age

In 1 Corinthians 4:6, Paul makes one more reference to the example set by himself and Apollos. "I have applied all this to Apollos and myself for your benefit . . . ," Paul writes, "so that you may learn through us the meaning of the saying, 'Nothing beyond what is written,' so that none of you will be puffed up in favor of one against another." The exegetical problems involved in the interpretation of this verse are notorious.[42] We have to be content here with the observation that Paul considered the model of leadership in mission that he and Apollos had presented to be in some way instructive for the Corinthian Christians. Certainly, the quality of cooperation Paul highlighted earlier in the letter with regard to his working relationship with Apollos (3:5-9) stands opposed to any behavior that divides by setting "one against another." Perhaps Paul also had in mind the subordinate-status terms of "servants" and "stewards" he had earlier assigned to himself and Apollos (4:1-2), when he urged his correspondents to avoid acting in ways that "puffed up" or increased their sense of self-importance at the expense of others.

In any event, Paul makes no claim in his letters to inimitability. In fact, he often commends his own conduct as a faithful pattern of Christian response to God's grace that could be emulated by others. Occasionally, he will even exhort his correspondents to model their behavior directly on his example, to imitate him (1 Cor. 4:16; 11:1; Phil. 3:17; 1 Thess. 1:6-7; cf.

---

42. Among these difficulties is a question about what, precisely, Paul means by "all this." Is Paul making reference to the whole of chapters 1–4, the part that begins to focus on Paul and Apollos at 3:4, or just the last few verses (4:1-5)? The full implications behind Paul's use of the verb μετεσχημάτισα ("to apply" as a figure of speech or allusion) are likewise elusive. Conzelmann, *1 Corinthians*, p. 86, echoes the frustrations of many other interpreters when he declares the adage Paul quotes in 1 Corinthians 4:6 ("nothing beyond what is written") to be "unintelligible" in this context.

2 Thess. 3:7). With this background in mind, I take 1 Corinthians 4:6 to be an invitation to consider how Paul's leading metaphors for mission could be appropriated by a widely dispersed, post-apostolic audience that extends into our own era.

Paul finished his missionary career with work left undone. A few isolated traditions may be adduced in favor of the hypothesis that he managed to reach Spain, but no hard evidence exists to support the contention that he succeeded in establishing the church there.[43] The Iberian peninsula was only one area out of many in the western European sphere of the Greco-Roman world that still awaited evangelization upon Paul's death. In the centuries to come, itinerant preachers and Christian travelers would revisit Spain and also make their way to innumerable settlements scattered across eastern Europe, proconsular Africa, Mesopotamia, and other places that had not yet been exposed to the gospel. If mission as an act of building and planting includes the idea of beginning work in locations where the church has little or no presence, then Paul left plenty of opportunities for post-apostolic missioners to follow his example by inaugurating new ventures in Christian witness.

There are still places in the world where pioneering mission work remains to be carried out. Even the "Great Century" of Western foreign missions, stretching from William Carey's arrival in India (1792) to the start of the First World War, during which time a truly global church took root on all six inhabited continents, by no means exhausted the possibilities for initial evangelization to be conducted among non-Christian people.[44] Those involved in the "frontier" missionary movement today point to a continuing need to initiate outreach among numerous groups of people for whom the gospel is largely unknown because they have no complete translation of the Bible in their own language or access to an indigenous expression of the church. The recently published second edition of the *World Christian Encyclopedia* provides a massive amount of documentation pertaining to the contemporary situation of the unevangelized.[45] In-

---

43. For a review of the evidence regarding the trip to Spain and a possible reconstruction of events near the end of Paul's life, see Murphy-O'Connor, *Paul,* pp. 361-63.

44. The designation "Great Century" comes from Kenneth Scott Latourette's massive opus, *A History of the Expansion of Christianity* (New York: Harper and Brothers, 1937-1945). Three of the seven published volumes were devoted to the nineteenth century.

45. David B. Barrett, George T. Kurian, Todd M. Johnson, eds., *World Christian Encyclopedia: A Comparative Survey of Churches and Religions in the Modern World,* second ed.,

cluded in the research presented there is a detailed analysis of the world's population that divides it into nearly 20,000 distinct cultural segments. Among these are some 1,240 "population segments" that the authors classify as "completely unreached."[46] The hundreds of thousands of living people who stand behind these abstract numbers represent a significant challenge for Christians willing to carry the Good News across formidable barriers of language, ethnicity, social status, and political identification, just as Paul and his first-century collaborators did.

Considerations of geography aside, the image of mission under discussion in this chapter also has some important things to say about *how* new efforts at missionary outreach might best be started. A key concept here is the idea of laying foundations. In his use of the building metaphor, Paul draws a basic distinction between the work he does and the contributions made by others that goes beyond the issue of sequence in time already discussed. Not only does foundation-laying take place at the outset of the project, but the product of this activity also stands in a particular spatial relationship to the finishing work that is added later. By design, the foundation is the lowest part of any building, its inmost feature. If pilings driven into the earth are used to provide additional stability, the foundation may extend all the way to bedrock, below the level of the ground on which the whole building appears to rest when viewed from outside. By characterizing himself as a layer of foundations, Paul suggests that he is a missionary whose primary attention is focused on *substructures*. In Cor-

---

2 vols. (New York: Oxford University Press, 2001). A companion volume of analysis and synthesis was published concurrently: David B. Barrett and Todd M. Johnson, *World Christian Trends, AD 30–AD 2200: Interpreting the Annual Christian Megacensus* (Pasadena: William Carey Library, 2001).

46. See Barrett and Johnson, *World Christian Trends,* p. 60, for a summary of these data. The figures and definitions used in the *World Christian Encyclopedia* have not gained universal acceptance by missiologists and other scholars, despite the decades of careful work that lie behind this impressive work of reference. With regard to some of the problems raised by the idiosyncratic nomenclature often employed in these volumes, see Gerald H. Anderson, "World Christianity by the Numbers: A Review of the *World Christian Encyclopedia,* Second Edition," *IBMR* 26 (2002): 128-30. Quibbles aside about exactly how one ought to define categories such as "unreached" or "unevangelized," few would dispute that one of these terms or something similar may still be appropriately applied to a considerable number of culturally distinct social units scattered around the world. The present status of world evangelization is also considered in Patrick J. St. G. Johnstone and Jason Mandryk, with Robyn Johnstone, *Operation World,* sixth ed. (Minneapolis: Bethany House, 2001).

inth, he labors below the surface of things, attending to fundamental matters that bear directly on the gospel of Jesus Christ. His special burden is to put that gospel at the center of the community's life, so that it can secure the integrity and unity of the entire spiritual edifice. The idea that mission is a task to be carried out from below, as a means to provide essential structures of identity for newborn communities of faith, clearly differentiates this image from the other four presented earlier in this study.

Complementing the spatial dimension of Paul's work is the way he portrays his approach to preaching and evangelism. In contrast to the rhetoricians of his day who sought to persuade their audiences with brilliant arguments that compelled assent while delighting the senses, Paul claimed that his goal was simply to present an unadorned gospel:

> When I came to you, brothers and sisters, I did not come proclaiming the mystery of God to you in lofty words or wisdom. For I decided to know nothing among you except Jesus Christ, and him crucified. (1 Cor. 2:1-2)

There is, of course, more than a hint of disingenuousness in Paul's assertion of forensic artlessness. After all, his protest of simplicity is embedded in a sustained and sophisticated argument that betrays at least some exposure to classical training.[47] Modern studies of communication and recently discovered insights regarding the process of inculturation make it impossible for readers and hearers today to take declarations of complete objectivity at face value, even from ancient sources. Similarly inadmissible is the contention that any person's message could convey a pure form of the gospel, untouched by the perspective of cultural location.

Yet, there is a difference between what Paul was attempting to do in Corinth and the approach taken by his more eloquent opponents. In the view of the Corinthians themselves, Paul's manner of argumentation failed to convince, precisely because it did not measure up to their expectations for oratory. At the same time, the rhetorical skills of his rivals bespoke access to wisdom that Paul seemed to lack. Paul acknowledges the difference, while asserting that the contrast in styles perceived by the Corinthian Christians was

---

47. Paul's educational background is discussed by Christopher Forbes at the end of his detailed study of Paul's apologetic strategies, "Comparison, Self-Praise and Irony: Paul's Boasting and the Conventions of Hellenistic Rhetoric," NTS 32 (1986): 22-24.

not accidental. As Duane Litfin has demonstrated, Paul consciously avoided using at least some of the rhetorical conventions likely to be held in high esteem by his audience, in favor of a more straightforward method of "placarding" the cross.[48] His motive for doing so could have been founded on a desire to accentuate the inherent power of the gospel to convict those whom the Holy Spirit had prepared beforehand to receive its truth. If this was indeed his intention, then Paul succeeded to a remarkable degree in bringing the form of his preaching into alignment with his understanding of its content and purpose. Preaching that stays focused on the heart of the kerygma appropriately attends first and foremost to basic matters and avoids calling attention to itself. Paul apparently believed there to be no better way than this to lay a foundation consisting of Jesus Christ (alone).

The action of planting that Paul pairs with foundation-laying reinforces the impression of working below ground level. To appreciate this, however, one has to be accurate with respect to the agricultural activity envisioned. Planting (φυτεύω) is not the same thing as sowing (σπείρω).[49] As we know from the familiar parable recounted in the Gospels (Mark 4:3-9 and parallels), one sows seeds by scattering them over a wide expanse of ground. Planting, on the other hand, is an operation that involves the fixing of a seedling, slip, rootstock, or sapling into the soil.[50]

As the accompanying pictures show, the postures implied by these different actions are quite dissimilar. The sower strides upright through the field, flinging handfuls of seed across the furrows that have been plowed in advance (fig. 26). The only equipment needed for sowing is a small bag in which to carry the seeds to be distributed. Standard depictions of this activity (and many popular songs) often communicate an al-

---

48. A. Duane Litfin, *St. Paul's Theology of Proclamation: 1 Corinthians 1–4 and Greco-Roman Rhetoric* (Cambridge: Cambridge University Press, 1994), p. 247. See also the extended analysis of Paul's rhetorical technique offered in Stanley E. Porter, "Paul of Tarsus and His Letters," in *Handbook of Classical Rhetoric in the Hellenistic Period (330 BC–AD 400)*, ed. Stanley E. Porter (Leiden: Brill, 1997), pp. 533-85.

49. A similar differentiation exists in Hebrew. Cf. H. D. Preuss, "Zara'" (sowing), *TDOT* 4:143-62, and J. Reindl, "Nata'" (planting), *TDOT* 9:387-94.

50. In both Testaments, planting is often associated with the cultivation of grapes (e.g., Matt. 21:33). Paul knows this usage (1 Cor. 9:7), but chooses not to identify the crop he plants metaphorically in 1 Corinthians 3. He does characterize the whole of the area under cultivation as a "field" (γεώργιον) belonging to God. This serves to highlight the corporate nature of the work he does with Apollos, a detail that corresponds to the community aspect of the building metaphor.

Fig. 26.
A Sower.
Photograph
taken near
Jerusalem
(early twentieth
century)

most casual, carefree, "Johnny Appleseed" attitude on the part of the sower, who is almost always male. In contrast to sowing, planting requires the cultivator to get considerably closer to the ground (see fig. 27; plate 4). This is backbreaking work, carried out on hands and knees or in a bent-over position, sometimes with the use of a small spade or hoe. In many traditional cultures, women are the ones expected to undertake the hard labor required by this kind of farming.

A final point to be discussed in this chapter concerns the way in which Paul handles the metaphors of planting and building as a matched set. He was by no means the first to combine these two figures. The idea of construing together the actions of planting and building was a commonplace in Paul's era, which may be found in both Jewish and Hellenistic sources.[51] Further back in time, one can find many places in the Old Testament where the two metaphors are laid side by side (e.g., Deut. 28:30; Isa. 65:21-22; Jer. 31:4-5; Ezek. 28:26).

A very natural explanation stands behind this literary convention:

---

51. For a representative sampling of source materials roughly contemporary with Paul, see Otto Michel, "Οἶκος," *TDNT* 5:137-38.

Fig. 27. *Red Rice Planting Women*, Nepal, photo by Jacob Holdt
(late twentieth century)

the activities of building and planting symbolize a settled existence. Only people who expect to remain where they are for the foreseeable future will devote the energy and capital necessary to construct permanent dwellings and to cultivate fields that may not immediately produce their full or best crop. The planting of trees for fruit and shade implies an even more distant temporal horizon. Israel was compelled to stay engaged with this set of metaphors over the long term, since together they bore directly on the nation's corporate identity at two decisive points in the Israelites' history. First, building and planting in the Promised Land represented an end to their nomadic existence as a people.[52] A second turning point was the catastrophe of the Exile, when Israel lost the accumulated benefits of many

52. The gravity of this shift in living patterns is signaled by the refusal of the Rechabites to build houses, sow fields, or plant vineyards (Jer. 35). The sect chose instead to honor the ideal of Israel's wilderness experience by practicing a non-sedentary lifestyle of herding and living in tents.

previous generations having invested themselves in the Land. Numerous passages in the prophets give witness to the ache that would be felt in exile at the thought of aliens and enemies enjoying the fruit of Israel's labor, living in cherished domiciles they did not build, while enjoying the sweet produce of vineyards they did not plant (cf. Amos 5:11). Such is the worst nightmare of the dispossessed.

In addition to the concept of community-building that lay implicit in the intertwined language of construction and horticulture, Paul had one more reason to appeal to the vocabulary of building and planting as he carried on his correspondence with the church at Corinth. This was the link that had already been forged in the Old Testament between these functions and the exercise of prophetic authority. The paradigmatic text comes from the prophet Jeremiah:

> Now the word of the LORD came to me saying, "Before I formed you in the womb I knew you, and before you were born I consecrated you; I appointed you a prophet to the nations." . . . Then the LORD put out his hand and touched my mouth; and the LORD said to me: "Now I have put my words in your mouth. See, today I appoint you over nations and over kingdoms, to pluck up and to pull down, to destroy and to overthrow, to build and to plant." (Jer. 1:4-5, 9-10)

In the context of an impending exile, the prophet is given here a two-edged vocational charge. Assuming continued disobedience on the part of Judah, his assignment is to destroy the nation in God's name, so that it may be rebuilt according to God's ways. He will do this by delivering a self-activating message of threat and promise, a prophetic word that will effect disaster and then engender hope. Not surprisingly, the prophet is led to expect resistance in the community to the terms of his call, particularly from those in positions of leadership and privilege (e.g., Jer. 26:1-11).

It is easy to imagine how the figure of an embattled but divinely authorized prophet like Jeremiah would have held special interest for Paul, especially as he faced growing opposition in Corinth and persistent questions from the congregation there about his performance as an apostle. By his own testimony, we know that an exasperated Paul could be driven to express strong feelings of anger, as he fought against the influence of the so-called "super-apostles" and their sympathizers within the community (cf. 2 Cor. 10:3-6). Yet, when pressed to define for himself and the church the ultimate purpose of the authority he sought to exercise in Christ's name, Paul deliberately chose to emphasize the *positive* functions of apostolic responsibility. He left behind any hint of destructive intent: "the authority that the Lord has given me [is] for building up and not for tearing down" (2 Cor. 13:10; cf. 10:8; 12:19). Here is the inner axis of Paul's missionary self-understanding, forced into view by the exigencies of circumstance. A profound sense of vocation compelled Paul to make known what God had accomplished on the cross, to seek to lay foundations for faith that could outlast the corrosive effects of Christian weakness, and to create new forms of community in the name of Jesus Christ. These are honorable ends that time has not diminished or made irrelevant. The pair of metaphors Paul used to frame his mission and ministry — building and planting — continue to be apt devices by which to conceptualize contemporary applications of an apostolic task.

chapter 7

New Testament Images
of Disciples in Mission

A Brief Recapitulation

From the outset of this project, my intention has been to discover a fresh way for the New Testament to inform contemporary thinking about mission theology by stimulating the renewal of mission imagery. This aim seemed to me to be justified by the current crisis felt by many in the field of missiology. As David Bosch and others have pointed out, much of what had seemed obvious and compelling at the beginning and heyday of the modern missionary movement seems in the present era to be losing its power to convict hearts and minds. In ecumenical circles especially, hard questions have been raised about past missionary attitudes toward non-Western cultures and religions. As a result, many of the images used to portray Christian missionary action in previous generations seem inadequate or even unacceptable today.

Creative attempts have been made recently to renew our stock of mission imagery. Briefly reviewing several of these studies, I noted how a certain kind of methodology had taken hold, which tended to proceed in a negative manner by recommending images and metaphors that corrected or compensated for particular errors felt to be widely embraced in current mission theology and practice. While acknowledging the critical value of these exercises, I proposed to do something quite different in this book.

My initial research question asked about the missionary roles assumed by apostolic-era disciples of Jesus. By framing my inquiry in this way, I expected that a substantial engagement with the New Testament would necessarily follow. After all, the New Testament is our most complete and sometimes the only source for much of what is known about the activities of Jesus' earliest disciples. No claim has been made that this procedure exhausts what the New Testament has to say about Christian mission. The decision to focus on Jesus' followers in the New Testament, rather than on Jesus himself or the church as a corporate body, does, however, present several advantages. One is that it brings into the foreground many examples of rather ordinary people involved in mission. These come from a variety of ethnic and cultural backgrounds. They are shown participating in different kinds of communities and social circumstances. While some of these had been specifically designated and to a certain extent were trained to become Jesus' agents of outreach, many others appear to have been more spontaneously moved to share their faith.

Besides the common factor of discipleship or devotion to Jesus, what links these New Testament demonstrations of Christian witness together is the experimental nature of the actions on display. These are followers of Jesus in the process of appropriating his mission and making it their own. They are attempting to emulate Jesus, but do not seem to assume that they have been called to repeat in specific terms exactly what their Lord said and did. In other words, while these disciples appear to consider Jesus a model of evangelistic behavior, they are not unreflective imitators of his example. As shifting needs and new opportunities arose, they had to adapt to the different conditions and situations in which they found themselves. The human character of the witness rendered by these first-century disciples is especially evident whenever it is shown as less than perfectly realized, which was often the case. Thus, what we have in these stories are *accessible exemplars* of New Testament witnessing, sometimes courageous and sometimes frail, often successful but not necessarily so.

Five different patterns of Christian witness emerged out of the exegetical analyses conducted above. In each case, a distinctive kind of action performed by a follower or followers of Jesus defined the image of mission under discussion.

We began by looking at mission as an act of announcing Good News. In this approach, the verbal aspect of Christian outreach predominates. Announcers of Good News are, first and foremost, proclaimers of a message they consider to be of the utmost importance. Ordinarily, they attempt to communicate that message in public settings, often in situations where crowds of attentive onlookers have gathered together. A high degree of self-confidence is needed to perform this kind of witnessing effectively. Not surprisingly, the ones most often shown exercising this ministry in the New Testament are the highest-profile members of the nascent Christian community, those widely acknowledged within the early church to be its most influential leaders. Like royal heralds, these emissaries went forth to speak on behalf of a commissioning power, whose authority far exceeded their own. Thus, in Acts especially, the boldness of the apostles is unmistakable. Nevertheless, an element of vulnerability persists even in this literary setting, since the earthly fate of the apostolic church still remained quite open in Luke's time. Fully fledged announcers of Good News must be prepared to operate in just this kind of environment, where personal risk and the possibility of rejection are potential entailments of faithful proclamation.

Another kind of missionary action takes place when Christ is shared with friends. Instead of orations and formal addresses, this image of mission pays special heed to more common forms of interpersonal communication. Christian witness here is more a matter of conversation within families and visits in the neighborhood than it is about posting declarations on public billboards for all to see. Beyond the glare of the spotlight, the scale of mission shrinks from what might be considered normal for announcements of Good News. This is eager, spontaneous, and sometimes persistent witnessing, which is driven less by command and commission than by a joy that will not be suppressed. The heroes of the early church could engage in this type of mission, but so did many lesser-known members of the community. As we discovered, to share Christ with friends does not mean primarily to transmit information to others about Jesus or the religion of Christianity. It is, rather, to make Christ present where he is not yet known, sometimes by word but just as often by deeds that express a heartfelt desire to incarnate and share God's love for one's kin and near neighbors.

Again and again in the New Testament, the Good News is shown crossing substantial boundaries of social difference. Interpreters of the gospel participate directly in this cross-cultural process, which continues to unfold today. At stake is the universal character of Christian witness. Standing in the way of its full expression are semi-permeable barriers of language and dialect, plus a wide variety of human distinctions based on cultural factors like race, class, gender, and social worldview. Interpreting the gospel is not about conquest or the imposition of one's customs and values on foreign peoples. Far more likely to unfold in connection with this image of mission are scenarios in which the spiritual aspirations of others receive courteous respect and in which invitations to explain the basis of Christian faith are extended to would-be interpreters of the gospel. As portrayed in the New Testament, the interpreter is a facilitating figure who enables communication to take place across the dividing lines of cultural insularity. Like simultaneous translators, interpreters are thus instruments of dialogue carried out principally by others. Not surprisingly, then, the role is meant to be temporary. Once contact has been made and the gospel becomes intelligible to this new set of hearers, the need for cross-cultural interpretation diminishes. Eventually, the interpreter is made redundant and then may disappear completely, just as Philip the evangelist did in Acts after introducing the Ethiopian eunuch to the Good News about Jesus Christ.

Shepherding can be a missional vocation, but only when the crucial function of gathering is given its proper due. If one's ultimate aim is to govern God's flock, then pastoral leadership inevitably centers on the tasks of ruling and discipline. Likewise, tending sheep can mean no more than trying to preserve the safety of the covenant community, to guard the faithful from outside threats. In contrast to these approaches, missionary shepherds seek out lost and disoriented sheep. Their attention is not focused on that part of the flock already safely ensconced within the protective enclosures of the visible church, but on other folds as yet cut off from the experience of Christian community. These witnesses dare to imagine the ultimate composition of God's people in the most comprehensive terms possible, with unexpected participants standing beside the long-affiliated and sharing with them equally in a sense of belonging. Accordingly, missionary shepherding requires one to stretch the traditional limits of pastoral care. No sheep is able to wander off so far that a relationship to God through Christ becomes absolutely impossible. Missionary shepherds are a way by which the truth of this assertion is tested and proved.

The cooperative nature of Christian mission emerges clearly in the concepts of planting and building, which together define metaphorically the heart of what Paul understood to be his own missionary identity. As the apostle explained, what he was trying to do could not be undertaken without reference to the actions of colleagues like Apollos, who labored alongside Paul in Corinth, or those who would follow after them in ministry there and elsewhere. In contrast to his co-workers, however, Paul concentrated his efforts on the substructures of evangelism, where critical supports for the future must be laid and where fragile seedlings either take root or die. His call was specifically to a vocation that included within it opportunities for pioneering missionary action. This implied a readiness to make adjustments in response to novel circumstances, since new ministries of outreach might not always be well served by conventional patterns, such as those Paul found in Jewish Christianity. Throughout, Paul was committed to a methodology for mission that emphasized the building-up of the Christian community. The first step for him was not to pull down or to uproot but to act in a positive fashion by laying solid foundations and planting carefully. Paul's approach assumed that everything he and his missionary associates and successors might venture to do was subject ultimately to God's oversight and judgment.

No book purporting to discuss mission imagery in the New Testament could do so adequately, in my view, without taking up the question of how to portray what one has discovered exegetically. For this reason, illustrations have been incorporated into each of the preceding six chapters. As representations of ideas and metaphors, these pictures were meant to exhibit and make more transparent what I considered to be the most crucial theological issues raised by this series of New Testament mission images. No doubt, others would choose their figures, drawings, paintings, and photographs differently, notwithstanding an intention to discuss the very same group of underlying concepts! The subjective nature of aesthetic preference cannot be avoided. Nor is it possible to standardize the results of individual perception. But these limitations need not cancel out the potential benefits to be gained by including graphic representations of more abstract concepts. To the extent that the pictures included here have been able to make the ideas lying behind them more vivid to the reader, they have served a useful purpose.

As indicated in the introduction to this study, many different kinds of media were used to create the artwork reproduced herein. More importantly, the illustrations included in this study have been drawn from a variety of cultural contexts and, in date, they range from the pre-Constantinian period of the church right up to the late twentieth century. The facts of geographic and chronological diversity implied by this selection of figures are not incidental to the purposes of this book. All along, the dynamic character of Christian mission and the enduring challenge of its depiction have been assumed, even as we have focused our attention on a single literary source (the New Testament) and a particular generation of witnessing disciples (those in the apostolic era). Down through history and across an expanding cluster of cultural matrices, Christians have been persistent in their efforts to re-interpret and re-appropriate the New Testament story of mission for themselves. Apart from the few secular scenes displayed, the illustrations thus show how a global sample of these interpreters of mission within the church has attempted to portray that story visually in terms that made sense in their own times and places.

Grasping the Big Picture

We began this study of mission images by considering a few of the ways they exert their power. At issue, in part, is the manner in which a given image is likely to impact potential readers, viewers, and hearers. Some images, for example, appeal especially to human emotions. That is, their effect is felt primarily as a kind of sensation or feeling. The most poignant images of this sort are ones that move or strongly motivate and so engender a deeper commitment to missionary action. Other images get our attention by stimulating more rational forms of cognition. This might mean offering up to the mind new and compelling insights about the basis, forms, or purposes of Christian mission. At a simple level, images of mission that provoke analytical thinking about evangelization often do so by focusing on one or two key concepts, which may be sharply expressed by a vivid metaphor or some other figure of speech. More complicated images, as we have seen, can function as visual fields through which several narrative threads may be passing simultaneously. As these different stories are allowed to interpret each other, the image placed before the mind's eye begins to acquire new textures and potential meaning, with the result that it becomes increasingly complex and so, perhaps, more subtly suggestive.

Yet another layer of signification is made possible when more than one mission image is considered at a time. This happens, for example, when several images of mission are presented together as a set, as they are here. What are the likely consequences of this strategy? A potential result is that a situation of interplay develops among the images, similar to what was described for single images functioning as narrative intersections, but on a larger scale. In this case, new aspects of meaning may be produced that lie beyond the capacity of any one image to capture or convey, especially as tension is created within the grouping as a result of factors of contrast. By the same token, when a group of images is presented conjointly as a body, the need for any particular image to bear the entire burden of representation is thereby reduced. At the same time, the whole collection becomes a crucial context in which each of the individual images may be read, considered, and evaluated. Meaning may also be added as a result of repetition. This might happen, for instance, when important motifs recur across a selection of images. Repetition, of course, is a tried and true way to signal emphasis, whether in painting, rhetoric, or literature.

The value of thinking about Christian mission in terms of multiple images considered together is easily demonstrated. Returning for a moment to the Brancacci chapel in Florence, for example, we may recall that the scene of St. Peter preaching (fig. 28; plate 5) reproduced earlier was but one of four scenes on the south wall of the chapel in which the apostle seemed to be engaged in missionary activities. Besides preaching, Peter is also shown baptizing new believers (fig. 29; plate 6), healing the sick and infirm with his shadow (fig. 30; plate 7), and distributing alms to a woman carrying a child, while others, also in need, wait their turn (fig. 31; plate 8). It is not unreasonable to assume that by placing these four scenes together in a defined zone within the decorative scheme of the chapel, Masaccio and Masolino were inviting the viewer to consider them together as a group.

What does this collection of images suggest about the nature of Christian mission as that may have been understood by these two artists and their patrons in fifteenth-century Florence? At the very least, we are bound to conclude that a case has been made here for an expansive definition of Christian mission, one that cannot be reduced to a single idea or task. In this part of the Brancacci chapel, both spiritual and physical needs are shown being addressed. Mission appears to be a matter of speaking and acting alike. It may involve an appeal to rationality, as implied in the event of preaching, but room is also left for the possibility of miraculous healing, wordlessly effected. Further, we observe in these four scenes a variety of pious responses to missionary outreach, including the rapt attention of those listening to Peter preach, a spontaneous gesture of prayer from the one just healed as a result of the apostle's shadow having fallen on him, and the conscious decision of the neophytes to be inducted into the church by baptism.

As for recurring motifs, the powerfully drawn figure of Peter clearly dominates the four-scene tableau. The apostle speaks with authority, dis-

Fig. 28.
*The Preaching
of St. Peter,* by
Masolino, with
Masaccio, Brancacci
Chapel, Florence
(1425)

penses grace through the rite of baptism, disburses the assets of the community with compassionate wisdom, and heals without even trying! Since
the whole chapel is dedicated to his memory, a high degree of respect for
the person of St. Peter is not out of place in this setting. But one suspects
that more than simple honor for the apostle lies embedded in these pictures
of mission. Peter's bearing is regal, almost detached. He commands deference, if not obedience, from all those with whom he comes into contact.[1]

1. Peter's competence to pronounce judgment on God's behalf is also implied by the
dead body of Ananias that lies at his feet in fig. 31 (cf. Acts 5:1-11). In another fresco scene,
painted on a sidewall in the chapel, additional homage is paid to the apostle by means of a
scene in which several Carmelite friars are shown venerating a tapestry with Peter's image
on it.

Fig. 29.
Baptizing the Neophytes,
by Masaccio, with Masolino,
Brancacci Chapel, Florence
(1425)

Fig. 30.
*St. Peter Healing with His
Shadow*, by Masaccio,
Brancacci Chapel, Florence
(1425)

Fig. 31.
*The Distribution of Goods
and the Death of Ananias,*
by Masaccio, Brancacci
Chapel, Florence
(1425)

Haloed and well-dressed, the character of Peter displayed in these pictures communicates both spiritual authority and social power. Not incidentally, these are the very same qualities that preeminently defined the aspirations of the late medieval papacy, whose incumbents were considered the successors of Peter, the first bishop of Rome. A single scene of Peter engaged in witness might have been enough to hint at an imperial style. By reiterating this theme over a series of different panels, the artists make it virtually impossible to ignore this aspect of their portrayal.

Turning back to the mission images featured in this book, a few concluding remarks may now be made with respect to the entire collection. What are the contours of the big picture that begins to emerge when this group of images is viewed as a whole? Fundamentally, mission has been defined here in terms of several actions: announcing Good News, sharing Christ with friends, interpreting, shepherding, and planting/building. The fact that these are multiple actions and not one, which are described serially rather than being placed in a hierarchy, means that no single approach has been allowed to monopolize our discussion of the Christian missionary vocation. The element of variation indicated by this result cannot be attributed to our (post)modern age and its preoccupation with difference. We know this because the exegetical analyses presented above effectively tie each of these mission images back to the first few generations of Jesus' disciples. In other words, the idea that Christian mission is a multifaceted undertaking is not at all foreign to the New Testament.

When the details of these several images of mission are examined more closely, the inherently pluriform nature of Christian witness is reconfirmed in a number of important ways. The first of these has to do with the "who" of mission in the apostolic era. As we have observed, not all those involved in the earliest period of Christian mission were expert evangelists or members of a specially trained cadre of witnessing agents. While it is true that Peter and Paul dominate the missionary record of the early church presented in Acts, many other individuals, not so well known outside their own local contexts, also appear in the narratives and are shown participating in various forms of Christian outreach.

The glimpses afforded us in the New Testament of these less prominent witnessing disciples are fleeting, to be sure. But enough detail is provided for us to know that the whole of the church's missionary story cannot be told through a too-small collection of images based solely on the larger-than-life exploits of its most forceful personalities. In order to fill out the big picture of disciples in mission that coalesces in the New Testament, it is necessary also to honor the parts played by the "minor" apostles, meaning figures like Andrew, Philip, Barnabas, and Apollos. In addition, space has to be made to recognize the contributions of even more obscure biblical characters, such as the unnamed woman of Samaria, whose halting testimony to the Messiah so profoundly affected her community, and the four believing stretcher-bearers who anonymously bore the paralyzed man into Jesus' presence.

This group of images also tells us something about the "where" of early Christian mission and does so in terms more comprehensive than might be expected on the basis of so few passages of Scripture. Thanks to the initial chapters of Acts, for example, we see the apostles at work in the cosmopolitan environment of Jerusalem, a city of great renown in the first century to which Jews from many different cultures were regularly drawn for cultic purposes. To the extent that the letters of Paul also presuppose an urban setting for his missionary activities, they supplement this perspective. Whether in provincial centers, such as Ephesus and Corinth, or in Rome itself, the figure of the orator would be instantly recognizable. Another profession highlighted here that probably assumes a Greco-Roman municipal context is that of the master architect or builder, whose great public-works projects were scattered across the Roman Empire. Planting and shepherding, on the other hand, are tasks that reflect the rhythms and priorities of life in small-town settlements, far-flung villages, and remote stretches of countryside.

Another way to describe the location of mission is to focus on the social circumstances or setting-in-life in which faith-sharing takes place. The New Testament passages we have studied portray an interesting array of situations in which missionary encounter may be imagined. We have seen Christian witness unfold, for example, in and around the marketplace of Athens, outside a small pagan shrine at Lystra, and among the pilgrimage crowds that flocked to the precincts of the temple in Jerusalem. In addition, Paul and other of the apostles are shown repeatedly in Acts offering up their faith testimonies in the context of legal proceedings brought against them or in circumstances of open debate. In such public settings, attempts to communicate faith would naturally tend toward some kind of formal discourse, appropriate for interactions involving large groups of strangers. In contrast, encounters taking place in domestic settings, in one's workplace, or in some situations of travel (such as Philip experienced for a time in the carriage of the Ethiopian eunuch) suggest the possibility of extended, informal conversations about ultimate concerns, conducted on a more personal basis.

Besides the "who" and the "where" of mission, there is also the matter of "how." In this regard, too, the collection of images presented in this study provides ready access to more than one way of visualizing Christian witness. As we have seen, some forms of missionary activity appear to be matters of individual effort only, but Paul reminds us that other individuals are often involved and that the total effect of any single person's evangelistic labor may not be realized until each witnessing disciple has had a chance to play his or her part in the larger missionary event taking place. When the many corporate images of mission found in the New Testament are also taken into account, the idea of collegiality in mission is further strengthened.

Related to the question of collaboration is the factor of time. Is evangelism the work of a moment or a process that develops in stages? Many of the passages featured here give the impression that conversion to Christian faith is a snap decision, triggered by circumstances of confrontation or the sudden perception of an extraordinary opportunity to change the course of one's life and destiny by abruptly shifting loyalty to Jesus. Paul's preferred image of mission as a building project proposes instead that Christian witness could be conceived in terms of many different individual performances, delivered over time but in coordination with each other. Less obviously, the idea of mission as interpretation implies a steady accumulation of patient effort, made necessary by the nature of cross-cultural communication, which poses to the goal of mutual understanding a variety of social and linguistic barriers not easily overcome or quickly brushed aside.

A few other differences in style also surfaced in the various images we examined. Already mentioned more than once is the fact that Christian mission encompasses both words and actions. Indeed, in the case of the paralyzed man, the forthright witness of his companions to the power and authority of Jesus was silently demonstrated in full view of those gathered together in the crowded house. This story and others also drew our attention to the importance of healing as an element of apostolic mission. Additionally, we have seen in these mission images at least two distinctive stances assumed by witnessing disciples with respect to their audacity. Interpreters of the gospel, it seems, require an invitation before they are able to take up their missionary calling. On the other hand, announcers and shepherds come across as assertive figures, who appear ready to act with little, if any, prompting from outside their immediate circle of faith. Even so, it should not be forgotten that most of the speeches recorded in Acts are set in situations where the apostles have been asked to explain themselves. First-century disciples who shared Christ with friends and family may be said to have inhabited a middle zone of importunity, where the sharp edges of zealous faith could be tempered by the long-term bonds of personal relationship.

The "how" and the "where" of Christian witness come together in the concept of spatial relations in mission, a concern that has informed the methodology of this study from the start. At issue here is the social dimension that defines different kinds of missionary encounter. Important factors in this analysis include the posture to be assumed by the witnessing agent, the relative positioning or connection of the characters to each other, and the tone of the exchange. By this criterion, each of the mission images highlighted in this study is unambiguously differentiated from all the others.

Thus, we saw announcers of Good News typically standing to face their audiences, whom they would be apt to address with declarations and other forms of direct speech. Friends sharing Christ with family and neighbors would not be expected to strike an orator's pose, preferring instead to sit near, to surround, or to embrace the person with whom they hope to communicate their joy in the Lord. For the act of interpretation, we have had to imagine three separate characters represented in this kind of scenario. According to this image of mission, the interpreter is a background figure, who strives to ease the crossing of a living, active Word into less familiar cultural contexts, in order that it might engage new conversation partners. Missionary shepherds seek after lost and disoriented sheep, reaching out toward fellow human beings who find themselves languishing in isolation far beyond the usual boundaries of Christian community. In Paul's case, his efforts to plant and build meant working below the surface of things, where critical foundations are laid and precious rootstocks must take hold to survive.

Finally, we may now ask about distinctive motifs that recur across this set of images and so describe its essential character as a group of approaches to Christian mission. The first of these has to do with issues of power. Throughout, whether acting assertively or responding creatively to an invitation to give witness, the New Testament missionary figures depicted in this study give no indication whatsoever that they considered the use of force a legitimate way to leverage the effectiveness of their appeals. In other words, there is no support to be found in these pages for the idea of compulsion in mission. Nor does the problem of proselytization arise, insofar as that distortion of biblical practice means to evangelize by coercion. To be sure, announcers may speak in an authoritative manner, but ultimately they are trying to persuade others with their speech. Likewise, the figure of the shepherd has been carefully interpreted to rule out the functions of governing and disciplining. As the Chinese paper cut of Fan Pu so gracefully illustrates, even lost sheep retain to the end their right to decide how to react to the beckoning gesture of the missionary shepherd. In sum, no matter how deeply felt the desire may be for others to know Jesus, it must remain up to them to act on whatever is received from one or more witnessing disciple.

A second defining theme that runs like a red thread through this set of images is the subordinate status for disciples implied by each of the missionary roles featured in this book. In some cases, the instrumental function of missionary action is treated as a foreground issue. We have seen this, for example, in the way that heralds, ambassadors, and even apostles are uniformly regarded in the New Testament as emissaries of some other more powerful person, who authorizes them to speak or act on his behalf. In addition, interpreters and others who hope to introduce Jesus to nonbelievers must be ready in some sense to stand aside once meaningful contact has been achieved. It is not theirs to expect to become permanent mediators of access to God through Christ. But it may be their hope to share with new believers in a mutual identity, to participate together in a fellowship of faith in Christ. Even shepherds must be viewed as subordinate characters, if Jesus' words about himself as the one true Shepherd of the whole flock are taken seriously (John 10:16; cf. 1 Peter 5:4).

Within the universe of material drawn from the New Testament on which we focused our attention, Paul provides the most explicit reference to God's part in Christian mission. As he put it in 1 Corinthians 3, his work and that of Apollos took place within the providence of God, who alone could produce the spiritual growth for which the apostles and so many others were exerting themselves. Paul's insight points to a third and final dimension of theological reflection that stands behind this set of mission images. It is that these first-century disciples consistently construed their activities to be part of a larger exercise of divine activity, which may be designated in a comprehensive way by the term *missio Dei*. The disciples shown giving witness in these five New Testament images of mission are rightly seen as instruments of a power greater than themselves. Regardless of the particular role to which each witnessing disciple was called, all were participants in a great movement of outreach they did not initiate. In this, they were truly followers of Jesus their guide and master, who likewise understood his own mission to be an expression of God's eternal salvific intention.

Bibliography

Achtemeier, Paul J. *1 Peter: A Commentary on First Peter.* Minneapolis: Fortress, 1996.

———. "'And He Followed Him': Miracles and Discipleship in Mark 10:46-52." *Semeia* 11 (1978): 115-45.

———. "The Lucan Perspective on the Miracles of Jesus: A Preliminary Sketch." *JBL* 94 (1975): 547-62.

Ådna, Jostein, and Hans Kvalbein, eds. *The Mission of the Early Church to Jews and Gentiles.* WUNT 127. Tübingen: Mohr Siebeck, 2000.

Ahl, Diane Cole. "Masaccio in the Brancacci Chapel." In *The Cambridge Companion to Masaccio,* edited by Diane Cole Ahl. New York: Cambridge University Press, 2002.

Allen, Roland. *Missionary Methods: St. Paul's or Ours?* Grand Rapids: Eerdmans, 1962.

———. *The Spontaneous Expansion of the Church and the Causes Which Hinder It.* Second ed. London: World Dominion Press, 1949.

Amity News Service. "New Wine in Old Bottles: Filling Traditional Papercuts with Christian Spirit." 2001.7/8.4. http://www.amitynewsservice.org/page.php ?page=712&p.

Anderson, Gerald H. "World Christianity by the Numbers: A Review of the *World Christian Encyclopedia,* Second Edition." *IBMR* 26 (2002): 128-30.

Andrews, C. F. *The Good Shepherd.* London: Harper, 1940.

Arias, Mortimer, and Alan Johnson. *The Great Commission: Biblical Models for Evangelism.* Nashville: Abingdon, 1992.

Avis, Paul. *God and the Creative Imagination: Metaphor, Symbol and Myth in Religion and Theology.* London: Routledge, 1999.

Bailey, Kenneth E. *Finding the Lost: Cultural Keys to Luke 15.* St. Louis: Concordia, 1992.

———. *Poet and Peasant: A Literary-Cultural Approach to the Parables in Luke.* Grand Rapids: Eerdmans, 1976.

Barram, Michael D. "'In Order That They May Be Saved': Mission and Moral Reflection in Paul." Ph.D. diss., Union Theological Seminary and Presbyterian School of Christian Education, 2001.

Barrett, C. K. *A Critical and Exegetical Commentary on the Acts of the Apostles.* Vol. 1. Edinburgh: T&T Clark, 1994.

Barrett, David B., and Todd M. Johnson. *World Christian Trends, AD 30–AD 2200: Interpreting the Annual Christian Megacensus.* Pasadena: William Carey Library, 2001.

Barrett, David B., George T. Kurian, and Todd M. Johnson. *World Christian Encyclopedia: A Comparative Survey of Churches and Religions in the Modern World.* Second ed. 2 vols. New York: Oxford University Press, 2000.

Baur, Ferdinand Christian. "Die Christuspartei in der korinthischen Gemeinde. . . ." In *Ausgewählte Werke in Einzelausgaben,* edited by Klaus Scholder. Vol 1. Stuttgart: Frommann, 1963.

———. *Paul, the Apostle of Jesus Christ, His Life and Work, His Epistles and Doctrine: A Contribution to the Critical History of Primitive Christianity.* Edited and translated by Eduard Zeller and Allan Menzies. Second ed. 2 vols. London: Williams and Norgate, 1875-76.

Beckwith, John. *The Andrews Diptych.* London: H. M. Stationery Office, 1958.

Bediako, Kwame. *Christianity in Africa: The Renewal of a Non-Western Religion.* Edinburgh: Edinburgh University Press, 1995.

Beker, J. Christiaan. *Paul the Apostle: The Triumph of God in Life and Thought.* Philadelphia: Fortress, 1980.

Bevans, Stephen. "Seeing Mission through Images." *Missiology* 19 (1991): 45-57.

Bevans, Stephen B., and Roger P. Schroeder. *Constants in Context: A Theology of Mission for Today.* Maryknoll, N.Y.: Orbis, 2004.

Blauw, Johannes. *The Missionary Nature of the Church: A Survey of the Biblical Theology of Mission.* New York: McGraw-Hill, 1962.

Blenkinsopp, Joseph. *Isaiah 56–66: A New Translation with Introduction and Commentary.* New York: Doubleday, 2003.

Bosch, David J. "The Structure of Mission: An Exposition of Matthew 28:16-20." In *Exploring Church Growth,* edited by Wilbert R. Shenk. Grand Rapids: Eerdmans, 1983.

———. *Transforming Mission: Paradigm Shifts in Theology of Mission.* Maryknoll, N.Y.: Orbis, 1991.

———. "The Vulnerability of Mission." In *New Directions in Mission and*

Evangelization, vol. 2: *Theological Foundations,* edited by James A. Scherer and Stephen B. Bevans. Maryknoll, N.Y.: Orbis, 1994.

Bowers, W. Paul. "Fulfilling the Gospel: The Scope of Pauline Mission." *JETS* 30 (1987): 185-98.

———. "Mission." *DPL*: 608-19.

Brown, Raymond E. *The Death of the Messiah: From Gethsemane to the Grave; A Commentary on the Passion Narratives in the Four Gospels.* 2 vols. New York: Doubleday, 1994.

———. *The Gospel according to John: Introduction, Translation, and Notes.* 2 vols. Garden City: Doubleday, 1966-1970.

Brown, William P. *Seeing the Psalms: A Theology of Metaphor.* Louisville: Westminster John Knox, 2002.

Bruce, F. F. "Paul's Apologetic and the Purpose of Acts." *BJRL* 69 (1987): 379-93.

Buchanan, Claudius. *Christian Researches in Asia: With Notices on the Translation of the Scriptures into the Oriental Languages.* New York: Richard Scott, 1812.

Bultmann, Rudolf. *The Gospel of John: A Commentary.* Edited by R. W. N. Hoare and J. K. Riches. Translated by G. R. Beasley-Murray. Philadelphia: Westminster, 1971.

Bundy, David. "The Syriac and Armenian Christian Responses to the Islamification of the Mongols." In *Medieval Christian Perceptions of Islam,* edited by John V. Tolan. New York: Garland, 1996.

Cachia, Nicholas. *The Image of the Good Shepherd As a Source for the Spirituality of the Ministerial Priesthood.* Rome: Editrice Pontificia Università Gregoriana, 1997.

Cadbury, Henry J. *The Making of Luke-Acts.* New York: Macmillan, 1927.

Caird, G. B. *The Language and Imagery of the Bible.* London: Duckworth, 1980.

Cassell's Illustrated Family Bible. London and New York: Cassell, Petter, and Galpin, [c. 1859-1871].

Castelli, Elizabeth A. *Imitating Paul: A Discourse of Power.* Louisville: Westminster/ John Knox, 1991.

Charlesworth, M. P. *Trade-Routes and Commerce of the Roman Empire.* Second ed. Cambridge: University Press, 1926.

Christiansen, Keith. "Masolino (da Panicale)." *DArt* 20:553-59.

Conzelmann, Hans. *1 Corinthians: A Commentary on the First Epistle to the Corinthians.* Translated by James W. Leitch. Philadelphia: Fortress, 1975.

Cooper, Henry R., Jr. "The Origins of the Church Slavonic Version of the Bible: An Alternative Hypothesis." In *Interpretation of the Bible,* edited by Jože Krašovec. Sheffield: Sheffield Academic, 1998.

Coote, Robert T. "'AD 2000' and the '10/40 Window': A Preliminary Assessment." *IBMR* 24 (2000): 160-66.

Costas, Orlando E. *Christ outside the Gate: Mission beyond Christendom.* Maryknoll, N.Y.: Orbis, 1982.

Culpepper, R. Alan. *The Johannine School: An Evaluation of the Johannine-School Hypothesis Based on an Investigation of the Nature of Ancient Schools.* SBLDS 26. Missoula, Mont.: Scholars, 1975.

Dahl, Nils Alstrup. *Studies in Paul: Theology for the Early Christian Mission.* Assisted by Paul Donahue. Minneapolis: Augsburg, 1977.

Dibelius, Martin. *Studies in the Acts of the Apostles.* Edited by Heinrich Greeven. Translated by Mary Ling. London: SCM, 1956.

Driver, John. *Images of the Church in Mission.* Scottdale, Pa.: Herald, 1997.

Dunn, James D. G. *Jesus' Call to Discipleship.* Cambridge: Cambridge University Press, 1992.

———. *The Theology of Paul the Apostle.* Grand Rapids: Eerdmans, 1998.

Dupuis, Jacques. *Toward a Christian Theology of Religious Pluralism.* Maryknoll, N.Y.: Orbis, 1997.

Dvornik, Francis. *Byzantine Missions among the Slavs: SS. Constantine-Cyril and Methodius.* New Brunswick, N.J.: Rutgers University Press, 1970.

Ein Afrikaner wird getauft. Stuttgart: Deutsche Bibelgesellschaft, 1983.

Eleen, Luba. *The Illustration of the Pauline Epistles in French and English Bibles of the Twelfth and Thirteenth Centuries.* Oxford: Clarendon, 1982.

Ellis, E. Earle. "Midrashic Features in the Speeches of Acts." In *Mélanges bibliques en hommage au R. P. Béda Rigaux,* edited by Albert Descamps and André de Halleux. Gembloux: Duculot, 1970.

Fermor, Sharon. *The Raphael Tapestry Cartoons: Narrative, Decoration, Design.* London: Scala, 1996.

Fitzer, Gottfried. "Τολμάω." *TDNT* 8:181-86.

Fitzmyer, Joseph A. *The Acts of the Apostles: A New Translation with Introduction and Commentary.* New York: Doubleday, 1998.

———. *The Gospel according to Luke: Introduction, Translation, and Notes.* 2 vols. Garden City, N.Y.: Doubleday, 1981-1985.

———. "The Languages of Palestine in the First Century A.D." In *A Wandering Aramean: Collected Aramaic Essays,* edited by Joseph A. Fitzmyer. Missoula, Mont.: Scholars, 1979.

Forbes, Christopher. "Comparison, Self-Praise and Irony: Paul's Boasting and the Conventions of Hellenistic Rhetoric." *NTS* 32 (1986): 1-30.

Fox, Robin Lane. *Pagans and Christians.* New York: Knopf, 1987.

Friedrich, Gerhard. "Κῆρυξ/κηρύσσω." *TDNT* 3:683-718.

Gannaway, Bruce F. "Mission: Commitment to God's Hopeful Vision." *Church and Society* 84, no. 1 (September/October 1993): 21-75.

Gärtner, Bertil E. *The Areopagus Speech and Natural Revelation.* Translated by Carolyn Hannay King. Uppsala: C. W. K. Gleerup, 1955.

Gaventa, Beverly Roberts. *From Darkness to Light: Aspects of Conversion in the New Testament.* Philadelphia: Fortress, 1986.

———. "The Maternity of Paul: An Exegetical Study of Galatians 4:19." In *The Conversation Continues: Studies in Paul and John in Honor of J. Louis Martyn,* edited by Robert T. Fortna and Beverly R. Gaventa. Nashville: Abingdon, 1990.

———. "Mother's Milk and Ministry in 1 Corinthians 3." In *Theology and Ethics in Paul and His Interpreters: Essays in Honor of Victor Paul Furnish,* edited by Eugene H. Lovering Jr. and Jerry L. Sumney. Nashville: Abingdon, 1996.

———. "Our Mother St. Paul: Toward the Recovery of a Neglected Theme." *Princeton Seminary Bulletin* 17 (1996): 29-44.

———. "'You Will Be My Witnesses': Aspects of Mission in the Acts of the Apostles." *Missiology* 10 (1982): 413-25.

Georgi, Dieter. *The Opponents of Paul in Second Corinthians.* Philadelphia: Fortress, 1986.

Gibson, Sarah S. "Shepherds/Shepherdesses." In *Encyclopedia of Comparative Iconography: Themes Depicted in Works of Art,* edited by Helene E. Roberts. Chicago: Fitzroy Dearborn, 1998.

Given, Mark D. "Not Either/Or but Both/And in Paul's Areopagus Speech." *BibInt* 3 (1995): 356-72.

———. *Paul's True Rhetoric: Ambiguity, Cunning, and Deception in Greece and Rome.* Harrisburg, Pa.: Trinity Press International, 2001.

Goodman, Martin. *Mission and Conversion: Proselytizing in the Religious History of the Roman Empire.* Oxford: Clarendon, 1994.

Goulder, Michael D. *Paul and the Competing Mission in Corinth.* Peabody: Hendrickson, 2001.

Gundry, Robert H. *Jesus the Word according to John the Sectarian: A Paleofundamentalist Manifesto for Contemporary Evangelicalism, Especially Its Elites, in North America.* Grand Rapids: Eerdmans, 2002.

———. *Matthew: A Commentary on His Handbook for a Mixed Church under Persecution.* Second ed. Grand Rapids: Eerdmans, 1994.

Haenchen, Ernst. *The Acts of the Apostles: A Commentary.* Translated by Bernard Noble et al. Oxford: Basil Blackwell, 1971.

Hahn, Ferdinand. *Mission in the New Testament.* Translated by Frank Clarke. Naperville, Ill.: A. R. Allenson, 1965.

Hare, Douglas R. A., and Daniel J. Harrington. "'Make Disciples of All the Gentiles' (Matthew 28:19)." *CBQ* 37 (1975): 359-69.

Hengel, Martin. *The Charismatic Leader and His Followers.* Translated by James Greig. New York: Crossroad, 1981.

Hock, Ronald F. "Paul's Tentmaking and the Problem of His Social Class." *JBL* 97 (1978): 555-64.

————. *The Social Context of Paul's Ministry: Tentmaking and Apostleship.* Philadelphia: Fortress, 1980.

————. "The Workshop As a Social Setting for Paul's Missionary Preaching." *CBQ* 41 (1979): 438-50.

Hogg, Rena L. "Martha J. McKown — 'The Elevation of Egyptian Womanhood.'" In *In the King's Service,* edited by Charles J. Watson. Philadelphia: Board of Foreign Missions of the United Presbyterian Church of North America, 1905.

Horsley, G. H. R. "Speeches and Dialogue in Acts." *NTS* 32 (1986): 609-14.

Hurtado, Larry. "Following Jesus in the Gospel of Mark — and Beyond." In *Patterns of Discipleship in the New Testament,* edited by Richard Longenecker. Grand Rapids: Eerdmans, 1996.

Hutchison, William R. *Errand to the World: American Protestant Thought and Foreign Missions.* Chicago: University of Chicago Press, 1987.

Hvalvik, Reidar. "In Word and Deed: The Expansion of the Church in the Pre-Constantinian Era." In *The Mission of the Early Church to Jews and Gentiles,* edited by Jostein Ådna and Hans Kvalbein. WUNT 127. Tübingen: Mohr Siebeck, 2000.

Jensen, Robin M. *Understanding Early Christian Art.* London: Routledge, 2000.

Jeremias, Joachim. "Ποιμήν." *TDNT* 6:485-502.

Joannides, Paul. *Masaccio and Masolino: A Complete Catalogue.* London: Phaidon, 1993.

Johnson, Luke Timothy. *The First and Second Letters to Timothy: A New Translation with Introduction and Commentary.* New York: Doubleday, 2001.

Johnstone, Patrick J. St. G., and Jason Mandryk, with Robyn Johnstone. *Operation World.* Sixth ed. Minneapolis: Bethany House, 2001.

Jones, E. Stanley. *The Christ of the Indian Road.* New York: Abingdon, 1925.

Jonge, Marinus de. *Jesus, Stranger from Heaven and Son of God: Jesus Christ and the Christians in Johannine Perspective.* Edited and translated by John E. Steely. Missoula, Mont.: Scholars, 1977.

Jongeneel, Jan A. B. *Philosophy, Science, and Theology of Mission in the 19th and 20th Centuries: A Missiological Encyclopedia.* 2 vols. Frankfurt am Main: Peter Lang, 1995-1997.

Kantor, Marvin, and Richard S. White, trans. and eds. *The Vita of Constantine and the Vita of Methodius.* Ann Arbor: Department of Slavic Languages and Literature, University of Michigan, 1976.

Keck, Leander E., and J. Louis Martyn, eds. *Studies in Luke-Acts: Essays Presented in Honor of Paul Schubert.* Nashville: Abingdon, 1966.

Kelhoffer, James A. *Miracle and Mission: The Authentication of Missionaries and Their Message in the Longer Ending of Mark.* Tübingen: Mohr Siebeck, 2000.

Kilgallen, John J. "Acts 17,22-31: An Example of Interreligious Dialogue." *Studia Missionalia* 43 (1994): 43-60.

Kingsbury, Jack D. "The Verb *Akolouthein* ('to Follow') As an Index of Matthew's View of His Community." *JBL* 97 (1978): 56-73.

Klassen-Wiebe, Sheila Anne. "Called to Mission: A Narrative-Critical Study of the Character and Mission of the Disciples in the Gospel of Luke." Ph.D. diss., Union Theological Seminary and Presbyterian School of Christian Education, 2001.

Kořán, Ivo. "Brokof, Ferdinand Maximilián." *DArt* 4:843-44.

———. "Brokof, Jan." *DArt* 4:843.

Köstenberger, Andreas J. *The Missions of Jesus and the Disciples according to the Fourth Gospel: With Implications for the Fourth Gospel's Purpose and the Mission of the Contemporary Church.* Grand Rapids: Eerdmans, 1998.

———. "The Place of Mission in New Testament Theology: An Attempt to Determine the Significance of Mission within the Scope of the New Testament's Message As a Whole." *Missiology* 27 (1999): 347-62.

Köstenberger, Andreas J., and Peter T. O'Brien. *Salvation to the Ends of the Earth: A Biblical Theology of Mission.* Downers Grove, Ill.: InterVarsity, 2001.

Kysar, Robert. *Stumbling in the Light: New Testament Images for a Changing Church.* St. Louis: Chalice, 1999.

Larkin, William J. Jr., and Joel F. Williams, eds. *Mission in the New Testament: An Evangelical Approach.* Maryknoll, N.Y.: Orbis, 1998.

Latourette, Kenneth Scott. *A History of the Expansion of Christianity.* 7 vols. New York: Harper and Brothers, 1937-1945.

Laws, Gilbert. *Andrew Fuller: Pastor, Theologian, Ropeholder.* London: Carey, 1942.

Legrand, Lucien. "The Areopagus Speech: Its Theological Kerygma and Its Missionary Significance." In *La Notion Biblique de Dieu: Le Dieu de la Bible et le Dieu des philosophes,* edited by J. Coppens. Leuven: University Press, 1975.

———. *The Bible on Culture: Belonging or Dissenting?* Maryknoll, N.Y.: Orbis, 2000.

———. "The Good Shepherd in the Gospel of Mark." *Indian Theological Studies* 29 (1992): 234-55.

———. *Unity and Plurality: Mission in the Bible.* Translated by Robert R. Barr. Maryknoll, N.Y.: Orbis, 1990.

Lehmann, Arno. *Christian Art in Africa and Asia.* Translated by Erich Hopka et al. St. Louis: Concordia, 1969.

———. *Die Kunst der Jungen Kirchen.* Second ed. Berlin: Evangelische Verlagsanstalt, 1957.

Lemche, Niels P. "Habiru, Hapiru." *ABD* 3:6-10.

———. "Hebrew." *ABD* 3:95.

Lipton, Sara. *Images of Intolerance: The Representation of Jews and Judaism in the "Bible moralisée."* Berkeley: University of California Press, 1999.

Litfin, A. Duane. *St. Paul's Theology of Proclamation: 1 Corinthians 1–4 and Greco-Roman Rhetoric.* Cambridge: Cambridge University Press, 1994.

Love, Richard D. "10/40 Window." *EDWM:* 938.

Lowden, John. *The Making of the Bibles Moralisées.* Vol. 1, *The Manuscripts.* University Park: Pennsylvania State University Press, 2000.

Luz, Ulrich. *Matthew 8–20: A Commentary.* Translated by Wilhelm C. Linss. Minneapolis: Fortress, 2001.

———. "Matthew's Anti-Judaism: Its Origin and Contemporary Significance." *Currents in Theology and Mission* 19 (1992): 405-15.

MacInnes, Rennie. "The Ancient Oriental Churches and Islam." In collaboration with Herbert Danby. In *The Moslem World of To-day,* edited by John R. Mott. London: Hodder and Stoughton, 1925.

Malbon, Elizabeth Struthers. *In the Company of Jesus: Characters in Mark's Gospel.* Louisville: Westminster John Knox, 2000.

Malherbe, Abraham J. *Paul and the Thessalonians: The Philosophic Tradition of Pastoral Care.* Philadelphia: Fortress, 1987.

Marshall, I. Howard. "Who Were the Evangelists?" In *The Mission of the Early Church to Jews and Gentiles,* edited by Jostein Ådna and Hans Kvalbein. WUNT 127. Tübingen: Mohr Siebeck, 2000.

Martin, Dale B. *The Corinthian Body.* New Haven: Yale University Press, 1995.

———. *Slavery As Salvation: The Metaphor of Slavery in Pauline Christianity.* New Haven: Yale University Press, 1990.

Martin, Luther H. "Gods or Ambassadors of God? Barnabas and Paul in Lystra." *NTS* 41 (1995): 152-56.

Mathews, Thomas F. *The Clash of Gods: A Reinterpretation of Early Christian Art.* Princeton, N.J.: Princeton University Press, 1993.

Mathews, Thomas F., and Alice Taylor. *The Armenian Gospels of Gladzor: The Life of Christ Illuminated.* Los Angeles: J. Paul Getty Museum, 2001.

McFague, Sallie. *Metaphorical Theology: Models of God in Religious Language.* Philadelphia: Fortress, 1982.

McGavran, Donald A. "Will Uppsala Betray the Two Billion?" In *The Conciliar-Evangelical Debate: The Crucial Documents, 1964-1976,* edited by Donald A. McGavran. Pasadena: William Carey Library, 1977.

Meeks, Wayne A. *The First Urban Christians: The Social World of the Apostle Paul.* New Haven: Yale University Press, 1983.

Meier, John P. "The Circle of the Twelve: Did It Exist during Jesus' Public Ministry?" *JBL* 116 (1997): 635-72.

———. *A Marginal Jew: Rethinking the Historical Jesus.* Vol. 3, *Companions and Competitors.* New York: Doubleday, 2001.

————. "Nations or Gentiles in Matthew 28:19?" *CBQ* 39 (1977): 94-102.

Mellinkoff, Ruth. *Outcasts: Signs of Otherness in Northern European Art of the Late Middle Ages.* 2 vols. Berkeley: University of California Press, 1993.

Messer, Donald E. *A Conspiracy of Goodness: Contemporary Images of Christian Mission.* Nashville: Abingdon, 1992.

Michel, Otto. "Οἶκος." *TDNT* 5:119-59.

Michelli, Pippin. "Crosier." *DArt* 8:193-95.

Minear, Paul S. *Images of the Church in the New Testament.* Philadelphia: Westminster, 1960.

Mitchell, Margaret M. *Paul and the Rhetoric of Reconciliation: An Exegetical Investigation of the Language and Composition of 1 Corinthians.* Tübingen: J. C. B. Mohr (Paul Siebeck), 1991.

Mott, John R. *The Decisive Hour of Christian Missions.* New York: Student Volunteer Movement for Foreign Missions, 1910.

Murphy-O'Connor, Jerome. *Paul: A Critical Life.* Oxford: Clarendon, 1996.

Mussies, Gerard. "Greek As the Vehicle of Early Christianity." *NTS* 29 (1983): 356-69.

Neirynck, Frans. "The Miracle Stories in the Acts of the Apostles: An Introduction." In *Les Actes des Apôtres: Traditions, rédaction, théologie,* edited by Jacob Kremer. Gembloux: Leuven University Press, 1979.

Nissen, Johannes. *New Testament and Mission: Historical and Hermeneutical Perspectives.* Frankfurt am Main: Peter Lang, 1999.

Novotný, Kamil, and Emanuel Poche. *The Charles Bridge of Prague.* Translated by Norah Robinson-Hronková. Prague: V. Polácek, 1947.

O'Connor, Daniel. *Gospel, Raj and Swaraj: The Missionary Years of C. F. Andrews, 1904-14.* Frankfurt am Main: Peter Lang, 1990.

O'Donnell, J. Dean, Jr. *Lavigerie in Tunisia: The Interplay of Imperialist and Missionary.* Athens: University of Georgia Press, 1979.

Okure, Teresa. *The Johannine Approach to Mission: A Contextual Study of John 4:1-42.* WUNT 2/31. Tübingen: J. C. B. Mohr (Paul Siebeck), 1988.

Ollrog, Wolf-Henning. *Paulus und seine Mitarbeiter: Untersuchungen zu Theorie und Praxis der paulinischen Mission.* Neukirchen-Vluyn: Neukirchener Verlag, 1979.

Osborne, Grant R. "John 21: A Test Case for History and Redaction in the Resurrection Narratives." In *Gospel Perspectives: Studies of History and Tradition in the Four Gospels,* edited by R. T. France and David Wenham. Vol. 2. Sheffield: JSOT, 1981.

Owen, F. Cunliffe. "The Warrior Monks of the Sahara: A New Order of Chivalry." *Harper's Weekly* 35, no. 1798 (June 6, 1891): 427.

Pelikan, Jaroslav. *Jesus through the Centuries: His Place in the History of Culture.* New Haven: Yale University Press, 1985.

Pogoloff, Stephen M. *Logos and Sophia: The Rhetorical Situation of 1 Corinthians.* SBLDS 134. Atlanta: Scholars, 1992.

Porter, Stanley E. "Paul of Tarsus and His Letters." In *Handbook of Classical Rhetoric in the Hellenistic Period (330 BC–AD 400)*, edited by Stanley E. Porter. Leiden: Brill, 1997.

Preuss, H. D. "Zaraʿ." *TDOT* 4:143-62.

Ramsey, Boniface. "A Note on the Disappearance of the Good Shepherd from Early Christian Art." *HTR* 76 (1983): 375-78.

Reindl, J. "Nataʿ." *TDOT* 9:387-94.

Renault, François. *Cardinal Lavigerie, 1825-1892: Churchman, Prophet and Missionary.* Translated by John O'Donohue. London: Athlone, 1994.

Ricoeur, Paul. *Figuring the Sacred: Religion, Narrative, and Imagination.* Edited by Mark I. Wallace. Translated by David Pellauer. Minneapolis: Fortress, 1995.

————. *The Rule of Metaphor: Multi-Disciplinary Studies of the Creation of Meaning in Language.* Translated by Robert Czerny et al. Toronto: University of Toronto Press, 1977.

Ross, Andrew C. *A Vision Betrayed: The Jesuits in Japan and China, 1542-1742.* Maryknoll, N.Y.: Orbis, 1994.

Ryan, James D. "Conversion vs. Baptism? European Missionaries in Asia in the Thirteenth and Fourteenth Centuries." In *Varieties of Religious Conversion in the Middle Ages*, edited by James Muldoon. Gainesville: University Press of Florida, 1997.

Sandt, Huub van de. "The Fate of the Gentiles in Joel and Acts 2: An Intertextual Study." *ETL* 66 (1990): 56-77.

Sanneh, Lamin. *Translating the Message: The Missionary Impact on Culture.* Maryknoll, N.Y.: Orbis, 1989.

Satterthwaite, Philip E. "Acts against the Background of Classical Rhetoric." In *The Book of Acts in Its First Century Setting*, edited by Bruce W. Winter and Andrew D. Clarke. Vol. 1. Grand Rapids: Eerdmans, 1993.

Schnabel, Eckhard J. *Early Christian Mission.* 2 vols. Downers Grove, Ill.: InterVarsity, 2004.

Schnackenburg, Rudolf. *The Gospel according to St. John.* Translated by Kevin Smyth. 3 vols. New York: Crossroad, 1990.

Schürer, Emil. *The History of the Jewish People in the Age of Jesus Christ (175 B.C.–A.D. 135).* Edited and revised by Geza Vermes et al. Rev. ed. Vol. 2. Edinburgh: T&T Clark, 1979.

Scott, James M. "Acts 2:9-11 As an Anticipation of the Mission to the Gentiles." In *The Mission of the Early Church to Jews and Gentiles*, edited by Jostein Ådna and Hans Kvalbein. WUNT 127. Tübingen: Mohr Siebeck, 2000.

Senior, Donald, and Carroll Stuhlmueller. *The Biblical Foundations for Mission.* Maryknoll, N.Y.: Orbis, 1983.

Sevenster, J. N. *Do You Know Greek? How Much Greek Could the First Jewish Christians Have Known?* Translated by J. de Bruin. NovTSup 19. Leiden: Brill, 1968.

Shanor, Jay. "Paul As Master Builder: Construction Terms in First Corinthians." *NTS* 34 (1988): 461-71.

Sharpe, Eric J. "The Legacy of C. F. Andrews." *IBMR* 9 (1985): 117-21.

Shearman, John K. G. *Raphael's Cartoons in the Collection of Her Majesty the Queen, and the Tapestries for the Sistine Chapel.* London: Phaidon, 1972.

Shenk, Wilbert R. "Henry Venn's Instructions to Missionaries." *Missiology* 5 (1977): 467-85.

Shiner, Whitney Taylor. *Follow Me! Disciples in Markan Rhetoric.* SBLDS 145. Atlanta: Scholars, 1995.

Shorter, Aylward. "Christian Presence in a Muslim Milieu: The Missionaries of Africa in the Maghreb and the Sahara." *IBMR* 28 (2004): 159-64.

Skreslet, Stanley H. "The Empty Basket of Presbyterian Mission: Limits and Possibilities of Partnership." *IBMR* 19 (1995): 98-106.

Smith, Eli, and H. G. O. Dwight. *The Researches of the Rev. E. Smith and Rev. H. G. O. Dwight in Armenia; Including a Journey through Asia Minor, and into Georgia and Persia, with a Visit to the Nestorian and Chaldean Christians in Oormiah and Salmas.* 2 vols. Boston: Crocker and Brewster, 1833.

Smith, F. B. *Radical Artisan: William James Linton, 1812-1897.* Manchester: Manchester University Press, 1973.

Soards, Marion L. *The Speeches in Acts: Their Content, Context, and Concerns.* Louisville: Westminster/John Knox, 1994.

Soskice, Janet Martin. *Metaphor and Religious Language.* Oxford: Clarendon, 1985.

Spencer, F. Scott. *The Portrait of Philip in Acts: A Study of Roles and Relations.* JSNTSup 67. Sheffield: Sheffield Academic Press, 1992.

Spicq, Ceslas. *Theological Lexicon of the New Testament.* Edited and translated by James D. Ernest. 3 vols. Peabody: Hendrickson, 1994.

Stark, Rodney. *The Rise of Christianity: A Sociologist Reconsiders History.* Princeton, N.J.: Princeton University Press, 1996.

Stott, John R. W. *Christian Mission in the Modern World.* Downers Grove, Ill.: InterVarsity, 1975.

Stuhlmacher, Peter. "Matt 28:16-20 and the Course of Mission in the Apostolic and Postapostolic Age." In *The Mission of the Early Church to Jews and Gentiles,* edited by Jostein Ådna and Hans Kvalbein. WUNT 127. Tübingen: Mohr Siebeck, 2000.

Sumney, Jerry L. *Identifying Paul's Opponents: The Question of Method in 2 Corinthians.* Sheffield: JSOT, 1990.

Tannehill, Robert C. *The Narrative Unity of Luke-Acts: A Literary Interpretation.* Vol. 2, *The Acts of the Apostles.* Minneapolis: Fortress, 1990.

Taylor, Richard W. "E. Stanley Jones, 1884-1973: Following the Christ of the Indian Road." In *Mission Legacies: Biographical Studies of Leaders of the Modern Missionary Movement,* edited by Gerald H. Anderson et al. Maryknoll, N.Y.: Orbis, 1994.

Theissen, Gerd. *The Social Setting of Pauline Christianity: Essays on Corinth,* edited and translated by John H. Schütz. Philadelphia: Fortress, 1982.

Thoburn, J. M. *Missionary Addresses.* New York: Phillips and Hunt, 1888.

Thomson, J. G. S. S. "The Shepherd-Ruler Concept in the OT and Its Application in the NT." *Scottish Journal of Theology* 8 (1955): 406-18.

Thrall, Margaret E. *A Critical and Exegetical Commentary on the Second Epistle to the Corinthians.* Vol. 2. Edinburgh: T&T Clark, 2000.

Trowell, K. M. *And Was Made Man: The Life of Our Lord in Pictures.* London: SPCK, 1956.

Uro, Risto. *Sheep among the Wolves: A Study on the Mission Instructions of Q.* Helsinki: Suomalainen Tiedeakatemia, 1987.

Vanguard of the Christian Army. Or, Sketches of Missionary Life. London: Religious Tract Society, [1882].

Venn, Henry. "Instructions to Missionaries." *Church Missionary Intelligencer* 14, no. 5 [May 1863]: 109-13.

Wallen, Burr. "Hemessen, Jan Sanders van." *DArt* 14:379-82.

―――. *Jan van Hemessen: An Antwerp Painter between Reform and Counter-Reform.* Ann Arbor: UMI Research Press, 1983.

Walls, Andrew F. *The Missionary Movement in Christian History: Studies in the Transmission of Faith.* Maryknoll, N.Y.: Orbis, 1996.

Ware, James Patrick. "'Holding Forth the Word of Life': Paul and the Mission of the Church in the Letter to the Philippians in the Context of Second Temple Judaism." Ph.D. diss., Yale University, 1996.

―――. "The Thessalonians As a Missionary Congregation: 1 Thessalonians 1,5-8." *ZNW* 83 (1992): 126-31.

Watson, Andrew. *The American Mission in Egypt.* Second ed. Pittsburgh: United Presbyterian Board of Publication, 1904.

Weder, Hans. "Disciple, Discipleship." Translated by Dennis Martin. *ABD* 2:207-10.

Westermann, Claus. *Isaiah 40–66, A Commentary.* Translated by David M. G. Stalker. Philadelphia: Westminster, 1969.

Wilkins, Michael J. *Discipleship in the Ancient World and Matthew's Gospel.* Second ed. Grand Rapids: Baker Books, 1995.

Williams, C. Peter. *The Ideal of the Self-Governing Church: A Study in Victorian Missionary Strategy.* Leiden: Brill, 1990.

Williams, Joel F. "Discipleship and Minor Characters in Mark's Gospel." *Bibliotheca Sacra* 153 (1996): 332-43.

————. *Other Followers of Jesus: Minor Characters As Major Figures in Mark's Gospel.* JSNTSup 102. Sheffield: JSOT, 1994.

Winter, Ralph D. "Are 90% of Our Missionaries Serving in the Wrong Places?" *Mission Frontiers* 15, nos. 5-6 (May-June 1993): 29-30.

————. "Editorial Comment." *Mission Frontiers* 24, no. 6 (Nov.-Dec. 2002): 4-5.

Witherington, Ben, III. *The Acts of the Apostles: A Socio-Rhetorical Commentary.* Grand Rapids: Eerdmans, 1998.

Wohl, Hellmut. "Masaccio." *DArt* 20:973-83.

Wood, Ian. *The Missionary Life: Saints and the Evangelisation of Europe, 400-1050.* Harlow, England: Longman, 2001.

Woods, Leonard. "The Ordination Sermon." In *Pioneeers in Mission: The Early Missionary Ordination Sermons, Charges, and Instructions; A Source Book on the Rise of American Missions to the Heathen,* edited by R. Pierce Beaver. Grand Rapids: Eerdmans, 1966.

Wuellner, Wilhelm H. *The Meaning of "Fishers of Men."* Philadelphia: Westminster, 1967.

Yates, Timothy. *Christian Mission in the Twentieth Century.* Cambridge: Cambridge University Press, 1994.

Index of Names and Subjects

Index of Scripture References

NEW TESTAMENT

Matthew

3:5	45
4:15	125n.8
4:18-22	39, 81
4:23	45
4:25	83
7:7-11	109n.34
9:1-8	101
9:9	83n.3
9:35	45
9:36	169, 187
10:1	42, 43
10:5	43
10:5-15	42
10:7	44
10:8	44
10:14-15	44
10:16-23	44
10:27	45
11:1	45, 49n.13
11:2-6	41
13:10	41
13:36	41
16:17-19	179-80
17:10	41
18:12-14	169
18:13	170n.24, 171
18:18	180n.41
19:16-22	84n.4
20:29	86n.7
21:33	222n.50
24:3	41
24:14	47
25:31-46	170
26:13	47
27:57	88n.11
28:8	87n.10
28:16-20	29, 46n.9, 126n.12
28:19	43, 47, 119

Mark

1:4	45, 48n.11
1:5	45
1:7	45
1:15	1
1:16-20	39, 81
1:17	1
1:21-28	101
1:28	83
1:32-34	99n.25
1:40-45	101
1:40-3:6	107n.32
1:45	45
2:1-12	30, 101-16
2:7	105
2:13-14	83n.3
2:18	80
3:6	106
3:22-23	99
4:3-9	222
4:34	41n.3
5:20	45
5:21-43	84, 99-100
6:6-13	26n.49
6:7-13	42, 155n.1
6:8-10	43n.5
6:11	44
6:12	44
6:12-13	49
6:13	44n.7
6:29	86
6:30	49n.14
6:34	169
6:55-56	98-99
7:31-37	100
7:36	100n.27
8:22-26	100
8:27-33	120
8:31-33	84
9:30-32	84
10:13-16	100
10:17-22	84
10:46-52	85-86
13:10	46, 47
14:3-9	86, 88
14:9	46, 47
14:27-28	169
14:28	170n.22

15:40-41	86
15:42-46	86
15:43	87
16:1	86
16:7	126n.12, 170n.22
16:7-8	87n.10
16:9	87
16:9-11	87n.10
16:9-20	47
16:15	119
16:17-18	48n.12
16:20	47

Luke

1:1-4	121
3:3	48n.11
4:16-30	45, 120
4:20	56
5:1-11	82, 83n.2
5:6	82
5:10	39
5:17	110n.35
5:17-26	101
5:27-28	83n.3
6:17	83
7:18-23	41
8:2	87
8:39	45
9:1-6	42
9:1-11	49n.14
9:2	44
9:5	44
9:6	44n.7, 49
9:57-62	85n.5
10:1-20	26, 42
10:9	44
10:10-11	46
10:10-16	44
10:17	49
10:23-24	41n.3
11:5-13	109n.34
12:3	45
15:1-2	173
15:3-7	169, 170
15:5	171